Collecting Toy Soldiers in the 21st Century

Picture 2: Haffner semi-flats, Franco-Prussian War
These beautiful but well used semi-flat figures must have been made closely following the events of the war. The wonderful set of flat tin backdrops depict a burning city with war damaged buildings and a citadel on top of a hill firing its guns. This might be the fortress of Sedan.

DEDICATION

This book is, as always, dedicated to my darling wife Mary.

Picture 1: Jacket picture: The drums and fifes of the Royal Welch Fusiliers
This special paint band I bought from the Pottier-Smith collection. H.L. Pottier-Smith was a leading member of the British Model Soldier Society from when it started in 1935, and was one of the few collectors with the desire and resources to take full advantage of Britains offer to make up models of customer's choice on request. It is all very well for people to grumble that Britains did not make this or that. What most of these people meant was that Britains did not include what they particularly wanted in their regular range, at their regular prices, because for most of the 1930s, 1940s and 1950s Britains were perfectly happy to quote the cost of anything anyone desired within reason. The beautiful little set, painted to an enhanced standard with black flashes behind the neck, is both a tribute to Britains best craftsmanship and an endorsement of the urge in collector communities to elevate quality and excellence onto the pinnacle of value and desirability.

Picture 3, opposite: Haffner vignette, semi-flat, Franco-Prussian War
Beautiful vignettes of this type, combining a number of figures in a single setting, became a traditional centrepiece for Best Quality flats, semi-flats and solid figures in Germany. No one can deny they have WOW! factor. This one comes from the same series depicted in the frontispiece.

Collecting Toy Soldiers in the 21st Century

James Opie

PEN & SWORD
Barnsley

First published in Great Britain in 2011 by
Pen & Sword
an imprint of
Pen & Sword Books Ltd
47 Church Street
Barnsley
South Yorkshire
S70 2AS

ISBN 978-1848843738

Typeset in Garamond BE 11/13 and Gill Sans
Copy-editing, design and typesetting by Henry Hyde

Printed and bound in India by Replika Press Pvt. Ltd.

Pen & Sword Books Ltd incorporates the Imprints of Pen & Sword Aviation, Pen & Sword Maritime, Pen & Sword Military, Wharncliffe Local History, Pen and Sword Select, Pen and Sword Military Classics, Leo Cooper, Seaforth Publishing, Frontline Books and Remember When.

For a complete list of Pen & Sword titles please contact
PEN & SWORD BOOKS LIMITED
47 Church Street, Barnsley, South Yorkshire, S70 2AS, England
Email: enquiries@pen-and-sword.co.uk
Website: www.pen-and-sword.co.uk

CONTENTS

FOREWORD
by Max Hastings

Throughout modern history until very recently, collecting toy soldiers was a familiar boyhood passion. In the twenty-first century, popular sentiment recoils from encouraging or even allowing children to play games of war. This seems silly, for many of us deployed much more imagination upon our small armies on the nursery floor than does a modern child self-imprisoned before a screen; nor did the cult of soldiers breed many psychopaths. Today, however, the privilege of playing with soldiers is largely confined to adults. On both sides of the Atlantic, fortunate grown-ups cherish this remarkable heritage, building collections of the finest achievements of European manufacturers, especially those made by Britains in the company's heyday between 1893 and 1973.

James Opie knows more about toy soldiers than anyone else on the planet. He built a personal collection which reached its zenith in 1984, when he had 65,000 figures, and he still boasts an army of 16,000. Through his work as a specialist adviser first to Phillips, today to Bonhams, he knows the auction salerooms intimately. He is the author of several definitive studies, notably *The Great Book of Britains*, an enchanting bedside companion for anyone who enjoys voyaging down memory lane, as well as an essential collectors' crib. No one is better qualified to explain the principles, opportunities and market lore of collecting, as he does in this new work.

I am a mere lover of toy soldiers rather than a collector. To me, they stir nostalgia for some of my own happiest days almost sixty years ago, and reflect my delight in recalling the great era of the British Army. When I was nine or ten, I spent every penny I could raise on my regiments, which embraced horse, foot and guns in 19th century parade uniforms as well as plastic soldiers of the World War II era, which proved most serviceable for battles. James, who comes from a family of distinguished academics and collectors, describes how he roamed his neighbourhood as a boy, in the days when every high street boasted toyshops plentifully stocked with soldiers. I did likewise, especially favouring Kenways in London's Brompton Road. There seemed almost as many fighting men in its showcases as this country today fields in Afghanistan. Today, alas, there are few dedicated toyshops and even fewer which sell such small works of art as Britains manufactured for so long.

But, for those who aspire to collect, the author remarks that beyond specialist toy soldier shows and salerooms, the Internet offers wonderful opportunities for purchasing gems. A new entrant can identify a niche he would like to fill, then set about creating his collection. He might choose the warriors of a given historical period, such as Romans and Greeks, the American Civil War or Zulu War; or he may prefer to focus on a certain period of manufacture, such as European flats and semi-flats of the 19th century, or Britains' pre-First World War designs. A rich man could spend £100,000 on making a collection of Britains' hundred most attractive sets. For those with modest budgets, however, it remains possible to pick up figures for a few pounds apiece. The market places a high premium on the condition of original boxes, which influence prices dramatically. But those who merely want to own soldiers for the enjoyment of the spectacle can build groups to arrange in a display case without much injuring their bank balance.

I have a modest little field force marching across a shelf at the top of our house that a connoisseur would sniff at, but which pleases me tremendously. It is made up of examples of

Britains' imperial splendours: running Highlanders; a Royal Navy gun team; several troops of cavalry; a battery of horse artillery; a fighting square of Sherwood Foresters; a Coldstream Guards band; and a platoon of Cameron Highlanders in firing positions. How I should love to have owned them half a century ago! Today, they do not make me a collector, but they reflect my sympathy and respect for those who set about the business in earnest. James draws a distinction between those who see their holdings as model soldiers – intended, like my own, merely to be looked at – and toy soldiers, which should be played with. He himself has been a champion wargamer.

In this book, he sketches the evolution of toy soldier manufacture since the 17th century, identifies the highlights of the craft and of collecting fever – which peaked in 1987 – and suggests a practical approach to starting a collection, of which the first line is: "Get stuck in!". He himself is attracted by what he calls 'the WOW! factor' – aiming to identify and purchase specimens that are conspicuous for their beauty or rarity. A really dedicated collector with deep pockets is willing to pay up to £3,000 for a single figure. The American billionaire Malcolm Forbes created an army of 65,000 which he kept at his home in Tangiers until it was sold in 1997 for $700,000.

Most of us would be – have to be – content with much less. I like James' philosophical reflection in this book: "What is important in life? To reach death with a rich experience". He himself has achieved this through his lifetime among toy soldiers, and here he distils his enormous learning for the joy and advantage of the rest of us. Happy collecting!

MAX HASTINGS
November 2010

ACKNOWLEDGEMENTS

Collecting toy soldiers would hardly work without all the collectors who enjoy it so much. I am grateful to all those with whom I have, over the years, discussed so ardently, and from whom I have learned so much. If I have left anyone out, forgive me for forgetting the names that go with the faces in remembering what a good time we had, it might well have been decades ago!

Peter Abbott, Daniel Agnew, Stuart Asquith, Walter Badusche, Steve Balkin, Roland Bamford, Colin Barber, John Begg, Georges Biettron, Charles Biggs, Mike Blake, Christian Blondieu, Barrie Blood, Robin and Elke Boyes, Sally Bowes, David and Margaret Bracey, Giles Brown, Bertel Bruun, Mike Buckwell, Jenny Burley, Pierce Carlson, Bill Carman, Ian Carrick, Peter Cole, Paul Collett, Bill Conolly, Richard Conte, Cyril Couts, Peter Cowan, David Cowe, Bill Cranston, Derek Cross, Neal Crowley, Ron Dawson, Bud Day, Jeremy de Souza, Philip Dean, Roy Dilley, Henri Doizy, David Ednam, Burtt Erhlich, Jay Facciolo, Peter Flateau, Colonel Sam Floca Jr, John Franklin, Gisbert Freber, John Garratt, Lionel Gaurier, Leigh Gotch, Freddie Green, Peter Greenhill, Ged Haley, James Hammond, John Hanington, Gus Hansen, Peter Harris, Brian Harrison, John Harwood, David Hawkins, Philip Haythornethwaite, Alan Hickling, Andrew Hilton, Bill Hocker, Brian Hornick, Bill Jackey, Jack Jenkinson, Peter and Anne Johnson, Verne Johnson, Peter Jones, Norman Joplin, Lenore Josey, Hilary Kay, Edgar Kehoe, Harry Kemp, Lynn Kenwood, Henry Kurtz, Philip Lane, Richard Lane, Lionel Leventhal, Allen Levy, Adrian Little, James Luck, Hugo Marsh, Ernie Marshall, Frederic Mathieu-Bloise, Michael Maughan, Sally Manson, Bill McDade, Bill Miele, Warren Mitchell, Andy Morant, Paul Morehead, Scott Morlan, Stephen Naegel, Andy Nielson, Bill Nutting, Richard O'Brien, George Palmer, Ted Pearce, Frank Perry, Alfred Plath, Don Pielin, Bill Pierce, Ken Pizey, Reggie Polaine, Jim Poulton, David Pressland, Julian Pritchard, Colonel Donald Pudney, Steve Pugh, John Randolph, Len Richards, Alex Riches, Edmund Roche-Kelly, Hans Henning Roer, Arnold Rolak, Andrew Rose, Ed Ruby, John Ruddle, Stewart Saxe, David Scheinmann, Michael Schreter, Max Schulman, Irving Seligman, Roy Selwyn Smith, Joe Shimek, Arthur Smith, Jo and Steve Sommers, Brian Starling, Peter Sturgeon, Edward Suren, John Teychener, Luigi Toiati, Hermione Todd, Ted Tookey, John Tunstill, Walter Vernon, Shamus Wade, Derek Wailen, Bob Walker, Richard Walker, Joe Wallis, John West, Kemble Widmer, Patrick Willis, Rob Wilson, John Norris Wood.

There is also a publishing team involved in the preparation of a book such as this, so my thanks must go to my editor and erstwhile colleague Phil Sidnell, my tireless copy editor Henry Hyde, the man who also made my pictures come out with suitable clarity, and Charles Hewitt, the man who put up the money. Long may the people at Pen and Sword continue to publish real books in support of the guys like us who so much need them.

Picture acknowledgements
Bonhams 2, 3, 36, 38, 45, 131, 161, 210, 217, 219, 220
Philip Lane 79
John West 111
Harry Kemp 107
First Gear Inc. 25, 75, 105
King and Country 76, 106, 221

INTRODUCTION

Toy soldiers in context: the importance of figurines and modelling as a universal experience

Made from the earliest times (see chapter 2), miniature figures are one of the most important parts of our cultural heritage. Browsing round the British Museum instantly shows the ubiquitous nature of the figurine, but the hundreds that are on display are diluted among the many ethnic and historical exhibits. Toy soldiers as such appear in smaller or larger numbers in most toy museums, although the Victoria and Albert Museum's collection at the Museum of Childhood in Bethnal Green seems curiously shy of being put on show. Are they wary of war toys?

The role of the figurine is constantly changing with the different purposes of manufacture envisaged by each generation, whether it is worship, grave goods, plaything or decoration. Together, from gods to soldiers and ninja turtles, they make up a complete microcosm of humanity, its concerns and fantasies. So why is there currently no public museum devoted to the figurine? Although there are a number of spectacular private collections of toy soldiers, they tend to be in relatively small spaces, and not readily accessible to the general public. Many collectors have pondered long upon this, and wished it were otherwise. But no one has yet fully succeeded in making permanent and public a comprehensive and important collection, and setting toy soldiers in their true context.

Picture 4: Reproduction ancient figurines

This type of figurine has been stock in trade in the tourist industry since the first visitor. Originally votive in character, who is to say that the figures of Foot Guards now offered in London in their millions are different in character to these, which I found in Crete, Cairo and Athens during a Mediterranean cruise, following in the footsteps of 2,500 years of travellers.

Picture 5: My great-grandfather's Gordon figurine

Presentation figurines are a splendid souvenir and can become family heirlooms, like this one handed down to me from my great-grandfather, who was chaplain to the first battalion of the Gordon Highlanders. He was given this magnificent 190mm scale silver figure as a wedding gift from his fellow officers. Until the advent of specialist toy soldier makers, silversmiths had traditionally been the source of toy soldiers for the rich and famous, and their work often still graces the tables of regimental messes. Unfortunately they need a lot of looking after as the silver tarnishes all too easily.

I should not neglect to mention that the person who came closest to achieving this, with the resources and the interest to perform such a service to humanity was Malcolm Forbes. His reputedly 70,000 strong toy soldier collection in the Palais Mendoub in Tangiers, curated by Peter and Anne Johnson, was an object lesson to us all from the early 1970s until its disbandment in 1996. I regret never having made the journey to see it. There are collectors who could well take up this mantle, but none has yet emerged a clear favourite. Peter Johnson wrote of his experiences in his book *Toy Armies* – see the Bibliography.

Reading on about my own path in exploring just a little of the recent history of the figurine, that part which is the toy soldier, will, I hope, enthuse you. Enter the charming world in miniature and be encouraged to discover a separate and as yet unrecognised branch of the arts, model making. So far, the almost universal fascination and participation that models and figurines provoke has not by any means received the acclaim from society that it deserves. Where is the National Modelling Gallery or the Toy Soldier Institute? For many years, the British Model Soldier Society National Collection, curated by John Ruddle, presented a good selection of toys and models at Hatfield House. Sadly, commercial considerations, apparently, have forced the closure of this exhibit, and although some of the figures have found a home at Blenheim Palace, as I write there is nowhere in the UK that people can turn up and see a substantial number of toy soldiers.

Yet there is also a point of view that would believe that models and toy soldiers are too intimate and personal to make a collective experience of them worthwhile. A public exhibit of toys and figurines that far outshone the endeavours of individuals might belittle each of us. Let such galleries contain things that us ordinary folk could not aspire to, so that it is a special occasion just to visit them and marvel. We, however, will be able to enjoy the creativity and iconography of our own miniature masterpieces, on display in private settings that we can cherish every day, and pass on to others in due course.

My own lifetime with toy soldiers

From the well-remembered time when I started manoeuvring twelve semi-flat lead cavalry at four years old, or maybe even earlier, I have been enthralled by military history. Lacking vast armies at an early age, I substituted the family jar of marbles, which usefully contained a large selection of

Picture 6: My first toy soldiers

Left to right: semi-flat cavalry from one of the same moulds used to produce the first toy soldiers I ever had. My first box of Britains, a Duofort box of Hussars and Infantry of the Line, and a large box of Crescent guards and Scots Greys. Extras such as the Crescent bandsmen (my first band), the Wend-Al Coldstream officer and the Johillco Foot Guard at the extreme right came through pocket money purchases at local toyshops or small gifts from friends and relatives. I remember my grandmother getting my first cannon for me, front centre, which turned out to be a rare mid-blue small Britains RA gun, still on sale at Harrods in 1949. Only a certain proportion of these figures are the actual ones I had when a small boy. I'm sure I have the actual twelve semi-flat cavalry, but I have lost them somewhere at my mother's house. I went through a phase of wanting to paint everything into Best Quality finish when I was eleven, and so I know that the kneeling and lying firing Crescent Foot Guards and the trombone player, front right, are my originals, down to the original piece of Plasticene I used to stop the trombonist, who had a casting flaw, from toppling over. I remember even then being annoyed that the Life Guards had a brown horse and red plumes rather than white, but only very recently have I connected the marching Foot Guards at the back, which have puttees, with the rare Reka doughboys dated 1920 which are the same figure (see picture 171). Apart from the nostalgia I feel towards these first three groups of toy soldiers, they form between them a good example of the sort of magpie collection that turns up at auction when a few childhood soldiers come out of the attic.

splendid glass marbles in different coloured swirls, providing various regiments with officers and large marble tanks, as well as pottery marbles which became enemy troops. Various methods of rolling the regiments around scattered the enemy to the four corners of the nursery. It was my first experience of wargaming.

My first box of Britains was given to me by my aunt, probably in 1948. Interestingly (I didn't keep the box) with all the catalogues and experience I have gained, I still haven't pinned down the number of this box. It must have been a Duofort box, and it contained three hussars with bright blue jackets, four infantry of the line on guard and three marching. I wasn't too enamoured with the hussars or marching infantry, but the infantry on guard were firm favourites, with their dual ability to shoot from the hip or stick their bayonets into the enemy. When I put on my exhibition in London in 1985, the exhibition title *On Guard* reflected my first Britains figures.

Every Christmas and birthday added to the ranks, and woe betide the relative who gave me, 'sniff', cowboys and indians or, 'horrors', a clockwork tinplate car. When I started wargaming with real toy soldiers of the Second World War era, it was the relatives who hadn't cottoned on to the idea that ceremonial troops were now a no-no who attracted birthday wrath.

As the forces of my imaginary country, Magmania, developed, squadrons of army Dinkys and aircraft were added to the inventory, and the Meccano set became a fortification more

Picture 7: My 54mm hollowcast wargaming figures

The first toy soldiers I used for boyhood wargaming were two series from Crescent and one from Johillco, mostly collected one by one from Woolworths. I thought that the bright green tin helmets on the British Infantry were tropical slouch hats, so I called them the Green Hats. As firepower was the main objective, I got as many with Tommy guns as I could find. The U.S. infantry were less interesting, as they were mostly kneeling and lying riflemen, but they did make good snipers. The Hill figures were the best, as they featured both standing and lying Bren gunners. The kneeling man with binoculars was Alexander, the CinC. I gave him a red helmet to make him more visible.

Picture 8: Magmania

At 11 years old I was busy equipping my imaginary empire of Magmania. This picture shows Marx unpainted 60mm soft plastic figures bought from Woolworths for 3d each, depicting U.S. Second World War G.I.s and British household cavalry. These figures were a revelation, half the price of painted figures, much more realistic, and pre-dating Airfix 1/32 scale unpainted figures by over a decade. Woolworths must have cleaned up, as they covered a fair amount of counter space for a time. I painted these in colours I thought appropriate (spot the three original examples) and added an Ideal half-track and a Benbros Land Rover as suitable transport for the M.P.s. I was considerably put out when I discovered much later that the flashes I had devised for the Magmanian M.P. helmets turned out to be almost identical to the flag of West Germany.

Picture 9: My plastic wargaming figures

My three favourite plastic regiments, again largely for their firepower, were all Lone Star. The paras in helmets came usually in grey headgear, but sometimes in green or U.N. blue. Magmania sent a contingent to the U.N. with Magmanian flashes. The large number of poses and the vehicles that went with them were very appealing to me. Included in this picture are examples of all the different paint variations and also three of the successor Swoppet style series, which is relatively rare. While the bren gun carrier and the trucks with weapons and trailers were common, the straightforward lorry and the Land Rover were for some reason difficult to find, even at the time. The Lone Star Harvey series were consistently well designed in a compatible style, even if the red berets seemed a bit reminiscent of the Herald combat infantry. In the picture, a few of the Harvey designed metal series are mixed in for comparison. The Australians at the right were also very original and I especially like the man trudging along with a slung rifle. At the back is the box in which three dozen pieces of each series were distributed for sale loose in the shops. As a final bit of intrigue, I have also included (in front of the larger Land Rover) the tiny miniature die-cast Land Rover that Lone Star made, possibly to go with their '000' trains.

impregnable than the Maginot Line. As a boy, and continuing on to university, I scoured London and Bristol on my bicycle, searching for different things as I grew older.

At first, it was to do with new and different World War II troops to add to the 54mm wargaming army. The most useful were the Lone Star paratroops that appeared in so many different guises from the 1950s onwards, complete with die-cast vehicles. Regiments of these were added to red beret paratroops and Australian Western Desert troops as the core of the Magmanian forces. They were all of satisfyingly homogenous design, and were widely distributed. I am still very nostalgically attached to them, although most of the hundreds I once possessed have departed.

Then came the period when I took on board the idea that hollowcast figures were finished, and it would be a good idea to collect such as I could find. I was ransacking back rooms of small shops and offering to relieve them of passé old metal toy soldier surplus stock for half the original price. At the same time, I was asking friends at school whether they had any old toy soldiers surplus to requirements – my collecting theme of the moment was to gain as many toy soldiers as I could afford. Although I made some good finds by these methods, my chronic lack of funds and the carrying capacity of my bicycle were limiting factors. Nevertheless, I look back with huge satisfaction at the Band of the Black Watch bought at

Picture 10: Dan Dare

Boxed set of Crescent Dan Dare figures from 1952, unfortunately missing the rocket launching ramp. In front are duplicate figures from the set – why oh why was there no figure of the Mekon? In plastic, U.N. Commandos, Eaglewall character figures and prototype Kentoy Terra Novans, my rarest plastic figures, a lucky highlight of my collection. To complete a Dan Dare figure cameo would need a rare set of the rather larger Southall figures.

Picture 11: Grenadier Guards Band

Charged up by my frustrated desire to own this set in 1956, I eventually acquired two. In fact the second set is short the unique drum major in state dress and one clarinet player. The standing drum major to the right is a later Britains Collectors Club figure. The 1956 series of bands was brought out by Britains during a final burst of hollowcast activity when everyone else had already converted to plastic. The major disadvantage of them was that they innovated to the extent of using plastic drums, decorated with beautiful but extremely fragile transfers. You can see the obvious damage to these flaky flimsy creations. I notice that the bass drums have deteriorated somewhat since the similar picture I did for The Great Book of Britains in 1993. Soon after Britains substituted paper labels for the drums, which were much more satisfactory, but annoyingly they never did a paper label for the tenor drummer. Another feature of this series of bands is the way that the crossbelts for the Guards drummers are gold with a black centre line rather than white over white frogging.

Allders in Croydon at half price, and the as far as I know unique three plastic prototype figures of Dan Dare Terra Novans never issued by Kentoys, which I had as a gift from the Kentoys proprietor as I was continually hanging around his shop in the Earl's Court Road.

Perhaps had I realised that I should have been buying ten times as much to invest at this point, I might have done even better, but one thing I have learned in sixty years of collecting is never to regret in hindsight what I was not perspicacious enough to foresee at the time. My grandmother always told me not to be too greedy, and refused to buy me the Grenadier Guards band in Hamleys just because I so badly wanted it. Now I have two, and enjoy them all the more because I never had one when I was small.

I was simply getting what I could, and thus in the 'Magpie' phase of my collecting. Before I left University, however, I had started, inspired by the late Len Richards, collecting (too late, even then) all the plastic toy soldiers ever issued. I joined the British Model Soldier Society, then considered too serious for under 18 year olds, and settled into an aspiration to collect all the British made toy soldiers that had ever been issued (even then I realised that a complete worldwide collection would be biting off far too much).

This aspiration was refined in 1973, when I decided to close a rather open-ended ambition by limiting the collection to 1893-1973, the period of eighty years that I still consider to have been the heyday of the British toy soldier. By 1984, my collection had peaked in numbers at

Picture 12: My beautiful cabinets

Mary designed and had installed these wonderful display shelves for my collection in 1988. There are sixty shelves of various sizes in a double room, with sufficient cupboards for the original boxes. The photograph is taken at eye level, and each bank of shelves has twelve levels from floor to ceiling. The depth of them is just right to take an infantry set of eight or five cavalry in a single row, with sufficient headroom to take things in and out quite easily. To take a picture like this, the glass doors slide back.

Picture 13: An expert teaching reference cameo: Britains Doughboys

This rather battered crew of U.S. infantry doughboys, currently included in my U.S. section of the Boxer rebellion display (see Chapter 9) demonstrates putting together a reference cameo of individual figures around a theme and also the various conditions in which figures can be found. Len Richards was the original master collector of individual varieties of figure, and his passion was finding different castings and paint variations. Unless a better example fell into his lap, he was not too worried about upgrading his examples, and much of his collection was actually in Fair to Poor condition. I have used the same principle here with this cameo of Britains U.S. Infantry 1926 to 1941.

In the back row figures 1 and 2 are the original marching Doughboys in Good condition from set 227, first produced in 1926. Figure 3 is the second grade fixed arm equivalent (this figure has broken legs, but I have propped him up for the picture), and 4 is the second grade drummer boy, in Fair condition, for which there was no Best Quality equivalent. Figure 5 is a rare second grade U.S. Marine in khaki. Perhaps from the subject of the cameo, it should not be here, but it fits with the other second grade figures. There was no full dress U.S. Marine in full dress. Then come figures 6 to 8, which are the U.S. infantry officer figure. This casting was used both for the second grade (6 and 7, with different paint versions) and for the Best Quality (8). If you can see the missing paint from figure 8 in the picture, particularly from the scabbard, this means it is only in Good condition.

To the left of the picture are three infantry on guard. The first is the second grade doughboy on guard, which is quite common. The second is the same casting, much rarer in best quality paint, since it was not a standard part of set 1251, and so may be a special figure. This is a good example of a figure in Poor condition with its rifle broken off and missing, which is still well worth having to demonstrate a point. Similar, and also in Poor condition and without its bayonet, is the khaki painted U.S. Infantryman using the casting from the second version of set 91. This may well be a figure used in a Beiser playset, and so could on those grounds be excluded from this cameo, but I find that including it makes for a useful extra talking point. Note the moustache, used in set 91, but all other Britains U.S. troops were clean-shaven, even before 1938.

The standing firing figure in blue has been repainted, but is my only example of the normal standing casting in puttees for set 1251. The other standing firing figure, in Poor condition with very faded paint, is second grade, but a rare casting with the doughboy hat but in full trousers rather than in puttees. The kneeling figures are second grade firing in gaiters, second grade firing in puttees and Best Quality firing in gaiters. The lying figures are feet together second grade in gaiters, feet together Best Quality in puttees, and feet apart second grade in gaiters. Although the possibility remains that there is a version feet apart with gaiters, it may be that the conversion to puttees took place before such a version was ever issued. Equally, in view of the casting on show with full trousers, were there ever kneeling and lying castings with full trousers? Such is the intrigue of putting together this type of cameo.

approximately 65,000 figures, and from then on, although there were still many acquisitions, the outflow of troops exceeded the inflow to an increasing degree. Today, I have about 16,000 toy soldiers remaining after twenty-five years of reduction. These intervening years comprise about ten per cent of the whole history of commercial toy soldiers, and twenty per cent of the history of Britains.

After putting everything I could reasonably afford of time and treasure into amassing such a substantial collection, why did I change course? Partially, it was that I had in my mind achieved what I had set out to achieve. The limiting factor of cash resources had become more apparent as the market for toy soldier collecting drove prices up. I was only ever able to collect the really rare and now become valuable pieces that I had acquired because I had come across them before the most substantial rises in their market price. The nature of rare sets is that they don't appear often, and the market funnels them towards the highest bidders, thus making it easier for those with larger funds to take their pick. I had been most fortunate in collecting for the most part well before this era arrived, and I knew that I could not compete in this arena. Over the next few years there were just a handful of occasions when I took a deep breath and spent money. Otherwise, I held my fire.

One reason that I had continued collecting from boyhood into my adult life was that I come from a famous collecting family, where such behaviour was encouraged. My parent's collections of childhood, and my brother's of mass-market ephemera are on a much grander scale than mine. I had rather selfishly concentrated on the actual collecting of objects that gave me intense pleasure, without doing much with them. The death of my eminent father in 1982 was a huge shock, and a reminder that I had better put all the effort I had expended in collecting and learning about toy soldiers to good use, if I could, before it was too late. My first book was published in 1983.

Building on the research I had done during my collecting, I produced ten publications over the next ten years, before temporarily retiring from most writing. More importantly, in 1979 I was able to take on the cataloguing of the toy soldier auctions at Phillips. Since then I have written 133 catalogues (in the 31 years to the end of 2009), and worked not only at Phillips but also at Christies and Phillips' successors, Bonhams. During that time, I have looked closely at about two million toy soldiers during the process of presenting them in the most attractive way possible.

In 1986, I wrote of my experiences to date in *Collecting Toy Soldiers*, published by Collins. The present volume is by way of a follow-up to the previous book. I have tried to keep

Picture 14: Characters that novices can recognise

The teaching tour for non-toy soldier people includes many icons from popular and childrens culture. Here, Charlie Chaplin, Asterix, Tintin, Mickey Mouse from a series exclusive to McDonalds, Madonna in the film 'Dick Tracy' and Mr Bump. The first five are made of softish plastic in the same style as today's most popular toy soldier figures, while Mr Bump is in resin (I once did a publicity tour of Scotland wearing a very hot Mr Bump suit).

Picture 15: Mr Pickwick to Harry Potter

I would defy anyone not to recognize at least fifty of the media related figures on the novice tour, from Mr Pickwick to Harry Potter via the Beatles. Here, in the 'Literary' section (my regular daytime job was with a book club organization) Harry Potter, newly set on his pedestal as most popular book series for children, looks over at past bestsellers such as Frodo Baggins from The Lord of the Rings, Peter Rabbit as a 1910 Austrian bronze and Mr Pickwick, part of a hollowcast series made by Heyde. The tin that Harry is seated upon contained sweets, and I have not come across the figure sold separately.

Picture 16: The Beatles

These Subbuteo Beatles I bought in Pontings in Kensington High St at the time they were selling them from a stack of about 200 boxes. They were, as far as I know, the only official Beatles models in 54mm scale. Then there is an unrelated small set of a pop trio, maybe Gemodels or Culpitt, designed by George Musgrave, with a nice set of drums, the only one in these four groups. The second box of Beatles has pictures but no names, hence probably unlicenced - I got it at a collector's fair in Avignon, France not so very long ago - don't know the maker. The bagged set 'Beatlemania' probably also unlicenced has the logo 'emirober' on the header card. I got this in Seattle, Washington US about ten years ago in an antique market - again, never heard of the maker.

duplication to a minimum, and the pictures in this book are all new. They feature just 72 of the soldiers pictured in the previous book, and those of you who have the last volume can (or may not) pass some time working out which they are! During these twenty-five years, there have been many changes for toy soldier collectors. Perhaps the most important are the advent of many more shows, the increased ease of international travel, the continuous improvement in methods of production and the effect of the World Wide Web. Any of these changes would have been reason enough to produce a new book. Putting them all together has made it essential to update such a collecting book for today's circumstances.

However, there have also been personal changes for me that have added much to my experiences. Thanks to the beautiful cabinets that my wife Mary designed for me, my collection has made its way out of its storage boxes and onto open shelves. Obviously there are many basics that I have re-stated here, but what I wrote then was before I had my collection on display, and largely before I had whittled it down in size. I can honestly say that I have derived more pleasure and good memories from this process, in the second half of my collecting career, than I have from the sometimes frustrating, frantic and frenzied first half.

Handing on the story

Collecting by type, manufacturer, subject and catalogue number is a very left-brain activity. Every soldier can be fitted into a number of significant slots in the scheme of things. This is initially a very satisfying way to organise a collection, but it is not the whole story. Once everything I had was out on display, which the reduction in numbers allowed, all sorts of other possibilities opened up. It was immediately much easier to put figures into different contexts, to compare styles and influences over my chosen eighty-year period. To me, the most interesting theme of *Collecting Toy Soldiers* was cameo collecting, and since my whole collection was available to arrange, I have been able to put a large part of my cameo collecting theory into practice. The main theme of this book will be the telling of the toy soldier story through these cameos. My interests have widened, and I am now more aware than ever that not only are there still many discoveries to be made from the past, but that over the last twenty-five years, more designers than ever have been busy making beautiful figures for our enjoyment, both for children and adults.

I have two tours of my collection on offer to visitors whose interests I don't know well – there is the tour for toy soldier aficionados, which assumes all the basics and tries to entertain with unusual stories and an exploration of their particular interests, and there is the tour for the friend or neighbour which assumes no prior knowledge and endeavours to engage their interest through scenes from military history, the history of commerce and war in the twentieth century and various well known icons from everyday life.

The important part about all this is the ability to tell the stories, for it is in contextualising the objects and explaining them to others that the importance and entertainment value of them lies. Together with the visual satisfaction and the capacity to re-arrange and demonstrate things from different angles, the toy soldiers supply endless fascination. This is even without venturing into the realms of model making, painting, restoration, gaming, research, militaria or military history that can add so much to the pastime. My collection is now a teaching and appreciation device for visitors. I intend to demonstrate in this book that you can do the same with whatever you have, in quantity or quality, to multiply the pleasure of the toy soldiers for yourself and bring that pleasure to everyone you meet.

CHAPTER 1
THE LURE OF TOY SOLDIERS

A little philosophy up front

Let me start with a truism. My collection of toy soldiers is the greatest in the world. But then for you, so is yours. Mine will remain so until the day, hopefully not too soon, when I cannot take even the last one with me to whatever happens next. Nor would I wish to, but there is the possibility that the happy memories of all of them will make it through to the afterlife, and that will be more than enough, especially if the little artefacts that have brought me so much pleasure and instruction in this life go on to do the same for others.

The WOW! factor

Given that toy soldiers have produced a WOW! response in me from an early age, I have tried to apply this in my collecting ever since. Certain figures, groups, sets or boxes tend to get a WOW! reaction when they are shown to others, even knowledgeable people, and this gives one of the most satisfying feelings known to the collector. If one wanted to provide this response as an acronym, it would go like this:

- **W**onderful
- **O**ut of the ordinary
- **W**ish I had that in my collection

Wonderful includes both the idea of visually exciting and the ideas of rare and valuable. Out of the ordinary discards everything common, overhyped or badly designed. Wishfulness is simply the aspirational aspect of the collecting urge that motivates us all. Which will shortly bring me on to money matters.

The one emotion that has to be guarded against is envy. To admire what people with greater resources than oneself have achieved is good. To join with them in appreciating their finds and add one's own knowledge to theirs is a great deal more satisfying than regretting that one could not have all the toy soldiers in the world. The objective should be to make the most of what one has, and reflect that good use of that (including disposals) provides all the justification for collecting that one could want.

Chasing the WOW! factor is no bad principle in collecting, so I do not hesitate to apply this charismatic description to toy soldiers on a scale of 0 (relatively boring) to 10 (almost unattainably WOW!). A collection based on WOW! would be regarded as iconic (see page 86), and would only need ordinary toy soldiers as a foil for the WOW! items.

The whole point of cameo collecting is to elevate low WOW! factor figures to a higher level of interest through pointing out what is WOW! about them, which can be done by harmonious grouping, telling a story or making a reference group unusually complete. Sometimes sheer scale can do the trick, such as presenting 1,200 Royal Welch Fusiliers in a single column. WOW! factor of a single figure 0, WOW! factor of all 1,200 maybe 5, enhanced to 8 or 9 when you point out the Germanic plug-handed set at one end and the Britains special paint fife and drum band at the other.

Picture 17: Early German and French made British fusiliers

The back row and the two larger figures are all German made, mostly hollowcast, while the rest in front, with one exception, are all CBG Mignot. Hidden in the back row are two of the first Britains figures, which shows how very German looking they were. These are the two third and fourth from the right. The firing figures in red greatcoats with green bases are rare early CBG Mignot. These are the bodies of French infantry with a British head, and the coats are painted in red when in real life they would have been grey. CBG Mignot had these same figures available without greatcoats as can be seen from the standing figure furthest on the left. The marching figure front right on the green base is a German made figure, to my mind looking rather better than the beige based later CBG Mignot marching figures next to it. Left back are some German firing figures which seem to have very small heads in relation to their bodies. The CBG final figure on the left, without a pack, is slightly better proportioned. Telling which of the German made figures come from which manufacturer is one of the most difficult identification problems in toy soldiers, here one might consider Heyde, Heinrich and Noris as the best candidates to have made some of these. Dr Hans Henning Roer, one of the top German experts, has written two books well worth reading on these and others. This group introduces my regiment of Royal Welch Fusiliers, and usually gets a good WOW! response, even though many of them are not in the best of condition.

Rather than going into the intricacies of my rarity rating system, developed for reference listings of Britains, I will give you my personal WOW! factors for various things throughout this book, and relate them to values in chapter 12. It should be remembered that WOW!

Picture 18: Box for Jones toy soldiers

Story book toys for girls and boys, as a toy, educational, a museum exhibit, instruction in tactics, a collector's hobby. The box says it all!

factor is highly subjective, even if there is general agreement amongst knowledgeable collectors as to which figures to gasp at the most.

Should you be intrigued by rarity rating, this is developed in my book *Opie's Pocket Price Guide to Britains Hollowcast Toy Soldiers*, and in the appendix listing to *The Great Book of Britains*.

Why begin collecting?

If you, dear reader, already possess toy soldiers, how did you start to collect them? If you do not, what reason might tempt you? A wise manufacturer, Jones in the United States, illustrated five different reasons on the front of one of his toy soldier boxes (see opposite), but the foremost is often nostalgia.

On nostalgia and other pleasant motives

As a young child, you might have been given some toy soldiers, as they are a traditional and ever present toy. Many years after the demise first of the old metal toy soldier for children and then the fully painted plastic ones in the same traditional 54mm size (see Scale, below) which for a decade supplanted them, they still continue to be on the market. Bully, Schleich and Simba from Germany, Papo and Plastoy from France have marketed extensive ranges of fully painted plastic historical and fantasy play figures of a very high quality (recently all made in China, naturally). Interestingly, the 80mm scale is similar to that of the 3¾ inch poseable action figures now routinely produced for any big screen adventure, starting with

Picture 19: Schleich, Simba, Papo, Plastoy, Revell

Over the last ten years, firms specializing in flexible plastic comic character figures such as Asterix, Tintin and the Smurfs have branched out into historical and fantasy figures. These have evolved into ever more elaborate creations, and are now nearly as good as adult models. Some chart unusual territory such as the Plastoy Inca (or is it an Aztec) and Samurai, others are slightly surreal, such as the excellent model of King Henry V right back, released under the Revell brand as 'Axel Hitman'. Darth Vader, a Star Wars action figure, is included for size comparison.

Star Wars. For collectors, series of ever more realistic toy soldier-like figures in nearer to 54mm scale continue to be issued, including, for instance, a breathtakingly beautiful 60mm scale set of Spartans and Persians from Conte to go with the film *300*.

The most pleasant way to start down this route is never to have stopped collecting from an early age. I count myself particularly lucky in having done this, as when I ask around among other collectors, the number of people who did not discard their toys around puberty seems fairly small. Others were able to store their toys for a time, and use them as the nucleus of a collection when taking up the adult pastime later. Many, however, needed to start again from scratch. At any event, nostalgia from a childhood involved with toy soldiers has perhaps been the key motive to enjoying collecting as an adult. It certainly has been for me.

Other additional sources of enjoyment in collecting toy soldiers include collecting personal souvenirs of people and places. Figures can be icons of family genealogy, such as my great-grandfather who was chaplain to the Gordon Highlanders before the First World War, and my grandmother who spent her childhood on an *estancia* in the Argentine. During the First World War, one of my grandfathers met my grandmother in Alexandria, my other grandfather was also there before starting his career in the Sudan, and my wife was born there, so Egyptian figures have a special resonance for me. My parents both served in the Second World War, and I was born during it.

Picture 20: Gauchos

These Gauchos, made by Industria Argentina, symbolize my grandmother's early childhood spent on her father's estancia on the pampas. Industria Argentina were a maker largely given to copying Britains, but these hollowcast figures are highly original and very nicely made. Kettle, stand, campfire, sausages on grill and side of meat are all separate individual pieces, and part of a much larger range of Gaucho figures and accessories. They are difficult to find in the UK, and apart from their personal WOW! for me seem also to do it for other people.

Other figures can be iconic in portraying military history, either in artistic but unrealistic toys or in today's beautiful collector models. The unashamed charm of form and paint style among various eras of toys is a great source of pleasure, comprising a naïve art not seen elsewhere. The story of the cut and thrust among manufacturers to seize pocket and present money from their young customers has its own intrigue, and setting out to complete a collection that very few children could have managed is a fascinating discipline.

At what stage is your collecting? Starter collector, specialist collector, satisfied collector

The best way to start

Get stuck in. I started when my grandmother gave me toy soldiers to play with at an early age. Many others started that way. Some gave up their soldiers at the end of their childhood, and returned to them later. Others, like me, never stopped. If you want to start, grab a bunch of what you like the look of (see Chapter 3) and get as many as you can reasonably handle, both from the point of view of room and resources. Congratulations, you are a collector. Easy, huh?

This is 'magpie collecting'. Collect the things that attract your eye, that are icons for you. Play with them, mostly by arranging them and re-arranging them in artistic displays. See what your friends think of them. Find out as much as you can about what you have acquired. My magpie collection was that which I had when I was a boy (see picture 6)

Becoming knowledgeable

Once you can start demonstrating your knowledge of your collection, you are beginning to add value to what you have. It is usual at this stage to start discovering favourite models, sets and manufacturers, and to feel the urge to 'fill out the line' and make complete collections of specific and difficult to find subjects. You are now a specialist collector, and setting your collecting ambitions for however long you stay with it. I set out to collect examples of the whole output of all British toy soldier manufacturers for the period 1893 to 1973. It took me twenty-five years to define this ambition, and another fifteen years to complete a collection I was satisfied with.

How large does a collection become?

At its height, my collection contained 65,000 pieces. By any standards this was fairly large, but I have known several larger ones. Quality is, after all, just as important as quantity. A gentleman in California was proud to advertise that he had 250,000 toy soldiers, and had made most of them himself, rather than collecting them. By contrast, a collection that concentrated on

Picture 21: Icons of 1893 and 1973

Of course I chose 1893 as the start date for my collection because that was when Britains started to manufacture toy soldiers. The icon for 1893 is straightforwardly one of Britains first Life Guard figures. Britains themselves did not for a number of decades worry unduly about their history, which is par for the course for any commercial firm whose first concern is earning profits this year and next. From time to time Dennis Britain would brandish an 1897 second version Life Guard as being Britains first model, but in fact this one is four years earlier, in all probability from a bought in German design. 1973 was the year when Britains and a number of the first manufacturers of New Toy Soldiers brought out their first new style figures, as well as being the date when I finally gave up on trying to keep up with the marketing of toy soldiers in several sizes of box for each series.

figures worth over £100 each would be able to concentrate a great deal of worth in a small space. From my experience, the collector who wishes to use a fair sized room to display a good collection of toy soldiers will end up with around 16,000 figures, which is where I have arrived. That would generally be considered a large collection, as would anything over 5,000 pieces.

Setting out to collect the hundred most attractive sets of Britains toy soldiers, for instance, where a standard set is five cavalry or eight to ten infantry, a collecting plan might be formed which involved no more than a thousand figures in a hundred original boxes. By representing the cream of available rarities, however, within that total there might be approaching £100,000 in value. By contrast, it would be perfectly possible to form a wide-ranging collection of a thousand individual pieces, each with its own story, for under £5,000. Collected without original boxes, this collection would fit into a medium size glass fronted bookcase, or could even be packed in a dozen shoe boxes. This would be seen as a modest collection.

Individual cameo collections assembled round individual topics normally amount from just a few figures up to two or three hundred. Anything larger than that would be seen as a themed collection in its own right. A collection of 10,000 figures would contain the possibility of hundreds of cameos, with the figures being capable of re-arranged in many different ways to illustrate different points of interest.

Famous collections from the last thirty years have been varied in size:

- Peter Cushing, who sold his collections at Phillips in 1969 and 1996, had 5,500 figures.
- Douglas Fairbanks Jr's collection, sold at Phillips in 1977, contained 2,500 soldiers.
- Henry Harris had a plan to collect 5,000 figures.
- H L Pottier-Smith's collection was 9,000, including 241 Courtenays and many Britains specials.
- Len Richards' famous reference collection comprised 17,000 soldiers.
- John Hanington had 24,000 figures, including 934 Lucottes.
- Burtt Erhlich sold his iconic collection in an auction of 6,000 pieces.
- Kemble Widmer's spectacular display collection showed about 16,000 figures.
- The Ruby family reference collection of Britains was around 12,000 strong.
- Arnold Rolak's icon collection of Britains amounted to just 3,400 figures, but was worth over £200,000.
- Malcolm Forbes collection in the Palais Mendoub, when auctioned, was 43,500 figures and sold for almost $700,000 in 1997.
- The Loraque collection of Spanish history was 12,000 figures.
- William C McDade's reference collection of Britains was about 5,000.
- Terry Hanly had a Britains style display collection of 16,000 pieces.
- Barry Blood has accumulated 60,000 individually different figures made in plastic from around the world.
- Brian Hornick's display collection was in excess of 100,000 pieces.

It is said that in the United Kingdom, one in three people collect things, and when talking about this I sometimes get the answer, 'that few?!' One has only to look on eBay or watch afternoon television to have an idea of how strong is the collecting motive. Sometimes the passion seems overwhelming and the desire all-consuming. There may be an element of 'I can do that' and 'I can do that better than you' in here. Collecting is, after all, only a matter of looking, selecting and purchasing. A good balance between collecting and everything else

that is going on in life would seem to be essential. What a collection does is to provide a personal possession that is safe to use according to one's needs. It is unique to the collector, reflects the best of his intellect and personality, providing entertainment and satisfaction for him and his friends.

Collecting toy soldiers is satisfying from a number of points of view. The history of the toy soldier is reasonably well understood, but there are plenty of areas still in need of research. The figures tie in to historical occasions and places, evoking heroic deeds and personalities. Collections can be assembled virtually ready-made or picked up piece by piece. They can cost from as little as a pound apiece to as much as fortune and space will permit. There are enough fascinating minutiae to investigate and acquire to enable each individual collection to explore a different direction. There are also numerous allied activities, which we will touch on in later chapters.

The satisfied collector

Some collectors decide they have had enough, and dispose of their collections. Some do this from force of individual circumstance, some because they have become bored with the subject. Numerous collectors I know have been through this cycle, and it seems to be quite normal for people who have written books or achieved collecting ambitions to release their collections back into the market place. A well produced auction catalogue, for instance, makes a very satisfying souvenir of a collecting career.

For my own part, having written several books on toy soldiers twenty years ago, I was able to tell myself that I had gone beyond parts of my collection, and indeed needed new specialities to conquer. My circumstances were such that releasing a large part of my collection made a great deal of sense, and the 'been there done that' stories were almost as good as the 'look what I've got' stories. I carefully chose to keep a few things to demonstrate each aspect of toy soldier collecting, which I am now sharing with you. The fact that this still amounts to 16,000 figures bears testimony to the huge diversity of it.

Picture 22: Reynolds historical figures

This is a small cameo group I am particularly satisfied with, the Romans and Vikings from Reynolds, also known as H.R.Products. The five different Vikings were available as a boxed set, and I have an original box (which was just a red box with an end label) and also an original individual box for Guthrum, the main Danish opponent of Alfred the Great, and one of the Roman figures. Designed by Norman Tooth, although these figures are not the world's most animated figures, they sit together beautifully as a group, and are also comparatively rare. WOW! factor 7.

Some introductory thoughts on toy and figure design

Toy Soldiers and Model Soldiers

- Soldier: member of an army.
- Toy: plaything, especially for children.
- Toy Soldier: A representation of a soldier for a child to play with.

The operative word here is play. Toy soldiers are meant to be manipulated through imagined scenarios by young minds getting to grips with this rather grim side of being human. Just as miniature figurines seem to have been a part of every society yet formed by humans, so playing at war has also. Much of the energy expended by the boy Winston Churchill in manoeuvring toy soldiers might well be the equivalent today of playing a shoot 'em up computer game. The characters in those games, therefore, should perhaps be counted as toy soldiers.

Model soldiers are attempting to re-create in miniature the actual appearance of the military through history, and their chief attribute is realism, or the artistic portrayal of realism. Boys may well become interested in models at quite a young age, but models are essentially created or collected and then admired and used to illustrate historical points of interest rather than to be played with.

Realism

Since the first iconic figurines of Neolithic times, the degree of realism in models has been to the taste and ability of the designer. The ability in sculpting to enhance specific detail has enabled aspects of uniforms or facial expression to stand out in models, or on the other hand to be simplified to give a better effect *en masse*. Toys generally tend towards simplification, in which lies much of their charm. The naïve art of the traditional late nineteenth century toy soldier is as if they were miniatures of the boys who dressed in play uniforms at the time, and thus about as far removed from real war and ferocity as it is possible to be. Instead, they were a spectacle of delight to the eye, formed up in their splendid uniforms, the epitome of a grand theatrical production.

A question I sometimes ask is whether, had the techniques of the time allowed, toy soldier manufacturers would have tried to make their figures more realistic than they did. I suspect that they would have, as the larger and more expensive products tended towards realism, even if they retained and intensified their antique toy soldierly qualities at the same time. It must also be recalled that flat, semi-flat and paper soldiers from the same period, where realism and fluidity was much easier to depict, had those qualities in plenty. In the period 1893 to 1973 that was the heyday of the toy soldier, few fully round solid or hollowcast toys were totally realistic. They had certain conventions of presentation that are similar in principle to the conventions that governed christian art from the end of the Roman Empire to the Renaissance. Within the conventions, as in medieval art, there has been room for a wide and charming range of delightful differences in style from the various manufacturers.

The more widespread advent of adults collecting toy soldiers over the last fifty years has blurred the boundaries between models and toys. Britains and other toy soldier makers had always been aware that there was an adult collector market. In earlier times, the accuracy of uniforms and intricacy of the figure was of great interest for adults purchasing for their young friends or relatives, and thus formed a major part of the sales appeal. As the toy soldier evolved, hollowcast and painted plastic figures in 54mm scale were left behind. The first modellers of military figures often used these toy soldiers as the basis of their creations, but as more

and more dedicated model figures came on the market from the 1950s onwards, the so-called 'conversion' of toy soldiers into models became less necessary. The term remained in use for collectors who 'converted' toys into positions, ranks or regiments different from those originally issued by the manufacturer, rather than making them into models.

Picture 23: Marlborough

The contrast between the Cherilea toy character figure of the Duke of Marlborough and the Del Prado cavalry troopers could not be greater, yet curiously they go together. Notice the medieval sword with which Marlborough has been provided. In this picture I have tried to disguise the fact that the Duke's horse is missing a leg by propping him up against one of the troopers. The Marlborough figure is rare (WOW factor 8 in good condition) and I have never been able to afford a complete one.

Collector's Toy Soldiers

Since 1973, vast ranges of toy soldier like figures have been produced by many hundreds of different makers specifically to cater for the mature collector of toy soldiers. As techniques of production have improved, allowing ever more intricate production of designs, with breakeven points for profit arriving at lower and lower runs for each design, so a trend towards additional realism has emerged. Perhaps the most telling divide between Toy style and Model style today is the style of paintwork. Toys, using the conventions of Toy Soldiers from their heyday, are painted stylistically in bright gloss colours, so there is no mistaking them for realistic models. The same design, however,

Picture 24: New Toy soldiers for collectors: Highlanders

A selection of toy style New Toy Soldiers. Front left, Canadian and Dunedin Highlanders from the Nostalgia series, back left, British Bulldog, front centre, Britains Royal Scots piper, unknown casting at ease in the Britains style, Fusilier Miniatures Gordon drummer at attention, centre back, Sarum Soldiers highland dancers, Black Watch with wounded comrade, Seaforth and girlfriend, Black Watch officer, back right, Imperial Productions colonial and Dunedin Highlanders.

can often be painted meticulously in matt and metallic colours to give a completely realistic model-like impression. This is more a matter of a collector's personal taste. Although the model style tends to cost more to create, prices for good looking models or toys today are not dissimilar. Decades ago, finished models used to cost many times more than toys, but this is no longer true, as the price of painting models in China, in particular, has reduced amazingly. I myself would not mix the two styles, but as the toy soldier style is usually used for re-creating ceremonial pageantry, while the models appeal more to historical battle scene re-enactment in miniature, they both have many followers.

Picture 25: Britains Museum Collection: Black Watch

Typical of the best of today's ready to display models are these historical figures of the Black Watch, that form part of a series currently of ten showing a history of the regiment's changing uniforms since the regiment was first formed in 1739. Left to right: 10003 French and Indian War, 1758, 10001 Crimean War 1854, 10009 Piper c.1910, 10013 Piper, Battle of El Alamein 1942 and 10014 Iraq 2006. Made and painted in China, they cost £24.99 each, which is relatively considerably less than comparable finished models were costing in the 1960s.

Scale

Scale is measured from the soles of the feet of a standing figure to the crown of the head. Because of the thickness of bases and the height of headgear, which should not be taken into account, the only true way to ascertain the scale of a figure is to measure it for yourself. Even the stated scales of manufacturers can be misleading.

The largest reasonably practical scale for toy soldiers is the 100mm (4 inch) figure. The major exception to this is obviously G I Joe, or Action Man as he was known in the UK. This very popular toy was 12 inches tall (300mm) ⅙ of real life. Today, the G I Joe trade mark is only available as a 3¾ inch scale figure, confirming that the smaller scale is a more convenient one for combat play, but attempts to re-introduce larger scale figures continue. The smallest scale for toy soldiers as children's playthings is 20mm, but of course in recent times these have not been recommended for children likely to swallow them. Most of the scales from 28mm or smaller are commonly only used for wargaming rather than as toys.

Picture 26: Scale, in two rows

A colourful double row of toy soldiers shows the many scales in which they have been made, from the 110mm scale Heyde size 0 firing British infantryman at the left of the back row to the 2mm figures being played with around the fort by the boys at his feet. At the right of the rows are the 54mm infantrymen that are Britains standard scale, best quality at the back, and second grade at the front.

Picture 27: Britains CBG scale I

Some scales of the most popular makers in England (Britains) and France (CBG Mignot). Left to right: Britains HH size, officially 83mm, Highlander shown is 80mm, CBG 4me grandeur, officially 75mm, infanterie a grande tenue shown (which is the only figure in this size I have) is 68mm, Britains H size, officially 70mm, infantry of the line shown is 68mm, Britains standard size is 54mm, as shown by the Norfolk Regiment example, CBG 3me grandeur, officially 55mm, supposedly slightly taller than Britains, actually these, a French Navy bugler and British Napoleonic era officer, turn out to be no more than 51mm, Britains W size, officially 45mm, is actually 43mm and finally, Britains first version small size is 41mm.

The most popular scale for toy soldiers has tended to be around 54mm, correlating to ¹/₃₂ of real life, and gauge 1 model trains. As this was the most popular scale for model railways in the late 19th century, this could have had an influence on both Britains and CBG Mignot, both of whom produced most prolifically in about this size.

The terms ¹/₃₂ and 54mm are sometimes rather loosely used to cover models which are strictly speaking anything from 51 to 62mm tall, but given the normal differences in height of personnel, as long as the design style is compatible, this need not be a problem.

Picture 28: Bowmen

A selection of toy and model medieval bowmen, mostly made of plastic. Left to right, figure one is a Britains Swoppet Wars of the Roses series crossbowman, with figure nine a longbowman from the same series. Figure four shows how it looks when the top of the crossbowman is placed on the legs of the longbowman. Figure two is an original Cherilea crossbowman from their Robin Hood series, with another repainted in a more model style behind him. Figure five is a Hinton Hunt model crossbowman from the late 1950s that I painted myself. Figures six and eight are de Agostini model style figures in metal. Figure ten is a late series Britains Herald figure made in Hong Kong. Figure eleven is a hollowcast Cherilea longbowman from 1952. Figures twelve and thirteen are repainted by me from Swoppet and Crescent longbowmen, and figure fourteen is a New Toy Soldier style bowman from Alymer. Although including such a diversity of styles, with scales varying between 48mm and 58mm, I myself find the grouping taken as a whole looks satisfactory. Compare it with other groups that are more obviously compatible, such as my Turkish detachment in picture 146. For a grouping of toy soldiers that are definitely not compatible, see picture 204.

Static and animated modelling

The archetypical toy soldier is usually portrayed in a drill position, such as marching or at attention. This portrays his position as part of an army, one of the characteristics of which is the management of men in a mass, which before the modern age often gave tactical advantages. More recent weaponry has given advantage to wider spread formations on the battlefield, thus leading to a more animated pose being suitable for models. This has been a dichotomy long evident in toy soldier design, more recently emphasised as the ability to produce wildly animated models has been eased by advances in technology. Peter Cole, in his second edition of *Suspended Animation*, contends that Britains led the way in drill styled toy soldiers merely for reasons of ease in production. This would ignore the amazing fluidity of much flat and paper soldier design from the nineteenth century, where there was always room for both the massed battalions of infantry and the much more active look of individual officers and cavalry. There were also a number of exceptions from Britains themselves.

Tradition in military history allows both for the individual hero, from Achilles or Alexander in ancient times to today's SAS trooper, and for the proud regiments that show their mastery in their ability to manoeuvre as one man on parade. In the 21st century, there has been a tendency to offer either individual figures that don't look all that good in massed groups, or more stylised sets in time-honoured toy soldier poses that don't look too wonderful individually. Perhaps there is a place for splendid individual figures that look

12

Picture 29: Animation – running figures

The tradition evolved in flat and semi-flat figures for animation and movement was somewhat lost in the period 1890 to 1930, when the majority of stylized toy soldiers were marching on parade, and could be accused of being stiff and unrealistic. However even with solid and hollowcast models, animation was never lost. Heyde and CBG Mignot had many cunning animations in their ranges, and when composition and French hollowcast figures became popular in the 1920s there was an outburst of fluid or even wild design. Here is a small selection to ponder, right to left Britains charging Highlander, 1903, Elastolin British Infantry First World War, 1923, Britains second grade charging Highlander, 1916, Britains charging British infantry in gas mask, 1938, Authenticast solid-cast French Chasseur a pied on guard, 1946 and Cherilea plastic first series combat infantry infantry in a swirled basic colour to simulate camouflage cloth, 1955

great in hundreds. Every now and again, these have emerged from manufacturers and often become the most popular of all models. Let's have more.

There is also a place for the more fluid hero figures of officer or standard-bearer to be portrayed in a more exciting pose while fitting in alongside traditional toy soldiers.

Pictures 30 and 31: Hastings

One of the nice things about well-animated figures is that they look good from different angles. I am particularly fond of this Hastings duel from the early plastic Elastolin series in hard Polystyrene. Hausser had pioneered well-animated figures in composition, and were able to do even better with the crisper finish achievable with the new material. Together with a great paint job, they look more like models than toys, and justified their premium price.

13

Picture 32: Britains French Foreign Legion with Deetail officer

One of the more nicely animated figures among the Britains hollowcasts was the charging French Foreign Legionnaire, a casting from the Paris factory that hadn't been used in the London range until 1954. Was it issued then under the influence of the new all action plastic figures? Anyway, it has always been one of my favourites, and later Britains brought out the perfect officer to go with it as part of the Deetail range. He works with Zouaves too.

Articulation and separate weapons

Dolls have generally been articulated since the earliest times. Traditionally, toy soldiers have not, but the articulation of arms was often introduced as an additional play feature. Artist's mannequins are traditionally articulated at the neck, shoulders, elbows, wrists, waist, hips, knees and ankles. Separate weapons have featured quite often in the evolution of the toy soldier, but much more so in the era of plastic and action figures.

In 1956, the 54mm scale Swoppet was patented by Britains, which included articulation at the waist and neck, with weapons that fitted in the hands, and this can be seen as the forerunner to the current 95mm media action figures which started with Micromen and became successful with the *Star Wars* franchise. G I Joe was first issued in 1964, and was essentially a doll for boys. As such, he was as completely articulated as an artist's mannequin. Action figures on the other hand have tended to be articulated at the neck, shoulders and hips only. The recent Conte models for the film *300* come with quite a high degree of articulation, with movable heads, arms and wrists.

There is a case for saying that highly articulated figures are actually small dolls, and derive their play value principally from this feature. Certainly, the tendency in playing with these is to use them to interact in relatively small groups. Toy soldiers, on the other hand, can be moved quickly around the play area in large numbers already in realistic poses, and so are easier for bigger wargames, as well as looking better on the shelves. A wise collector, Howard White, once said that 'all toys are extensions of children's limbs, but toy soldiers are extensions of their minds'.

Picture 33: Articulation – Star Wars

Compare the rather stilted appearance of the Star Wars so called 'Action' figures back right with the well animated poses of the metal A New Hope series in the front and the slightly larger plastic figures left back. Even the fully animated artists manikin at the back is unable to replicate the action in the smaller models. The action figures are just little dolls with little movement to them, no better than Lego or Playmobil. It is only when reaching the size of the original G.I Joe that properly articulated figures are easily possible.

CHAPTER 2
FROM FIGURINE TO TOY SOLDIER

How toy soldiers have evolved

Pre-history

Although collecting toy soldiers is seen today as just a fun hobby, small figures have played a long and distinguished part in the development of human culture. It seems to be a basic aspect of our awareness to try to understand and control the world through reproducing it on a smaller scale. Miniature figures have featured in every society known to archaeology. Simply walking through the British Museum brings

Picture 34: Maltese figurines

The Maltese figures from which these are reproduced date back to about 2,500 B.C. It is conjectured that they represent tribal leaders, and that plug in heads were used to show a likeness, replaced on succession. This would pre-date the popular method of plugging different heads into toy soldiers by nearly 4,500 years! In the centre is a model of a figure from the terracotta army of the Chinese emperor Qin Shi Huang (died 210 B.C.). These figures were originally made life size.

at every turn the discovery of objects that would not look out of place on the shelves of the toy soldier collector.

They were made from stone or pottery or probably other less durable materials, for all sorts of reasons. Some of these reasons may remain hidden to us, but using small models as icons of gods was probably the most popular. Others we know about include providing hoped-for realities in the after life, and most certainly also as playthings. All in all, as some of these figurines have survived from up to 100,000 years ago, they represent the earliest surviving evidence of our artistic activity. Toy soldiers are part of an ancient record of humanity!

Before the industrial revolution

In ancient and medieval times the uses of figurines for votive, iconic, instructional and recreational purposes continued. Before methods of

Picture 35: Crucifix

Probably the most instantly recognizable figurine in the world, shown here with a model of the virgin Mary.

mass production became available they had, perforce, to be made by individual craftsmen. Naturally, this meant that they could be commissioned only by the relatively better off, but lead figures that have the feel of toys have been found throughout the Roman world. This never prevented people from making their own representations whenever they felt the inclination.

In medieval times, jointed instructional toys to do with fighting on horseback helped the young nobility to learn about the essential skills of their heritage. When ruling included the need to be able to lead armies and understand tactics, young princes were taught with the aid of toy figures, as is well documented for the French royal family in the seventeenth and eighteenth centuries. Jewellers and metalworking craftsmen in particular were well able to supply the demand from the aristocracy for the toys felt to be suitable for their boys, and provided many miniatures that were fine enough to decorate tables or shelves besides.

Picture 36: Wooden soldier

This typical early nineteenth century 80mm scale wooden toy soldier was found recently behind the paneling underneath a window in a regency house in Cheltenham. Courtesy Bonhams

The advent of the toy soldier trade

The first signs of the making of toy soldiers for speculative sale, rather than to commission, emerged in the late sixteenth century in Germany. Although held back for decades by the Thirty Years War, by the early eighteenth century the manufacture of flat figures for distribution throughout

Europe was well established. These are also often called tin soldiers, after the metal from which they are made.

Flat figures (flats for short) are so called as they are virtually two dimensional, usually less than two millimetres thick from front to back. In terms of scale, they might be almost any size, but early figures were often quite large, up to 160mm. The constraints of materials and transportation meant that sizes were usually smaller than this. The figure shows the soldier from the front, and when it is turned round, the view from behind is seen. Essentially there are thus two complementary pictures of the subject, fitted to the same outline. Flat figures were made by engraving each side of the figure and flow channels into flat slates, fitting the two sides together and pouring a tin and lead mixture through the mould, which would also incorporate a base on which the figure would stand.

Picture 37: Flat Romans

The charm and artistry of the flat figure are simply shown here by these Roman soldiers. Flats look good in masses, as with these eight legionaries marching, which when looked at closely are actually in three different positions. The slingers at the back demonstrate the front and back view of the figures, which are normally double sided. The barbarians to the right and their opponents show all the animation of today's models or plastic figures. With the exception of the two foremost figures with the green bases, which may well have been repainted, these are in a typical manufacturers painted finish of about 1870. They are quite fragile, as can be seen by the missing pilum heads and sword.

These figures largely formed the basis of the first trade in toy soldiers, as they were cheap to make, and the expertise of design in two dimensions was akin to drawing rather than sculpture. Designs rapidly became intricate and attractive, and distribution of the figures was as both unpainted and painted, perhaps using very willing child labour for the colouring in much the same way as for contemporary prints. The flat figure was developed in the eighteenth century by the Hilpert family, and continued through the endeavours of such as Besold, Ammon, Heinrichsen and Allgeyer among many others. A 'standard scale' of 27mm for flats was agreed in the nineteenth century, and most flat figures by far are in scales between 27mm and 30mm. These figures continue to be manufactured and collected today, in ever improving intricacy of design, with most recent editions being in 30mm scale.

At the same time as flat figures were establishing their popularity, as is the way of the world, competitive products established themselves both cheaper and more expensively alongside the flats. If an ounce of unpainted tin soldiers did not cost very much, an unpainted sheet of paper soldiers cost even less. Strasbourg in northern France was the birthplace of the trade in sheets of beautifully drawn paper soldiers that could be coloured and mounted on card or wood. A little later, the Pellerin family made the town of Epinal synonymous with paper

Picture 38: Haffner semi-flat vignettes
A close-up of some of the figures and vignettes from the frontispiece picture brings out the quality of them. Courtesy Bonhams

soldiers. As with the flat figures, reverse views of the soldiers were often included in the sheets. Once lithographic colour printing was established in the 1830s, sheets could be sold colour printed, which made them even more attractive. Some soldiers made of plaster also appeared, notably those distributed by Giroux in France.

The progression of the commercial metal toy soldier from flat to semi-flat and finally to fully round figure is not well documented. Various larger lead soldiers appeared occasionally in the eighteenth century, but the general distribution of them had to wait until the better marketing and production methods of the later nineteenth century. These new styles were easier for children to play with. Top quality semi-flat figures such as those by Haffner, had a decade or so of popularity around the time of the Franco-Prussian war (1870-71), the most widespread scales being 40mm to 50mm (see

Picture 39: Heyde Knight
Larger scale Heyde figures are much sought after. This rather fanciful knight makes a splendid icon. The provision of a shield in much the same shape as that of a Roman legionary gives it a slightly unreal look.

19

Picture 40: CBG Mignot solid cast Highlanders

These splendid Highlanders are not totally in the correct uniforms, as the cuffs are green rather than yellow, as they should be if they are Argylls, which might be inferred from the tartan of the kilt. No highland regiment had green cuffs. The Black Watch had dark blue collars, these are painted light blue. Also, the sporran is painted as it should be for the Camerons. The Lucotte First World War Highlanders are shown far left, and a CBG Mignot Highlander in khaki is far right. All the CBG Mignot Highlanders in the picture, officer, bugler, colour bearer, advancing and marching, some with the rifle on the right shoulder, are exactly the same basic figure. The arms are bent according to the position needed, and then the appropriate weapon or colour is soldered to the hands. Although this saves on design work, it is actually rather labour intensive.

frontispiece). Toy soldier manufacture in Germany probably received a boost from this war, with a feel good factor from a relatively short victorious campaign. The firm of Heyde, which started in 1872, was to dominate the German manufacture of the fully round models that were the next development in commercial production. The cut and thrust of bringing out new models, scales, styles and novelties must have been just as intense at this time as later on. The main role of semi-flat figure design gradually lapsed into the production of home casting moulds, and by 1910 very few top quality figures were being made.

Towards the end of the nineteenth century, solid lead alloy toy soldiers from 20mm scale up to 100mm dominated the upmarket end of the toy soldier market, with the most popular scale being No.2 size, or 48mm. Germany had by far the largest export trade to Britain and the United States, the leading exporters being Heyde, and Heinrich. The Germans manufactured solids in various scales, while in France CBG Mignot (including Lucotte), without exporting a great deal, was making most of its output officially in 55mm (actually in 51mm) scale.

The Britains revolution – 1893-1899

At this point, in 1893, the family firm of William Britain and Sons entered the toy soldier market based in London, taking advantage of a number of innovations in manufacture and distribution. Experimenting with moulds designed in Germany, but rapidly moving forward with William Britain Junior doing the design work, the Britains produced the first range of toy soldiers using the hollowcasting method. One major innovation was to do away with all the additional parts that needed to be soldered onto the solid figures produced by their competitors, although movable arms for some figures gave additional play value. The range was kept small and concentrated on high volume, well presented boxed sets at half the price of imported solid cast figures of a comparable size. Distribution was through the well developed

British toy wholesale trade and individual major department stores such as Gamages, which soon devoted a whole department to the new product. Over the course of a few years of aggressive marketing, the foreign competition in Britain was mostly eliminated. In Germany, Scandinavia and Spain, particularly, the traditional solid cast figure from Heyde and native manufacturers persisted until the Second World War and, in some instances, beyond.

Picture 41: Britains early sets: Turks

It is not at all clear why Britains made Turkish Cavalry as early as 1897. It was their first foreign, as opposed to British Empire, set. The infantry set was only created to join the cavalry in 1912, after war had broken out between Turkey and Italy. These were the only sets Britains made of the Turks, and the opposition to them in a series of wars 1911 to 1913 included Italians, Bulgarians, Serbians, Greeks and Montenegrins, all of which were represented in the Britains list. No wonder I decided to add other Turks to the badly outnumbered Britains sets. One feature of the dated version of the Turkish infantry is the officer, who only appeared with this set until 1915.

Entering the 20th Century – 1900-1914

Success in the UK soon bred indigenous competitors, and Britains had to keep on their toes to stay ahead. They went for a highly innovative strategy of new lines, as well as fighting off competitors by marketing cheaper products alongside their standard best quality 54mm range. By 1906, they were ready to try a major foray into the French market, but although they opened a factory in Paris in 1912, they were unable to make many inroads. Possibly the Britains name, not much in evidence on the boxes containing French factories' output, was as counter-productive in France as it was appropriate in England. One likely result of

Picture 42: French hollowcasts 1920-1940

The French mounted officer in the kepi is on the same horse as the Imperial Guard Horse Grenadiers, but the horse furniture has been altered. Not all manufacturers would have taken the trouble to do this. The figure with his head turned to the left in the front row could well be the Emperor Napoleon III, and the mounted figure at the back right is the emperor Haile Selassie.

Picture 43: Hill Austrians?

These splendid early figures are marked JH Regd and an indecipherable design number. I have always thought of them as John Hill figures, based on the JH, and hope that they are meant to represent Austrians. I am perfectly willing to entertain other opinions, however.

Britains' French activity was that after the First World War, a number of French craftsmen had been taught the hollowcasting techniques. Many of them seem to have started to manufacture during the 1920s and 30s, particularly after Britains closed their Paris office in 1923. Of course, the rising cost of raw materials because of the world war was another major incentive to hollowcast.

Ex-Britains employees in London were also setting themselves up in business to see if they could carve themselves a share of the cake. Britains were forced to avail themselves of the Copyright Act of 1814 to prevent these new competitors from pirating their designs. As a result, all new Britains models from 1900 to 1912 were identified and dated. In 1913, the law changed and the date was no longer needed. Although this meant that competitors making hollowcast figures had to design their own, many bit the bullet and produced a number of excellent models. The chief contenders in the UK were Hill, BMC, Renvoize, Reka, Hanks and Fry. Some of these are shown in pictures 43, 95-6, 99 and 108.

At this time, a further new method of making toy soldiers was being developed, from a material called 'composition'. This is composed mostly of sawdust and casein glue, moulded and cooked around a wire armature. The material is light and surprisingly strong, although the paint can flake, the material can chip and is susceptible to damp. Above all, larger scale figures could be made cheaply, which meant that much of Britains' competitive advantage was eroded.

War toys go out of fashion – 1915-1941

After the trauma of the First World War, war toys were out of fashion with a vengeance. In England, all enthusiasm for things military had been pounded out of the population by four years of gruelling blood-letting. So much was this so that the first time that Britains summoned up the courage to put figures of soldiers engaged in trench warfare on the market was in 1938. This was probably in response to the vast range of British troops in the trenches

Picture 44: Elastolin and Lineol

By the 1930s in Germany, Hausser-Elastolin and Lineol had settled in as the main producers of composition toy soldiers. Their best quality ranges were around 70mm scale, and much of their production was devoted to the soldiers of the First World War, as here. The square based figures are Lineol, whereas Elastolin favoured oval bases. The animation was superb, and probably had considerable influence on other makers worldwide.

by then being marketed in the UK by the German manufacturers Hausser-Elastolin and Lineol, in addition to the many British manufacturers who had not been so squeamish. Britains had been put off the trenches by the outcry that had followed their issue of an 'Exploding Trench' toy in 1916, at the very time that so many people's loved ones were experiencing the real thing. Naturally they withdrew it in short order, and it is now one of the rarest Britains items known.

Britains' response was to produce a higher proportion of toy figures from the civilian world, thus creating the Home Farm, zoo, Miniature Gardening and other lines in addition to the footballers, Boy Scouts, civilians and railway figures they had already issued by 1914. With the inevitable competitors, as well as those continental manufacturers whose similar products were mostly already on the market, this opened up a whole world of collecting for non-military enthusiasts which has continued with unabated fervour into the 21st century.

Picture 45: Hill Civilians

Many of Britains competitors followed them into civilian subjects, and many collectors specialize in these peaceful equivalents of the Toy Soldier (Could well be the subject of another book later). My collecting taste has remained largely in the military, but the increasing popularity of old civilian models means that I have handled vast quantities through the auctions. These Hill figures show a vigour and imagination not so often seen in the Britains models of the time. Left to right, miller with flour scoop, priest officiating at wedding, groom, bride, two lady tennis players and golfer. Courtesy Bonhams

Alongside this new development, Britains continued to expand their range of military items outside the contentious subject of trench warfare. Motor vehicles and aircraft made their appearance. Lines were specifically created for export to south and north America. When the coronation of King George VI took place in 1937, not only was there a huge revival in demand for ceremonial troops, but re-armament was happening, and toy soldiers were no longer so traumatic. In Germany, Hausser-Elastolin and Lineol had been harnessed to the Nazi propaganda machine and were churning out vast numbers of party figures as well as German army soldiers and beautiful tinplate vehicles in 70mm scale. Other European countries, particularly Belgium and Italy, also had makers of composition figures.

Britains responded with large ranges of anti-aircraft equipment and army buildings, along with new models in battledress. By 1941, when the company went over to munitions production, their range of hollowcast figures was the largest in its history. Similar developments among their competitors, notably John Hill and Co (Johillco), Crescent, Charbens and Taylor and Barrett, continued the British hollowcasting tradition, along with some very diversely designed hollowcasts in France.

In the United States, this was the period when the so-called Dime-store figure was at its zenith. In a scales which varied around 70mm, the same size as Elastolin and Lineol, these were usually hollowcast figures of the US Army of World War I and contemporary US troops, and sold through outlets such as Woolworth. Manoil and Barclay in particular developed a rather chunky style unique to the USA.

The period between the two world wars were vibrant times, and there were social developments that laid the foundations for even better times to come. The British Model Soldier Society was founded in 1935. At this time, almost all model making was based on the converting of toy soldiers to something more realistic. Model figures to assemble and paint were almost unheard of. The toy manufacturers had branched out into almost every corner of society, including popular media characters such as Mickey Mouse, Snow White and Buck Rogers, and even into marketing premia such as the hugely successful Cococubs, manufactured on behalf of Cadbury by Britains.

Picture 46: Dime store

The figures on foot are typical Dime store figures in around 75mm scale. To the left are a Manoil hostess in khaki and a wounded U.S. soldier. To the right are two of Barclay's 'pod-foot' figures. With their bulky bodies and large heads they look a little crude compared to the similar scale Danish made Royal Canadian Mounted Policeman at the back, but they have their own charm and are widely collected in the U.S.

New materials – Die-cast, Aluminium and Plastic 1945-1973

Once the war was over, there was a worldwide struggle to get back to enjoying life once more. Toys were in short supply, as were raw materials, and much of British production was devoted to exporting to help reduce the immense debts run up in defeating the Nazis. Some of the demand was fulfilled through home made products, and it was a time of exciting experimentation to see whether new methods could produce traditional toys more cheaply. At no time recently was there more creativity, and if some of the experiments resulted in ugly curiosities rather than beautiful masterpieces, these figures record both the diversity of endeavour and the desperation to have something rather than nothing.

Picture 47: Post-war boxes

Typical colour illustrated boxes of the early 1950s in Britain.

Most of the British hollowcasting manufacturers re-started making their traditional figures and designing new ones, with some new manufacturers entering the field, notably Timpo and Cherilea. A brief but intense flowering of the hollowcast toy soldier maker's art took place from 1948 to 1954, a sort of Indian summer of the golden age of the matchstick mendable toy. Egged on by the authorities, much of the output was aimed at export to the US.

A few enterprises that never turned to making hollowcasts did thrive for a time, however, one in particular being a true precursor to the New Toy Soldiers of today. Authenticast was a maker born of a Swedish, American and Irish connection which started to manufacture solid toy soldiers in 54mm scale in neutral Eire in 1945. They were

Picture 48: Post-war hollowcast G.I.s

The famous Timpo G.I.s designed by Roy Selwyn-Smith march in a squad of ten behind a Charbens colour bearer and escort. To the rear is a group of plastic Timpo West Germans from the same design. In front is the equivalent Crescent figure marching with the rifle carried in the hand. All these were vigorously exported to America.

Picture 49: Crescent U.S. Infantry series

This Crescent subject came in two sizes around 1950, and directly competed with the rather nicer Timpo figures, which cost 1/3d. These ones had almost as much variety and cost just 6d each. I am particularly fond of the anti-tank gun in the smaller size series, which came in its own box. A little later, this series changed its uniform from olive green to khaki with bright green helmets, which is how I bought them in my boyhood (see picture 7)

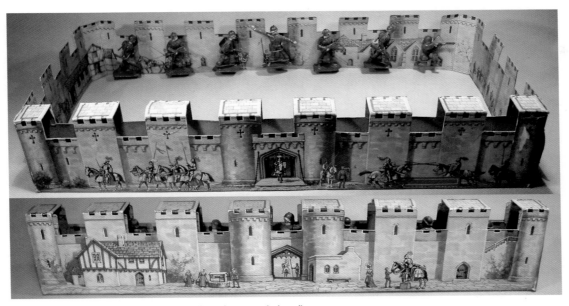

Pictures 50 and 51 : Crescent Castle packing (open and closed)

Extra play value was given with this cardboard castle box for Crescent toy soldiers. Perhaps most appropriate for toy knights in armour, Crescent packed plenty of their other series in the same box, as with these U.S. Infantry. The Castle itself was ingenious, with all the product information on the lower edge of the box, out of sight when the castle was set up. Each wall of the castle was colour printed on both sides.

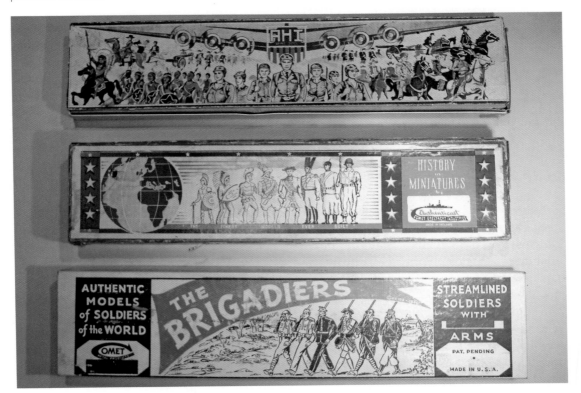

Picture 52: Boxes immediately post-war in the U.S.

AHI, Comet (Brigadier) and Authenticast (made in Eire) were all made for the U.S. market in the immediate post-war years. These are typical of the boxes they appeared in, AHI (made in Japan) being a little later than the others, around 1955.

designed by Holger Eriksson, a Swedish sculptor of some note, and judging from the number that survive, they had a wide distribution for a few years. Many of the figures are striking and beautiful models which stand comparison with many of much more recent years.

Picture 53: Authenticast Highlanders

The solid metal marching and at ease Highlanders were both very popular for a while. The Highlanders at ease in feather bonnets at the back are by Malleable Mouldings in early plastic acetate, and are somewhat prone to melting.

Die-casting in zinc alloy rather than lead had been developed during the 1920s, and Meccano in particular had introduced their Modelled Miniatures from 1934, soon to become the famous Dinky Toys, and in the 1940s and 50s led the world into an addictive trip on model vehicles. Britains had used die-casting machinery during their ammunition production in World War II, and were soon using die-cast parts in their own vehicles, but as far as toy soldiers were concerned, after a shortlived experiment, they stayed with the traditional hollowcast for the moment. Others, particularly Crescent, also experimented with die-casting, but the impurities in the early zinc alloy made the models extremely fragile and prone to 'metal fatigue'.

In due course, die-casting was to become a force in model soldier making, but for the time being the cost of the moulds and the problems with the metals meant that no toy soldier company took it up successfully. As die-casting was the pre-eminent method of manufacturing vehicles, however, serious collectors of military models necessarily included the whole paraphernalia of mechanised warfare in this form. Some series of models, notably Lone Star, were particularly suited to fit standard scale.

Late in the 1930s, aluminium had been another new wonder material, ductile enough to enable figures to be made in sand moulds. The advantage of this was that the models could be almost unbreakable, but only if the mouldings were of sufficient thickness to prevent them bending like foil. This meant that the modelling of thin parts was extremely difficult. Quiralu and an offshoot of CBG Mignot trade named Mignalu, with some others in France, started producing aluminium figures in the early 1930s. In 1947, Edgar Kehoe started a make entitled Wend-Al to produce aluminium toy soldiers for the British market. He was allied to Quiralu, who provided some designs and the expertise. The onset of the third new material, plastic, swept away the market for aluminium toy soldiers just a very few years later.

During the 1930s, one of the most exciting developments had been plastics. Although prefigured by composition, the search for a truly mouldable non-metallic material was solved, and became commercially available in the late 1940s. Many early plastics were disastrously fragile, melted, or snapped easily. Malleable Mouldings used some of the

Picture 54: Aluminium Quiralu colonials

Although necessarily somewhat chunky, aluminium toy soldiers such as these North African colonial troops in a drum and fife band with bugler and mascot with escort could look extremely good. Visiting Paris with my Grandmother in 1958, the large stores were still full of sets like this. The mounted Spahis were especially splendid, better in their way than the Britains ones which came out in this year.

Picture 55: Quiralux plastic

Quiralu tried to continue the success of their aluminium series by converting to plastic, changing the name of the series to Quiralux, but it was not to be. The future in France was with Starlux, who had originally made models from composition and converted to plastic early after the Second World War.

Eriksson designs (see above) adapted for plastic production from 1946, but they didn't take off, perhaps because the early acetate plastic that they used was so brittle and sometimes unstable. After these first experiments, more flexible and durable plastics became available in the early 1950s.

Picture 56: Starlux minis

On my trip to Paris in 1958 I was collecting French military Dinky toys, and to my delight I found that Starlux produced scaled down versions of their French combat infantry to go with them. Unfortunately pro-rata they were incredibly expensive. The French Dinkys have not worn well, and I have managed to get them covered in mould, but they still look brilliant with the miniature Starlux.

Incredibly quickly, and with Britains virtually the only exception, the entire British toy soldier market switched to plastic. From 1953, Herald, Timpo, Lone Star, Charbens, Cherilea and Crescent all started producing painted plastic figures. Within a year, Britains had made the decision to acquire Herald. Collaboration and then consolidation produced the famous series of Herald, Swoppet, Eyes Right, and Deetail which were as successful in their day as the hollowcasts had been before them. Traditional hollowcasting at Britains finally came to an end in 1966, after several years of much reduced production. At the same time, in continental Europe, an identical transformation had been overtaking the major manufacturers, with both Elastolin and Starlux successfully converting to plastic from composition.

In Britain and Europe, where well painted toy soldiers had been traditional, plastic toy soldiers were marketed in very similar ways to the metal toy soldiers that had come before. Most were distributed for sale loose, in

Picture 57: Herald Infantry

Four groups of the Herald Infantryman which was without doubt the best representation of a Briton on National service ever produced. I was so pleased with the appearance of these men on parade in numbers that I have eighty-seven of them. Here are some of the ones not done up in different coloured berets. Left back are four of the first ones, with fixed arms. Then come six of the 'proper' Herald ones nicely painted, which cost 1/3d. Then four of the reduced paint version which cost 9d, and finally two of the ones made in Hong Kong, 6d. The vagaries of the plastic and moulding means that along the ranks are various heights and expressions which give an almost lifelike appearance to them. Quite strange, really.

Picture 58: Plastic Herald Trojans

Within this group are the five original Herald 'Trojans' (they are all Greek warriors of a rather later date) on foot, with the lone mounted figure, designed by Norman Sillman. The easiest way of picking them out is to spot the light green of the bases. They are: bowman with orange plume, Paris, spearman, Hector, yellow plume Achilles, blue cloak Odysseus, red cloak Ajax. The horseman is Agamemnon. The bowman with the yellow plume is a late version Hong Kong produced Herald figure. The swordsman with the yellow plume front right is a pirated figure also made in Hong Kong, note the different base colour and flaking paint. I thought these figures looked good without their plumes, as with the spearman, so took off those on the extreme left and right of the picture, repainting them with smooth helmets. The swordsman in blue front left is a repainted figure by someone else.

Picture 59: Elastolin copies

The top models of the western world in plastic were considered fair game for reproduction in the Far East. Here are the regular 70mm and 40mm scale Elastolin plastic Romans with smaller size copies made in Hong Kong, the very smallest being sold unpainted. The Elastolin figures are made of a hard but rather fragile Polystyrene, with the copies in softer plastic.

Picture 60: World wide plastic, Turkey-Brazil

My mother got the plastic soldiers from Turkey for me around the same time as the light green types in hard plastic were found by my friend Jeremy in Brazil: 1956. The Brazilian ones seem to me to bear a family likeness to the metal U.S. dime-store figures of Barclay and Manoil.

Picture 61: Elastolin Men at Arms

I like these late issue 70mm late medieval men at arms from Elastolin because they are all similarly equipped in workmanlike armour, the foot soldiers without whom the fancy knights would be unable to win battles. The halberds they are wielding were battle-winning weapons in the hands of the Swiss on a number of occasions. In production terms, by this stage Elastolin have adopted a rather softer plastic, which is more durable than their original Polystyrene. The halberds are made of a harder plastic to avoid warping, and the paint finish is kept to a minimum to keep the price down. Hitherto, Elastolin figures had been a great deal more expensive than British made figures, but these were rather more competitive.

Pictures 62 and 63: Starlux, Pipe Band of the French Navy and musicians of the Italian Bersagliere at the double.
From the 1950s to the 1990s Starlux brought out many imaginative models in plastic of contemporary European troops, visually very satisfying. Furthermore, until recently they could be purchased for unintimidating amounts of money second hand.

Picture 64: Marx Japanese

Marx was producing bags of fifty 1/32 scale troops for a dollar in the U.S. by the early 1960s or earlier, sounding the eventual worldwide death knell for mass market painted plastic toy soldiers. The animation in these figures was amazing, sometimes the figures were jumping about in an unbelievable fashion, but then I suppose that everyone knew that the Japanese military were a bit over the top. Banzai!

There were twelve poses in this fifty-piece bag, and they were not on sale in the UK. I got a friend of my mother to send me bags from Chicago. Note the wishful thinking of the man surrendering back left – I hadn't realized the Japanese did that. Curiously, when the giant six-inch version of some of them came out (see right back and the pose immediately in front of it) they were on sale in UK Woolworths for a while. The paint on the weapons is not original, they all came completely unpainted. The Marx guys also had a sense of humour, as with the cartoon figure of a Japanese officer on the left.

boxes of three dozen mixed figures of each series, and for the sake of convenience, six different figures to the series was the norm. 6d was a normal price for a single figure, with premium painted figures such as Herald costing 1/3d. In the US, by contrast, Louis Marx, as well as his superb playsets, was selling polybags of fifty unpainted 54mm scale toy soldiers, brilliantly modelled, for a dollar a bag. The disparity between 6d a figure and about a penny a figure was all too obvious. Woolworths imported a rather larger scale of Marx figure and sold them unpainted at 3d each, evidently making themselves a fortune, as for a few years they devoted quite a lot of their open top counter space to them. The wonder was that no one had yet seriously started to produce unpainted plastic toy soldiers for sale in Great Britain.

In 1958, Airfix started to manufacture boxes of about forty 00 scale figures for two shillings a box, and from then on, it was only a fairly short step to issuing 54mm scale sets. In spite of a long rearguard action, by 1973, only Britains and Timpo were still issuing fully coloured toy soldiers, which rapidly became a relatively niche premium product compared to the large variety of single coloured figures available from Airfix, Matchbox and others, including the ubiquitous bags of green combat soldiers (or green army men, as they were known in the US). Essentially, the age of the painted toy soldier for children was over, although the age of the model soldier for the collector had only just begun.

In this age of opportunity and commercial expansion, the role of the hobbies closely allied to collecting toy soldiers should not be forgotten. At first just in metal, sculptors such as Charles Stadden, Greenwood and Ball, Russell Gammage and Hinton Hunt offered a large variety of ready-made models, painted or unpainted, for the first time. This enabled a huge increase in people interested in military modelling. While I might not go quite so far as Henry Harris in putting their number at half a million, I might certainly think it to be well into six figures. While the membership of the British Model Soldier Society never rose much above a thousand, the circulation of *Military Modelling Magazine* was in excess of forty thousand, and this was essentially just a British magazine. Later in this period, suppliers of plastic model kits, in particular Historex, simply increased the appetite of the addicted.

Nor were wargamers neglected. Here the 00 scale (20mm) figures of Airfix played a central role in starting historical wargaming as a hobby for children. From this beginning, various makers in metal, usually to a scale of 25mm, supplied all those armies which Airfix did not, in a smaller image of the large amount of modelling castings also by then available.

In the 1950s, with the burgeoning of commercial modellers, techniques and materials, came the people who would research motives, history and current activity in the marketplace. Foremost among these were John G Garratt, an antiquarian bookseller in Farnham, Surrey, for both toys and models, and L W Richards, the acknowledged pioneer of classifying and researching the output of commercial toy soldier manufacturers.

Picture 65: Airfix Paratroops

Many years later than it might have been, the first unpainted set of 1/32 scale troops hit the shops in the UK. The shrinkwrapping was so strongly shrunk that it distorted the shape of the box. I couldn't understand why so many of these solders were shooting up in the air – were they trying to shoot down their own reinforcements? In any event, this was the end of the painted plastic figure.

The end of the classic Toy Soldier 1973-1993

1973 was a pivotal year in the history of the toy soldier. Britains launched its first New Metal Model, a die-cast guardsman, extended at first to just three London souvenir figures, but from 1983 broadened to a series of collectable and souvenir models which were to serve the company well right through to the present day. For the first two decades they had some success in the regular toy market as well. Thereafter, they really only appealed to the souvenir and collector market. With this came the launch of the William Britain Collector's Club in 1993, the centenary of Britains first toy soldier production.

Picture 66: Blenheim Waterloo

In 1973 I happened to be in the Portobello Road when Jan and Frank Scroby were unwrapping the first Blenheim figures, British Waterloo infantry at the slope (Coldstream Guards) to put out on display on their stall. I immediately bought the first eight from them, and asked them to promise to reserve the first eight from each new figure for me. Eventually, including some officers and the second versions with the longer, more realistic bayonets, I ended up with this cameo of what I consider to be the first of the wave of 'New Toy Soldiers' which has delighted most adult toy style soldier collectors ever since. Left to right: Rifle Brigade, Black Watch (there was no first version figure of these), Gordons, Coldstream Guards and French Imperial Guard.

Simultaneously from 1973 there was a sudden emergence of makers of solid metal models in the old toy soldier style. These were swiftly named New Toy Soldiers. The first generation of these new makers included Blenheim and its commissioned offshoot Nostalgia, Mark Time, Soldiers Soldiers, Trophy, British Bulldog, Steadfast and Dorset. By 1991, when Stuart Asquith published his *Collector's Guide to New Toy Soldiers*, he was able to list one hundred and eighty makers.

Within the toy industry itself, however, the decline of the toy soldier continued. Toy companies were already creating figurines for children's collectables such as Lego, Playmobil and action figures. There is a case for saying that action figures, which really took off from the launch of the *Star Wars* range of 95mm scale models in 1977, are the main successor to toy soldiers, but then one might on the other hand say that they are in a different league of figurine altogether. It is a matter of taste as to whether they should be included in the evolution of toy soldiers or not. For certain, displaying them with traditional toy soldiers is not effective. I am interested in them as part of the history, but not as part of my collection, so I have a few examples to show what they are.

Picture 67: Fisher Price Knights

It amused me somewhat to see these comic Knights on sale from the highly reputable firm of Fisher Price, as part of their range of toys, which are marketed as stimulating childrens intelligence. Aimed at 3+, these seem to be a straight forward invitation to violence, but of course children do not take such toys as literally as that, using them only for fantasy play.

Action figures are largely the product of media merchandising (although Lego has also indulged in this). Lego and Playmobil figures are, of course, caricatures, echoing in this, and taking to further extremes, the earlier stylisation of the traditional toy soldier. In the age of mass media, the heroics associated with films and television are more than ever prime sellers in the marketplace. The Wild West, Robin Hood, knights, pirates, Romans and Vikings, good sellers

Picture 68: Traditional TOY soldiers

For centuries there has been a tradition of lightening the grim load of war by making caricatures of soldiers as toys, such as the little wooden figures front right (see above, picture 39, for an early example of this style). Toy soldier manufacturers often make such figures themselves, indeed the Britains ones, never issued commercially, are some of the rarest there are. CBG Mignot made the large figure back left and Quiralu made the rocking horse soldier, the drummer and the cantiniere in a series also marketed by Wend-Al. In Germany, nutcrackers are often made in the form of toy soldiers, a miniature version of which is front left, next to the Britains Uruguayan cadet who is in the nearest equivalent to a Toy Soldier uniform among the regular Britains sets. Mid-left is a plastic toothbrush holder, and mid-right a wooden eggcup with bearskin egg cosy. The rest are all doll like toy soldiers, except for the Lego and Playmobil figures, which come from their pirate series, but are obviously in this same tradition. The 110mm British Infantryman of the Line behind the front row of little wooden soldiers looks very like the Schoenhut U.S. figures shown in Richard O'Brien's Collecting Toy Soldiers no.2.

Picture 69: Manga Heroine

This feisty character I picked up in Tokyo – you can just see her eyes under her fringe, a case of fashion outweighing good sense in swordplay.

in the heyday of the classic toy soldier, are now represented for children by Lego and Playmobil along with the action figures of science fiction, fantasy and other film tie-ins.

There have been extensions of this type of figure into the adult market as well, catering to fans of comics, manga, films and other popular media. When in Japan a few years back, I visited 'Manga City' in Tokyo, and they take models very seriously. Apart from the models of Alexander and Caesar (see pictures 127 and 132), I also bought this lovely little manga heroine that cheered me up on my desk at work for the next few years. Equivalent models from Western films such as *Sin City* can be bought in various scales from specialist outlets in London.

Souvenirs and Collectors 1994-2010

By 1994, the market for toy soldiers had mostly shrunk to production for souvenirs and collectors. I say shrunk in just the one sense, that of volume, for as the mass market for children vanished, so the variety of form and subject burgeoned out of all recognition. Whether in metal or plastic, traditional stylised figures or the most realistic of models, and in whatever military historical or fantastic subject, it is now likely to be available, painted or unpainted.

In most countries, and often supplied by former toymakers such as Britains or CBG Mignot, there is probably a small range of souvenir figures available for tourists. Those who travel widely could, in all likelihood, make up an interesting collection of these just from current production. One category of children's toy has remained and expanded, the 80mm scale figures marketed by the French companies Papo and Plastoy, and the German companies Bully, Schleich and Simba. These are historical and fantasy figures of a high standard intended for the age range 3 to 6 (see picture 19) To my mind, it is a shame that the Britains range of 54mm farm and zoo figures are no longer marketed, since the larger, more expensive Schleich range moved immediately into the market gap they left and now seem just as essential as Britains used to be, even in such small, independent toy shops as are left. Even in the premium and novelty market, there are today just as many figures as ever for children to collect, among others from Kinder eggs or with a Happy Meal from MacDonalds, which is now the world's largest toy distributor (see pictures 14, 201 and 204).

However, it is in the market for collectors that most expansion has taken place, and here it is that just about every need can be satisfied. Because of the plethora of new moulding techniques (and the promised revolution in 3D printing may take this yet further), it is now possible to produce virtually any style of figure in any position.

Picture 70: Recent developments in plastic toy soldiers

The earliest figure in this picture is the Britains Superdeetail S.A.S. figure in the centre, dating to 1983 the year following the Falklands War. Another S.A.S. figure, a metal model by Frontline, is centre rear. The six U.S. troops in 'Fritz' helmets to the right came in a header bag, and are painted just with faces and some splodges of desert camouflage on the front of the figures. I bought them in Brent Cross shopping centre in 2005. At about the same time I got the green unpainted Mujahedeen fighters at a show. The U.N. infantryman at the back is a late series Britains Deetail figure, and the two crawling figures at the front I recently found in a local toy shop. You can wind them up and they will crawl along. I have seen toys like this before, but these are the smallest so far, almost down to 54mm scale. In due course I look forward to toy soldiers that will move around by radio control.

Picture 71: Toy Story

Green Army men are some of the heroes of the Pixar Toy Story series, and with the release of the third film in fifteen years have achieved star status with their own Disney store presentation and Lego derivative set. Lego for many years tried to distance their product from the military, so these are the first twentieth century soldier figures to feature in the Lego universe, arrived by the back door. Congratulations!

Picture 72: G.I. Joe

I wonder if G. I. Joe collectors are picking up the latest Rise of Cobra manifestation of the brand, which is effectively yet another series of Star Wars style action figure in 90mm scale, aimed, it says, at 4+.

For those who wish to add to the traditional style Britains, foremost for collectors are Hocker, Fusilier and Asset. Makers that have produced a substantial body of subjects in their own distinctive style include Tradition, Mark Time, Blenheim/ Nostalgia/Marlborough, Trophy, Steadfast, Bastion, Dorset, Ducal and a host of others. A concise list of leading and interesting current and recent producers is compiled as an appendix on page 195. For those now pursuing the path of models, the current leading manufacturers are Britains itself, Conte and King and Country. King and Country started in 1984 as one among the New Toy Soldier manufacturers, and later saw a market for ready made, more realistic models. Richard Conte started in 1999, following the traditions of the Marx playsets, designing brilliant new models, issued painted in matt finish or reproduced in unpainted plastic for those who cannot afford to collect painted metal.

A relatively new addition to the marketing of collectable soldiers recently has been the subscription collection from the collectables and part work marketers such as del Prado, de Agostini and the

Picture 73: Today's Action figures

These Action Force Fighters turned up in my local newsagent the other day free with Action Combat, a not entirely PC publication aimed at boys of about six to eight. Toy soldiers are alive and well!

Picture 74: New Toy Soldier Royal Scots Greys

From the vast array of available or discontinued New Toy Soldiers since 1973, the ones I personally have liked best are those which followed the old hollowcast Britains but in different poses and the ones which are in a similar style but stand out through the excellence of their design and finish. Here are examples of both. Back left is the original set 32 of Britains mounted Scots Greys from 1957. At the centre of the front row of three is the Britains dismounted Scots Grey from set 2119, produced in the same year, and one of my favourite figures. Surrounding it are two similar cast and painted by David Bracey of Lancer, with a row each of the same figure with carbines and lances, which he did to add to my regiment of Scots Greys. Back right is a set of Bill Hocker's Scots Greys, very neatly finished and attractive figures at the halt, with the officer and his horse in a subtly different pose to the troopers. Bill has followed a Britains tradition in giving them fusilier rather than the standard Scots Grey headgear, thus following his avowed principle of making his output as toys rather than models. The beautiful mounted officer front left is more in the enhanced style of Freddie Green, and I apologise to whoever made it that I don't remember who they are. It has no identifying markings.

original pioneer of such offerings, the Franklin Mint. These, through spending large sums on television and magazine advertising, have greatly popularised model collecting. While the earlier product here has been not uniformly of the highest quality, recent collections have often been remarkably excellent, if tending to be more towards a 65mm scale than the 54mm which would probably have made them much more acceptable to most existing soldier collectors.

Exactly the same trends are discernable when the material is plastic. As well as many manufacturers such as Conte, Replicants and Armies in Plastic who have been designing their own new figures, more or less stylised or realistic, for collectors, there are numbers of firms such as Toyway that specialise in producing earlier figures from old moulds or designs. In this way, much of the design heritage of the 1950s to 1970s is preserved and available.

All of them rely on a relatively small market of enthusiast collectors putting together substantial accumulations of these figures, rather than on any kind of mass market for children's toys. The future looks bright for toy soldier collectors. Whatever style they enjoy most is there for them to acquire.

Picture 75: Britains American Civil War models

Officers and colour bearers, including Generals Robert E. Lee (left) and George McClellan (right), show a high degree of artistry in these models of the war between the states. There is now a huge amount of interest in this formative period of the history of the world's greatest super-power, reflected in the number of people collecting models of the struggle world wide. As the years have passed, and the issues have receded with time, so the romance of the blue and the grey has felt more striking, and the model makers are able to do it more and more justice.

Picture 76: King and Country American Civil War models

Federal cavalry under Major General John Buford arrive and dismount to form a skirmish line, showing off the super detail in these models, each individual, yet together forming something very like a diorama. It is possible to buy striking backgrounds and bases on which to pose figures such as these from manufacturers such as J G Miniatures.

As ready to display figures become more and more realistic, and nearer to diorama standard, it rather begs the question, are they too new and shiny? Although the bases look churned up, the figures themselves seem to me to cry out for a bit of wear, tear and mud. It is as if the pristine shininess of the traditional toy soldier has persisted in the journey towards realism, and has still not caught up with the reality of war often depicted by great modelers. But maybe we don't want to get that close to reality!

Picture 77: Du Guesclin

This is a recent model from a series by del Prado with a very acceptable degree of realism for a relatively mass market. As a key historical figure leading the French fight-back after Crecy and Poitiers, Du Guesclin is an excellent personality to grace the medieval section on the shelves.

Picture 78: Armies in Plastic Boxers

The firms that manufacture in plastic for collectors now produce just about any subject you might desire, such as these attractive Boxer figures. Were I to have the time to paint them up, they could join my Boxer display, but in the meantime just the potential of them and the colourful box art make them a satisfying possession. Twenty figures in ten poses currently cost under £10.

CHAPTER 3
COLLECTING TOY SOLDIERS
IN THE TWENTY-FIRST CENTURY

At this point, I would like to share my observations about the changes to collecting toy soldiers over the last twenty-four years. There has been much progress on all sorts of fronts since I wrote *Collecting Toy Soldiers*, and although many changes are discussed in detail in other chapters, summarising it is useful to highlight just how much has happened.

The changes in the production of toy soldiers, and their evolution towards more realism from 1987 to 2010 I have covered in the preceding chapter. I shall not repeat these here, although in many ways, that has been the most important change of all. It makes a huge difference to the many aspects of collecting I shall discuss in later chapters.

Searching for toy soldiers can now include a much wider range of sources. While in 1987 I was of the opinion that as a collecting hobby the subject of toy soldiers was not fully mature, today in 2010 for certain it is. There is enough recognition of toy soldiers that most people know what you are on about. Specialist shows for toy soldiers (see below) are now a much more fruitful source. Specialist auctions are relatively plentiful, with larger sections in local auctions of toys and collectables. The search round junk shops has by now really died the death, with car boot sales, charity shops and eBay taking up that role. All of this helps in funnelling the available supply from the general public towards the specialist dealers and auctioneers, who are now all on the Internet.

Changes since 1985

The increase in reference material
There is now a great deal more information available, thanks to the very many new publications devoted to the subject, the successful continued production of existing periodicals and the widespread use of the Internet, which didn't exist for public exploration in 1987. It would now be possible to have a virtual collection online comprising vast numbers of images and references, and many collectors and experts have set up websites sharing their knowledge and enthusiasm.

In 1987, I was able to recommend sixteen books. Now, in 2011, I can list nearly three times the number (see select bibliography page 189) even while leaving out many of those I recommended then. In 1987, the *Old Toy Soldier Newsletter* had only been in existence for eleven years, and *Plastic Warrior* for just two. Since then, they have been issued regularly, either six times a year, or quarterly, and just in those two magazines there has appeared a plethora of detailed information that has not been included in any book. It would not surprise me that there is fifty times as much written material about toy soldiers out there now than there was twenty-four years ago – I myself have written well over a million words during that period, even if most of it was in writing descriptions of soldiers for sale in auctions. When I look back through the catalogues I have written, I sometimes astonish myself with the soldiers that have been through my hands that I have forgotten all about. I wonder who is enjoying them now.

The other major sources for toy soldiers are the manufacturers' original catalogues and these auction house sales catalogues, many of which have more recently become much better illustrated in colour. Current production and sales are available online, and some auction houses keep back catalogues available. Otherwise it is a question of looking out for original catalogues, and reprints of older ones, both from manufacturers and auctions.

Nostalgia moves on to the plastic toy soldier

Nostalgic memories of childhood tend to take hold around thirty to forty years after the age of ten. Boys during the golden age of plastic toy soldiers (1953 to 1970) are now in their fifties and sixties, and many started adult collecting avidly over the last thirty years. Collecting plastic toy soldiers has come of age with a vengeance, with prices to match. Acquiring a complete collection of Herald and Britains plastic has become as difficult and aspirational as the equivalent in hollowcast.

I can lay some claim to having been the first adult collector of plastic toy soldiers, having started collecting British distributed plastic toy soldiers systematically in 1966. I thought I had made a fairly good job of it, but the minute detail of mould changes and packaging on top of the knowledge of scores of countries of origin displayed by many collectors nowadays takes the subject to a much greater depth.

Where will nostalgia move next? *Star Wars* would be a good bet, and other character figures both of that sort and the straightforward (and to my mind more attractive) models. I suspect that there will not be the same sort of nostalgia around for the metal figures made for the adult collector market, although there might be some for the New Metal Models made by Britains from 1973 onwards.

The effect of the Internet

Putting the words 'toy soldiers' into a search engine can now provide weeks of fun trawling all sorts of information and purchasing opportunities. I myself spent a fortnight recuperating from a minor operation setting up my own website. It has 350 pictures on it, more than I can include in this book.

Another huge advantage of the Internet has been in the amazing ease of corresponding. I know I very regularly used not to respond to people who wrote me often very interesting letters. With email, while I haven't always come back on everything, nevertheless I probably have replied to 95% of my messages, which I know is a great improvement on letter writing. A big apology to all those who never got a letter back from me!

Apart from connecting with friends and collectors, the effect of being able to look at prospective purchases on the Web is an incredible improvement. I have never been in the habit of purchasing without looking at something in my hand, but when a photograph comes in from a trusted source, were I in the acquisitive phase of collecting, I would certainly be tempted to risk it.

Digital photography

Colour photography has now become available to everyone. I now take about a thousand or more pictures each year just in the normal course of my auctioneering work. I used to promise myself that I would learn photography, and it was hugely expensive. Now one can just point and shoot with one's mobile phone. Thus it is a simple matter to attach pictures to an email, and send it to a friend or an appropriate website to find out about particular queries. And the websites of auctioneers and dealers, let alone eBay, are stuffed with pictures.

Fewer retail shops selling toy soldiers

Since 1987, the trend against toyshops has continued, and one disadvantage of the Internet is that it has put some small independent shops out of business. The advent of category killer out of town shops such as Toys R Us has meant that even Selfridges cannot afford to sell toys at Christmas, and where toy soldiers used to be on the shelves of every corner shop, today even Woolworth has folded in the UK, leaving us with nowhere to go but the specialists.

Rummaging around whole high streets, as I used to do in Alton, Hampshire, as a boy, was a delight. First there was Atkins, who sold Johillco and a few Britains, then Woolworths and Wymans, the newsagents half way up Crown Hill and the town's other toy shop, Gamley's who had some Britains and Wend-Al. If I was feeling especially energetic, there were two further newsagents to try before getting to the train station at the top end of the town. I was just eight years old. I think I would be hard put to it to find a single toy soldier for sale in Alton today.

More shows

While general toy fairs were well established in 1987, the first specialist toy soldier fair, which I organised in 1975 in Staines, had been the only one in the UK until that point. Shortly thereafter, the series of shows now known as the London Toy Soldier Shows started up and has been running at the Royal National Hotel in London ever since, currently three times a year. The British Model Soldier Society also puts on annual shows in London. Along with the shows in the USA and Germany, these are the starting point for anyone who has ever been thrilled by toy soldiers.

Some shows even specialise, for instance, in plastic toy soldiers, or soldiers produced more than twenty years ago. As this specialisation has proceeded, the amount of toy soldiers turning up at the general toy fairs has drastically diminished, so hardly anyone interested in them bothers to go any more. The Internet makes it easy to look up where the toy soldier shows are.

These days, many shows allow keen collectors an 'early bird' entry for a premium price, allowing them to start from 6.00 a.m. watching like hawks while everyone unpacks. Or indeed one may have arranged to meet with someone to look at something you already talked about earlier.

Searching for toy soldiers today

Shows are undoubtedly the best place to start collecting, as it is possible to get a feel for the huge variety of figures available to collect. And I do mean feel, for it is only by picking them up, turning them round and weighing them in the hand that you will learn to appreciate their art and charm, as well as which ones attract you the most. Shows are also the most useful for price comparisons of individual figures, although it is unlikely that any items but the most extremely common will have multiple choices on offer. Auction viewings have always been another good place to acquire an initial hands-on experience, while being careful to replace everything viewed in the right order.

The proper old junk shops (i.e. downmarket antique shops) have for many years been a dying breed, and largely replaced by car boot sales. These can be great fun to go round in any case, and the very occasional find at probably low prices can be a nice surprise. Upmarket antique shops usually pass on any toy soldiers they find to specialists. Where dealers have shops, these are also a great day out, particularly if they have special open days, and many dealers count their customers among their best friends. In London, sadly, there are fewer dealers to go and see than there used to be, with the passing of Under Two Flags and the retirement of Shamus Wade and Stephen Naegel. Luckily the Internet soon uncovers those that remain.

British Model Soldier Society 75th Anniversary show
April 24th 2010, Holiday Inn, Coram St

The BMSS shows are somewhat different to the general run of toy soldier collector shows. For a start, they cater for modellers as well as collectors, something that has annoyed people in the past. But it would be a great loss if it became too much the one or the other, and now that there are far more model collectables, the two sides are rapidly coming together. Apart from the modelling competitions, the tradition is that many of the dealers bring their most damaged junk. BMSS members are noted as converters of figures, rather than for their deep pockets. This does, however, often bring to the surface broken figures for which no known intact example exists, and therein lies the interest for people such as myself.

I have a Bonhams table inside the entrance, rather badly lit by halogen lights in the ceiling. Next to me is Philip Lane, who arrives late, but brings a card of 19th century Franco-Prussian War semi-flats very similar to those I have just received from the States. His price of £375 for about 20 figures confirms my estimate of £1500 to £2000 for 250 figures. I muse that the Franco-Prussian War may mark the apogee of commercial popularity for semi-flats, with life moving on rapidly to solids thereafter – maybe solids were Heyde's big innovation?

Philip has brought along a box full of Heyde No.2 size Delhi Durbar, complete with five elephants, anti-elephant stilt-men and the Gold Gun of Baroda, plus palanquins and attendants. Not often seen, and worth thousands of pounds.

Picture 79: Phillip Lane's Durbar medley

To discover that the old cardboard box next to you actually contains a heap of Heyde treasure worth thousands of pounds comes as quite a shock!

Picture 80: Stilt men

These were an attempt to get men up high enough to engage the enemy riding on elephants. They must have been quite skillful. By the time of the Delhi Durbars they were a regular feature of the Indian ceremonial, not expected to take part in combat. These ones have green bases as opposed to the more common beige.

Jenny Burley is next to me on the other side, and lends me a batch of photos of CBG Mignot large boxes, many tiered with figures presented standing up in scenes in the way that CBG excelled. I look forward to having a closer look at these later. Towards the entrance is Alex Riches, the fair organizer, and Harry Kemp, an accountant with a toy soldier habit as obsessive as mine, who has brought his teenage daughter. She is not at all sure what to make of the show, but has dressed quite attractively for a predominantly male audience.

Harry shows me several models I have never seen before, and tips me off that he already sold Alex a German made hollowcast British infantryman at attention. He has bought a tray full of early miniature and gilt figures, and brought along some larger gilts as well, in addition to his twice yearly clear out of things he has no longer room for or got tired of. As his tastes are very similar to mine, this is a table I should examine in detail.

I garner a die-cast Bugs Bunny (£4) for my media shelf (I am overloaded with Disney but don't have much Warner Brothers). Highly recognizable media figures are a good way of engaging visitors who are not into toy soldiers, especially children. There is also a large size highlander that we agree looks as if it was used to advertise whisky (a common use of highland figures, see picture 201). When I return to Harry's leftovers later, I find a best quality semi-flat highland piper in 40mm scale. This is quite a discovery, as I don't have any of this type of figure as highlanders. Harry seems a little reluctant to part with it and charges the full £6 on the label (see picture 81). Also from Harry came a Britains infantryman of the line, spiked helmet, standing firing in gilt finish, on an early dated oval base. He is at pains to point out that it is not intact, but neatly repaired (£2). I have the Britains master figure for this, and hope to use it in a small cameo.

Picture 81: Semi-flat Highlanders

Highlanders were popular from the early days. These examples, dating perhaps from the 1880s, show as much design flair as any figures in any medium since then. The one I had from Harry is on the right.

47

Harry also has a rather out of place figure for him, which is a 52mm scale standing firing figure in khaki with a pack. On its head is something that could be a Japanese pith helmet or a British steel helmet. For £10, it is worth a go, and turns out (looking in Blondieau's CBG reference) to be a Mignot WWI British infantryman, although Blondieau has none standing firing to show in a picture, so maybe they are rare. I have never seen any before. Anyway, one more for my Brits by the French cameo (see below).

Another figure that catches my eye is a truly splendid pewter finish English Civil War musketeer, with the distinctive lobster-pot helmet, which makes him look much more a cavalryman. This is marked Westair, and I seem to remember that this company had a short run of making figures as souvenir items. A quick Google at home and I come up with Westair, and they seem to have been going since 1972. Why have I not been more aware of them before now? Turns out I already have quite a few of their products, mostly die-cast, which are sold through museum and tourist locations. Their figures are mostly pewter finish in 40mm scale and fifteen in what they call 55mm scale. My Civil War figure is actually in 52mm scale. They also do a few resin figures in 70mm or 80mm and some cavalry in 25mm. They currently do four Celts, twenty Romans, five Vikings, two Saxons, a Norman, seventeen medieval figures, six Tudors, nine English Civil War, Trafalgar Royal Marine, Wellington, four Victorians, nine Second World War, two London and eight Highlanders, three of which are 55mm figures I don't have! Total, eighty-nine models!

Picture 82: Westair and other souvenirs

The Westair English Civil War 'Arquebusier' that I found at the BMSS 75th anniversary show is just in front of the Scottish Pipe Band. To the right is a group of five 40mm Romans sold at the Ashmoleon Museum in Oxford for £2.00, and front left is a pack of individually packed similar 'Scots' figures for £1.99. These figures have been available for nearly forty years and so cost a little more in tourist outlets today. The 'Scottish Pipe Band' with all of two members is extortionately priced at £8.00, while the twelve mounted Mexican cavalry are a somewhat crude but in their own way charming reminder that figures are a good way for locals to make some money from tourists all over the world. These came from the Pacific coast in 1982. At the back are some of Britains own hollowcast tourist items, left to right, 2157 Life Guard Drum Horse with Buckingham Palace backdrop, 2168 Gordon officer with Edinburgh Castle backdrop, 2169 12th Lancer officer with Trafalgar Square backdrop and 2158 Royal Canadian Mounted Police officer, which has a plain interior.

In addition, they import and distribute the ubiquitous Play-me antique finish cannon and war machine pencil sharpeners made in Spain that I have always rather liked. Anyway, the Civil War musketeer (in their catalogue it is an arquebusier – could be, if a little behind the times) costs £2.50 from them, in original box. Harry sold his to me for £4. Shows how little toy soldier people go to tourist venues.

Peter Flateau turns up with a small size figure not by Britains. It has a white spiked infantry helmet, and is marching with the right leg forward, as opposed to the Britains figures which march with the left foot forward. This kicks off a long discussion with Harry about whether the right foot forward is more common among German figures and therefore whether the figure we are looking at could be a small size German hollowcast. Once at home, I rush to have a look at my non-Britains small size hollowcasts, and find a whole squad of the BMC infantry and six other unknown figures with their right foot forward. Evidently British makers were not too particular. Probably Peter's figure is British after all.

Looking around for a few things, I spot

Picture 83: Carcassonne

The nicely printed header to this tourist set commemorates the apocryphal occasion on which a pig was hurled at the besiegers to show that the garrison could spare pigs and were in no danger of starving. Castles are becoming a fashionable collectable thanks to such specialists as Allen Hickling (see also pictures 50 and 51). Carcassonne is an unbelievable spectacle to visit, a cross between real history and Disneyland!

something I actually have on my acquisitions list, a set of eight Britains Waterloo Camerons at attention, on Lynn Kenwood's tables. Lynn's wife lets me have them for £35, a small discount. These are supposedly done from old moulds, but have used the mould for the very rare second version Waterloo Highlander at attention with only one movable arm. Not many of these latter can have been made – I have only one rather battered example (see picture). The new set looks very well in my Britains Waterloo cameo. If a set of the original one movable arm Gordons turned up, I would be very tempted, but it might well be priced out of my reach.

Picture 84: The slaughter of the innocents

Elaborate cribs in Spain show scenes from events surrounding the story of the birth of Jesus, here with traditional figures (now made of resin in China) depicting Herod's soldiers killing babies. Acquired during a visit to Caceres in western Spain.

Picture 85: Santons

Traditional Provencal figures include a French Revolutionary drummer, several examples here shown with a priest and a stone Borie. These figures remind me of the many happy holidays we have spent there.

49

Adrian Little always has good things on his stall, although most of them are too expensive for me these days. He has brought some broken figures along, however, and so I find one thing I have been actively looking for for the last few months, an example of a Britains cross-legged lancer. When I sold my original sets of these, I didn't have any left over, and I should have at least one for my reference cameo of Britains' early figures. This (£10) one has the lance tip missing (which often happens) and some retouching to it, but doesn't look too bad at all, with all its legs intact. He also has something else I am a bit of a sucker for, which is a French hollowcast representation of a British dragoon guard (£3). It is broken in two places, but the wildly galloping horse still stands up, and the rider is carrying a typical French version of the Union Jack, all red with blue crosses. I am putting together a cameo of French representations of British soldiers, which should shortly be great fun to contemplate, including examples of how the Brits were seen by Britains' Paris office. He also has some Heyde Gordon Highlanders which I like the look of, but are too expensive, but he can let me have one without a rifle for £2, which will go into my Highlanders by foreign makers cameo.

Picture 86: German and Brigader solid cast Highlanders

The larger scale firing group on the right could well be Noris, although I am not at all sure. They have very long rifles, and the way the sporran flows down the knees of the kneeling ones is superb craftsmanship. These are only in fair condition, and as happens with many solid German figures they have caught a touch of oxidation, and feel a little gritty between the fingers. Both the waving officer and the marching officer have lost their swords, the waving one has had a sliver of something soldered on as a replacement. Looking as good as they do in the photograph, one can only imagine how wonderful they might have appeared when new. The two pipers at attention are fairly common, and turn up from time to time. The group front centre are Heyde No.2 size Gordons in good condition, and then at the back left are battered Seaforths by other makers, three of which have lost their heads. I pick up figures in this condition to find new Highlanders without having to pay a fortune for them. The one I picked up at the BMSS 75th show is the third headless figure along. Left front are marching and action Gordons by Brigader-Statuette, the Danish maker who continued in the tradition of Heyde after the Second World War.

Another stall good for oddments is Peter Harris. He always has a chunk of stuff out of the ordinary. This time my eye is caught by a rank of British dragoons from Marlborough's time. They turn out to be made by Del Prado. Not often that you see these figures in quantity, when with this figure they actually look very good, better than as an individual piece, which is by no means true of all of them. He offers me one for £3, which can't be bad, so I buy it, and it will add nicely to my eighteenth century cameo, even if it is a little bulky.

From the British Model Soldier Society's own sales stand I pick a small set of New Toy Soldiers (£12), a scene of Winston Churchill walking round London blitz damage with King

Picture 87: The '45

Bonnie Prince Charlie by Carman presides over two of the same maker's clansmen, another with a standard bearer from Johillco's plastic Monarch series and a New Toy Soldier clansman at the back. The English forces are represented by a Cavendish sergeant, designed by Stadden, and two Del Prado dragoons.

George VI and Queen Elizabeth, and chatting to a rescue worker in tin helmet and gum boots who is having a cup of tea while resting on his pick. The figures are by a manufacturer I don't recognize, and although they are not very realistic, they have a certain charm, and should add neatly in to my ARP cameo (see picture 153).

Back to chat with Harry again. He is going through this tray of about thirty miniature cavalry he has got, costing £20, which contains quite a lot of different types. There are Britains miniature cavalry, a few the fully painted sort that are really hard to get, with at least four different non-Britains household cavalry figures either painted or gilt. In among all these are the small size Abel cavalry with the bases that must fit into some sort of special tray for moving them about. Similar German made trays were on offer at Gamages in 1902, and it is quite possible that Abel was importing these or similar items and then made their own. Anyway, here are five of the Abel cavalry, one of which has a movable arm, something I have not seen in this figure before, yet another excitement.

Next job for Harry, checking through his large box of mostly broken gilt cavalry he has acquired as a job lot from Ged Haley. There must be forty or fifty of them, and he very kindly asks me to take three for my collection, as a thank you gift for telling him about the Abels. These are all the standard Reka cavalry, marked Reka, British Make under the horse's belly. There is a lancer, a Scots Grey and a general officer, but they all have arms with lances, which is rather incongruous for the general officer. When I get them home, I look at the best quality finish equivalents in my shelves, which are all exactly the same casting, but the general has an arm with a sword, and the Scots Grey has an arm with a carbine.

Later. My step-grandson, apparently, likes to play with toy figures; he is four, about the age I was when I started. After a rapid think, I can't come up with any figures I would be happy for him to get his hands on, so I shall have to see what next week's *Plastic Warrior* show can produce suitable for him! All in all, the BMSS show has been a huge success for my collecting. Not only have I got twenty-five figures which fit into several current cameos, but I have seen quite a lot of things I had never come across before. What with chatting to many friends and doing some business for Bonhams, all in all, a great day.

Plastic Warrior 25th Anniversary Show
8th May 2010, Richmond

While space does not permit me quite so much detail in describing this show, it was another hugely fascinating occasion. I purchased 75 figures for £75 (co-incidence, the prices varied from £10 to 10p each), eleven of them in metal. Actually, if you do come across metal figures here, they are often cheaper than at other shows, as people are concentrating on plastic. I found a perfectly good long rein Britains Scots Grey that I could not resist at a fiver. Peter Harris gave me another of the Del Prado Dragoons. I found nine quite nice plastic knights at 10p each for my step-grandson. Another find was a blanked base Herald fixed arm Foot Guard at attention to go with my Zang cameo (see pictures 88 and 159). In fact, with the other three first Herald figures, it makes up a neat little four-figure cameo of its own.

Picture 88: Herald first figures

These first four models of the Herald range have an iconic fascination. Were one to look underneath the bases of these examples, the infantryman has the Zang trademark, the Highlander and Sikh have the famous Harrogate herald trademark, and the Grenadier Guard has a completely blank base with no indentation. An early Zang cameo might want to have all four figures in all three variations. When shown in the first Herald catalogue in 1953, they were given the identifications K1 (Khaki one) S1 (Scotsman one) I 1 (Indian one) and G1 (Guardsman one).

Auctions

The advantages of auctions

On expensive items, the price will, on average, find its level, so you will be likely to be paying a fair current price. On cheap items, you should be able to buy in bulk and end up paying much less than in shows or shops per figure. I may have mentioned already that I write catalogues for toy soldier auctions, currently for Bonhams. I hope I can say that lots described by me may be confidently purchased from anywhere in the world by reading my description carefully and looking at the website photograph. All the Web photography not included in the catalogues is taken by me while I am describing the lots.

The disadvantages of auctions

Occasionally you may find yourself in competition with someone determined to have something, in which case the bidding may exceed a sensible price. The only defence against this is to have the knowledge of what a sensible price is (see chapter 12), and drop out at anything above it. In general, each lot will involve a substantial expenditure, so if you just want one thing out of a lot, it may be better to look for it at a show or shop. You can always see if you can spot who buys and ask them if they will sell the piece to you, but that piece may have been the reason they bought it too! Some collectors buy a lot, take the piece, and re-enter the lot in the next sale without it.

Some advice for buying at auctions

- Examine everything that you are interested in carefully to see how good the condition is of each item.
- Work out what you would like to bid on.
- Allow for the addition of any buyer's premium and sales tax such as VAT.
- Estimate how much each lot is worth to you – i.e. how much would you be prepared to pay for it if you saw it at a show. To give it some excitement, add a few lots which you are not desperately interested in, and work out at what price you would be really delighted to get them as bargains.
- If you are present at the auction, you can work out how much of your budget you have taken up as you go along.
- **CAUTION** – try not to get involved in auction fever, i.e. bidding up against someone else because you MUST have it – they may well be doing the same!
- If you are not present at the auction, and the auctioneers are reputable, leave maximum bids on the auctioneers book, and they will bid only to your maximum for you. You will often secure items for less than your maximum. **CAUTION** – if it turns out that you never get it for less than the maximum, question the reputation of the auctioneers; they may not be fairly running your bid against the other bids they have.
- If you are leaving bids, the sum of all the bids you leave should be what you can afford to spend in total at the auction, as you could get them all.
- If you are not at the auction, the glossary in the catalogue should give you a reasonable idea of the condition of the figures (see Chapter 5).
- Be aware that some people will endeavour to reduce competition for their bids by denigrating the quality and condition of the figures. Judge for yourself, although it is always possible to talk to the auctioneers in person or by email if you are in any doubt.
- Sit where you can best see and be seen by the auctioneer. Some people enjoy sitting at the back to see who else is bidding. I prefer to rely on my preparation to decide my actions for me.
- If as the auction starts, the general level of prices seems to have risen or fallen, you will need to think quickly as to whether (if falling) you might want to pick up some extra bargains or (if rising) you might want to hold off some items in order to be better sure of obtaining the lots you want most.
- The auction will proceed quickly, maybe one lot every 20 seconds, so concentrate to make sure you are ready when the ones you want come up. The auctioneer will be looking around for your bid, so a straightforward wave of your hand or your paddle will record your bid. If he seems to be ignoring you, he is using increasing bids from others, but at some point (if you are still in the running) the bidding will stop and you

will be able to attract his attention.

- The bidding will normally go up in increments of about ten to twenty per cent.
- Don't be tempted to bid for anything that seems cheap but which you did not examine before the auction – there is probably a good reason why the bidding is not moving.
- Sometimes when bidding is strong, you may not be sure whether you were the successful bidder. If you are not sure, ask the auctioneer immediately 'Was that mine?', as the bidding can be re-started if there has been genuine confusion, but once the sale has moved on it will not be possible. In these events, the auctioneer's decision is final, but he will not wish to leave buyers unhappy.
- When you collect lots you have bought, check them out to see if they contain everything you saw in them at the view. If not, tell the auctioneer immediately. Reputable auctioneers will refund you or compensate you accordingly.
- Bring your own packing material unless you know from experience this will be provided.

Online auctions

The great new thing to hit the whole of society since my last collecting book has been the Internet, and one of the major commercial opportunities has been seen to be the ability to put auctions online. Now I haven't myself ever bid for anything on eBay, but I have heard from many who have. It is perfectly possible to find great things on eBay, bid for them and buy them successfully without anyone else having spotted them. All it takes is some time trawling the 30,000 or so offers that come up when you enter 'toy soldiers'.

It is a good thing to have an idea of what something might be worth, and also to regard descriptions and photographs with some caution. Some of the items will be genuine repaints, and some intriguingly talked about as 'really old toy soldiers' with fuzzy photos to match. Every now and then, however, up pops a previously unknown to exist Britains set. I have heard about more of these sets in the last ten years than I did in the previous twenty, as a direct result of eBay being available. Generally, however, these things have to be winnowed from the chaff of perfectly ordinary Britains, Timpo *et al* from the last few decades being sold individually by collectors or dealers at anything from one to twenty pounds each. By and large, this sort of material is what works best on the net, and anything really tasty will sell better at a traditional auction where more attention can be focussed on it.

Today, every auction has some sort of online component, even if it is only online viewing, and this has meant that the competition for lots even at obscure country auctions is now fiercer than ever. Bonhams is now moving with the times and has real-time auction bidding online.

Time is money

This old saying is more true than ever in this day and age. Tramping the streets in search of a bargain has been exchanged for the less exhausting but just as time consuming trawl through the Internet. Attending endless provincial sales and following up every lead pays off in the end, but you will spend a lot of time doing it. It is a lot easier to first make your fortune, and then employ agents to look for your preferred requirements, or commission them to be made. At the other end of things, you will sell most advantageously by going direct to collectors at shows, but ticketing, transport, unpacking, layout, packing up again and wondering at what price you will actually see the last of them is much slower than putting them into auction and paying someone to present them world-wide in the best possible light.

54

The joys and sorrows of collecting

At this point I would like to share with you two stories, one from the old days and one from the recent past. I am sure that the morals of these stories will be self-evident.

The old days

Imagine the excitement of going to a show, when I was in my acquisitive stage. Get up early, really early, the early bird catches the worm. If a show opens at 10.00 a.m. all the good things will be gone by 10.05. I well remember one of the Slough shows on 3rd June 1978, put on by the Maidenhead Static Model Club. Before the days of specialised toy soldier shows, there were only a dozen tables out of maybe 300 which had significant toy soldiers, but this time I picked up, for £150 the pair, two superb early sets of Britains, both Middlesex Regiment set 76, one in a lovely old un-numbered box with a naïve illustration of a soldier resting arms in front of two tents. This was a very rare early variation, of which quite possibly very few were issued, as I have never (until recently, see below) seen or heard of an equivalent set. It was composed entirely of wasp-waisted figures, and included an officer, two pioneers and five men at the trail. The other was a standard set of valise pack figures marching at the slope with a pioneer and a wasp-waisted officer, in a numbered printer's decorated box, which had Boer War battle honours included, so it could not have been before 1903. As the new box pack came into production from 1905, the set is unlikely to date from any later.

I cannot imagine any more glorious moment than the discovery and acquisition of such beauties. The figures were in good condition, not by any means perfect, but very acceptable considering how old they were. Ever since I saw a beautiful group of throat-plumed cavalry officers in Gloucester, and had missed out on an amazing collection of early Britains in Colne, Lancashire, I had been more than ever desirous of adding nice early Britains to my collection. Every collector will remember for the rest of his life the generally few occasions where by dint of patience and search he comes to some real gems for sale, which he can at that moment afford.

The Middlesex Regiment sets became the centrepiece of a Middlesex Regiment cameo. The Middlesex set 76 was one of the sets which lasted from the very early days right through to the end of hollowcast production, so it is possible to assemble a sequence of the different versions in their packaging which amounts to up to eight different sets showing the evolution of Britains hollowcast British infantry. As the Middlesex was a London regiment, Britains were always keen to represent it; it appeared in a number of display boxes as well as in the Parade series, and there was a special Band produced for it as set 1458. Later, Britains featured it in the Eyes Right plastic series and in the Metal Models sets.

When I put together *Britains Toy Soldiers 1983-1932*, I used the more common of the two sets to illustrate in the book on page 80, at the top. Looking back, I am not sure that I got the right box lid to go with it, as I never made a note of what type of box lid it came with. Swapping over box lids, of course, is the easiest thing in the world to do, either inadvertently or on purpose.

All these gave opportunities to extend the cameo, the sequence being the easiest to achieve, so I did that, and proudly presented the result at a British Model Soldier Society old soldier competition evening. Now, this competition cannot be won simply by putting out a display, no matter how rare. The entries, usually cameos, have to really engage the imagination and have interesting commentary to match, so I didn't win. However the rarer sets attracted much attention, particularly from some light-fingered gentleman who made off with one of the wasp-waisted figures at the trail (you see, I did promise you sorrows as well!) Of course, such events are not insured, so there was no way I could be compensated or even consoled.

So that was that – but there was a sequel. Some years later, in my role as cataloguer for Phillips, I came across an interesting cache of extremely rare single figures in the posthumous property of a gentleman which had come in for sale. Among these, was the wasp-waisted Middlesex figure. As the gentleman concerned had been one of the forty or so enthusiasts present the evening of the loss, I was forced to conclude that he had in all likelihood been the culprit. One is always saddened when one hears of instances where people succumb to temptation of this kind. Of course there was no way I could prove it, and in any case I had already sold the incomplete set in disgust.

I have spent two or three hours delving into such records as I have to try and find when and for how much I purchased these sets. I had thought they must have come to me around 1974, but I had to go to 1978 to find them so that I could put in my date of acquisition above. I won't say that every collector will want to keep exhaustive records of buying and selling, because it is quite laborious, but my father always used to urge me to keep meticulous records of where and when everything, new from the shops or second hand, came to me. I haven't been nearly so meticulous as perhaps I should have been, but the fact remains that every time I come across notes to myself, or look through the three red purchasing books that I kept from 1972 onwards, I have blessed every entry I have ever made.

On 26th October 1988, after just over ten years of possession, at auction I sadly parted company with my two early Middlesex Regiment sets. A prominent American collector paid £1,540 for the incomplete wasp-waisted set, and £1,320 for the valise pack set. Again, there is a sequel. On 5th October 2002, a set of wasp-waisted Middlesex Regiment turned up at a top Bertoia auction in the US. Here, there are six at the trail with pioneer and officer, so it looks as if this should be a different set, since mine had two pioneers and one at the trail missing. But hang on a minute, looking at the box lid, the label is slightly torn in precisely the same places as with my original set, which is illustrated on page 66 of my book, *Phillips Collector's Guides: Toy Soldiers*. So what is going on here?

My guess would be that during the intervening fourteen years, an additional wasp-waisted figure has been found, and appropriate arm changes made, to make the set look more complete. This is not at all evident from the Bertoia catalogue, but may be more visible on close examination, where any colour mis-matches or arm swops might show up. In any case, the price that was paid on the day for the completed set was $1,320, a considerable discount from the price I obtained for it, incomplete but untampered with, fourteen years previously. Maybe somebody noticed. It is actually by no means impossible, this figure being so rare, that the missing figure was re-united by a circuitous route with the set!

Recently

I always go round the shows looking for the odd thing that I can't resist buying to round out my examples of things to show people. My budget is extremely limited these days. Usually the most expensive things I buy are books on soldiers.

However, last year I found someone who was selling individual Britains Honourable Artillery Company pikemen, of which there is just one in each limited edition set 5291 issued in 1991. Looking at these more closely, he had them in original Britains bulk boxes, nine to the box, with the catalogue number 5852, which never appeared in the Britains catalogue. He wanted £3 each for the figures, or £20 for a box of nine, which I felt to be a bargain, so I bought a box.

When I got them home, they actually fitted quite well with my display of English Civil

War figures, if a touch tall, being on rather thick bases like all the Metal Models series from Britains. However, their red uniforms seemed evocative of Cromwell's New Model Army, and with their London connection, the London trained bands having played an important role on the Parliamentary side, I was very happy with them. When Sky News rang me to do a piece to comment on a new 11-inch Action Man style figure launch approved last year by the Ministry of Defence, I thought of incorporating them as the first models of a short history in toys of the British Army, which would end with the new figures.

With all this activity, I became more and more fond of the figures, and thought, why didn't I get more of these when I had the chance? I rushed back to the same place at the following show, but of course they had all gone, and the best price I could find was £6 a figure, which felt a bit steep considering what I paid before. Never mind, I was very happy with my nine stalwarts, as I was never otherwise going to be able to collect nine individuals from nine Limited Edition sets from 1991. When I went to the *Plastic Warrior* 25th Anniversary Show (see above) the dealer with the £6 figures was there and still hadn't sold them, so I was able to make a price with him on another seven to bring their numbers up to sixteen.

On this occasion, I noticed that here Britains had not gone to the expense of making a die-casting mould for these, but must have done them in a solid casting mould, maybe even outsourced to someone like HM of Great Britain, who produced the Mountain Battery centenary set. Unfortunately, this means that the models are not quite as crisp and clean as the regular Metal Models. In addition, there is sometimes a problem with the pike heads, and when I got the seven new men home, I discovered one of the pike heads was missing! One just has to live with such little annoyances.

Picture 89: Honourable Artillery Company see text

This sixteen strong squad of the Britains model of the famous City of London unit could, I imagine, have stepped straight out of the New Model Army with their red uniforms. I think they fit in well with the Britains English Civil War pikemen and others. The Rose musketeer front left, and the beautiful converted cavalryman with the pistol back right are also just the kind of models to add interest to otherwise straightforward groups of the famous Britains ECW figures.

Things to come

How have I found my attitudes towards collecting changing over the years? First of all comes the realisation that not all things are possible. Then there is the comfort of having done most of it, either in my own collection, or by proxy through having seen, or sold for them, an awful lot of other people's. The top collecting moments among the memories become brighter, more interesting and more significant with hindsight.

Thinking about Faudel Phillips and James Renvoize and which figures belonged to whom, or maybe James Renvoize made all of them and some went into Faudel Phillips boxes – that sort of thing can be an ongoing debate that is never necessarily totally resolved. All that can be known, unless illustrated documentation is discovered, is that there are these incredibly evocative toy soldiers with broad shoulders, big heads and loads of nicely sculpted equipment, painted neatly in the turn of the century conventional best quality style, which might belong under one or the other maker's name. They are obviously based on the same body or by the same designer (see picture 108).

As one part of the collection becomes reasonably well understood, so comes the urge to investigate and collect something new. Britains are now very well known, and so the most exciting parts of this world-beating company today are the very hard to get items, the pre-First World War sets and versions, the recognised WOW! factor top sets of the interwar and postwar hollowcast period, the Paris office production, the special paintings and the rarities among the more recent production for collectors. All of these have also held up well in price and may expect to continue so to do.

Apart from this, the areas of most excitement are the equivalents in the other major firms, Heyde, Hausser, Lineol and CBG Mignot, and the times of change when things were moving fast with no one really recording what was going on. I cite 1893 to 1916 and 1946 to 1960 in particular, but every period still produces its own surprises and fascinations, with plenty yet to research, reveal and collect. Not least in interest is the current diversity, with collectors being able to choose between the charmingly stylised toy soldier and breathtakingly realistic models or almost anything in between. I learned the other day that Del Prado had gone into administration. Who might eventually start making further figures from their moulds? The story continues. In chapter 12, I reveal what I think the future trends will be in values and collecting.

CHAPTER 4
TOY SOLDIER IDENTIFICATION AND RESEARCH

Finding out about toy soldiers is a most interesting part of collecting them, and can be taken to extraordinary lengths. Why is it that we have the urge to know more and more detail about each and every toy soldier that we come across or even hear about? It seems for me to be a thirst for knowledge, to be the person who knows. So you have a toy soldier in your hands, and you want to know what it is, what do you do? Close observation should be able to tell you much about what you are looking at.

First question – what type of figure is it? If you have read through this book this far, you should have a good idea of the possibilities. The most likely will be flat, semi-flat, solid or hollowcast metal, composition or plastic. All other materials are relatively uncommon. Solid metal figures can be old, usually having quite a high proportion of lead, and therefore weighty for their bulk, aluminium or die-cast, in which case they will be much lighter – the aluminium ones make a musical clink when tapped with each other – or New Toy Soldiers, made for the collector either in the old stylised toy soldier conventions or as more realistic models. These new ones usually have a relatively high tin content, and so are midway between the die-cast zinc ones and the old lead-rich ones in weight.

After this initial classification, the next question is to establish who made it. For this, the easy first action is to spot if it has any identifying name on it, often underneath the base if there is one. If not under the base or the horse's belly, lettering may be embossed down a trouser leg or across a back. Examine from all angles, just in case. In the absence of a Britains' or other useful maker's name, any lettering can be informative. 'England' or 'Made in England' can indicate or rule out several manufacturers, for instance. Initials can point towards a French maker. If there is packaging, this can also yield the manufacturer's name or clues to identity, but be careful of figures in the wrong boxes.

If no lettering evidence presents itself, first establish in your own mind what the toy soldier is made from and the method of manufacture, explained in chapter 2. Then try looking at the base, design and moulding, to see if they match up to any soldiers you have that you know the manufacturer of. Base shapes can be very distinctive, for instance, particularly with flats and semi-flats. The following list will be useful as to which manufacturers to consider and which to rule out, before going on to paint style, below. If the manufacturer can be established, then the figure can be researched in the manufacturer's catalogues, if any. Reproduction catalogues (as well as originals) are in wide circulation and always provide interesting reading. As original source material, they often give information to verify conclusions.

Major and selected manufacturers, by material and method of manufacture

These are the leading manufacturers within each style of manufacture. Some, of course, have manufactured in various different ways and so appear in more than one group. I have annotated the list with comments on the wording or trade marks visible on the model where I know of them. Most manufacturers other than Britains were not totally consistent about markings, particularly before 1946. Part of your collecting career would be adding to this relatively short list with all your favourite manufacturers. The most extensive compilation of manufacturers is that by the late John G. Garratt in his *World Encyclopedia of Model Soldiers*.

- NO = not usually marked.
- OCC = occasionally marked
- YES = usually marked – with comments
- CAT = catalogues produced
- H = I know of models of Highlanders available in range (I may well be ignorant of some where I don't put an H) (see chapter 8)

Flats

Often have distinctive base shapes (not necessarily mentioned below). High tin content.
- Besold Germany OCC base curves in from both ends to centre
- CBG Mignot France CAT NO
- Heinrichsen Germany H OCC
- Hilpert Germany NO
- Neckel Germany NO
- Ochel (common trademarks Kilia or Oki) Germany CAT YES sometimes long diamond shaped bases

Picture 90: Flat Napoleonic mounted

Look at this group of 28mm scale flats showing troops of the Napoleonic period. Notice that the bases are shaped differently. The group on the left which could be Wellington and Blucher at Waterloo have irregular oval bases. The British dragoons in the centre have bases with concave edges, and the cavalryman on the right has a diamond shaped base. Heinz Schenzle issued a compilation of base shapes and marks for flat figures in 1987 that seems to me to be definitive. However, many makers used similar base shapes, and there were a distressing number of figures made without any initials or marks on top or underneath the bases. Many flats remain a puzzle, at least to those such as myself without a deep lifelong familiarity with them.

In terms of the painting, the group on the left are painted in modern matt collector style, which when well done can make them into tiny works of art, for instance the work of the late Jim Woodley. The British dragoons are in gloss, which could well be a manufacturers finish, but does not look particularly early, more like the 1930s. Notice that there are two different figures among these, but only one of the second figure, with the sword arm held high. One of these also has a repaired base. One of them is turned end on to show how thin the figures are. The cavalryman on the diamond shaped base could also be a manufacturer's original finish, perhaps a little earlier than the others. Very few flats of this sort are worth more than about fifty pence each.

Semi-flats

High lead content
- Allgeyer Germany YES thin base with wide side supports
- Besold Germany OCC
- CBG Mignot France CAT NO
- Haffner NO some bases have double pointed side spurs
- Ideal CAT NO (Moulds)
- Prinz August CAT NO (Moulds)
- Spenkuch NO long thin base with slope ended side supports
- Schneider H NO (Moulds)
- Unknown NO
- Wollner NO

Picture 91: Semi-flat Highlanders

These small German semi-flats were affordable in quantity around 1880. Spot which two are by a different maker to the main body.

Clue: their kilts are a little shorter than might be comfortable. I'm afraid I have no idea of the names of either manufacturer.

Solids

High lead content
- Authenticast Eire CAT H YES marked Eire
- Bertrand et Vertunni France CAT NO
- Brigader-Statuette Denmark CAT H NO
- CBG Mignot France CAT H YES post 1950 only CBG Made in France
- Capell Spain NO
- Castresana Spain NO
- Figir Italy NO
- Haffner Germany H NO
- Heinrich Germany also trademark Noris H NO
- Heyde Germany CAT H NO
- Krause Germany H NO oblong base

- Lucotte France H OCC Imperial Bee stamped under base
- Prinz August Sweden CAT NO Moulds
- Spenkuch H NO
- Swedish-African Engineers South Africa CAT H YES

Picture 92: Heyde Charge of the Light Brigade

Heyde No.2 size (48mm scale) British 4th Light Dragoons at the battle of Balaklava. The matt painted finish tells us that these are later figures, maybe the 1930s. Earlier figures were in gloss finish, the reverse of Britains, where the earlier figures, before 1900, tend to have a more matt appearance than the later ones. probably because there was less varnish mixed into the paint.

Hollowcasts Pre-WWI

Hollow, often with a small hole in the head
- Abel UK H NO
- BMC UK H NO
- Britains UK CAT H YES but not if model first created before 1900
- Faudel Phillips UK H NO
- Fry UK H NO
- Hanks UK H NO
- Heinrich Germany F H NO
- McLauchlan USA NO
- Reka (C.W.Baker) UK H YES
- Renvoize UK H NO
- Simon & Rivollet France NO

Picture 93: Bischoff

I was once told that the charming marching Prussians on the left were the work of an obscure maker named Bischoff. From the paint style, they pre-date the First World War. The equally interesting rather larger scale figures to the right look as if they are French hollowcasts from the 1920s. I currently have them in the German section of my Boxer rebellion display, but they could equally be shown in the nineteenth century European section or Franco-Prussian War.

Picture 94: Charging Highlanders: Lord Roberts

These Highlanders were probably all to a greater or lesser degree inspired by the Britains original plug handed Highlander, shown third and fourth from the right, without the plugs, as usually found. The nearest copy is the Hanks figure at the extreme right – you can see how Britains would have got irritated by this one, the only real difference is the rather dangerous looking fixed bayonet. Behind the Hanks figure is a very similar Reka figure, sufficiently different not to be confused. The rather crude figure to the left of the Hanks is of unknown origin. The rest of the figures are supposedly from Lord Roberts Workshops, and include charming men in bonnets and field caps, with a running piper who must be extremely clever to keep playing while he jogs along. Even if found headless, like the only one here painted as a Seaforth, they are worth picking up at reasonable prices, since they are extremely rare.

63

Picture 95: British hollowcast Infantry of the Line on guard 1900 to 1930

If the marching figures were bad enough, those on guard are a real headache. Back row, left to right, two Hanks second grade, Hill, Britains Best Quality, Britains second grade, unknown, Hill second grade and three unknowns, some of which may be earlier figures by Hill, who seemed particularly fond of the on guard position. In the front row, only the third figure along, which is a later Hill model, is established. The first and fifth figures could be Faudel Phillips, but the others remain unidentified. One of the final reference books yet to be done is of military hollowcast figures other than Britains, organized by subject rather than manufacturer. Whether such a book would help find the origins of many of the above, I cannot tell.

Picture 96: British hollowcast marching Infantry of the Line 1900 to 1930

Identification photographs of this kind can be found in a number of reference books on toy soldiers. Starting from the back row (rifles on the right shoulder), and working from left to right, Reka Best Quality, Reka second grade, three unknown maker, Britains fixed arm, Hanks Best Quality, Hanks second grade, Renvoize (rifle missing). Front row (rifles on the left shoulder) unknown, Hanks gameboard (note the odd shaped base, which fits the gameboard), Abel, unknown, Britains Best Quality, Wellington Toy Company, Russell and BMC.

Hollowcasts interwar

- Britains UK CAT H YES
- Charbens UK NO
- Crescent UK CAT H
- Johillco UK CAT H OCC often marked Proprietors or Props
- Taylor and Barrett UK H sometimes marked T&B
- Unknown French often have initials of the maker underneath the base
- Warren USA

Picture 97: BMC Boxes (earlier)

Identifying figures is sometimes made easier by the presence of an original box. BMC issued many of their soldiers in Union Jack Series boxes.

Picture 98: BMC Boxes (later)

When BMC were in their heyday they issued their figures in boxes with full colour labels, here using the artwork from the famous History and Traditions series of postcards, and other art for the North American Indians box.

65

Picture 99: BMC types of European armies

BMC was a maker with a very distinctive style. Here, round the front of the Russian mounted Cossacks, are examples of Belgian, French, Serb and Russian infantry, with an Italian Bersagliere, a Belgian kneeling which looks rather like a BMC but is actually probably by Fry, an Austrian in field grey with two probably meant to be Austrian Foot Guards in front of him. The splendid Cossack officer is to the right rear.

Hollowcast post-WWII

- Britains UK CAT H YES
- Charbens UK H YES
- Cherilea UK CAT H YES
- Crescent UK NO often marked Made in England
- Johillco UK CAT H OCC
- Lone Star Harvey UK
- Timpo UK CAT YES

Dime-store hollowcast

NB Dime store is not a term that defines the method of manufacture, but can be applied to any figures originally sold in dime stores in the USA.
- Barclay USA
- Jones USA NO
- Lincoln Logs USA
- Manoil USA
- Minikin Japan

Composition

Made of a sort of pliable plaster on a wire frame and then baked.
- Brevetti Italy YES
- Durso Belgium YES
- Hausser-Elastolin Germany CAT H YES except very early models

- Lineol Germany CAT H YES
- Preiser Germany
- Timpo UK H NO
- Tippco Germany tinplate vehicles to accompany composition figures

Plastic, painted

- Britains UK CAT H YES
- Charbens UK CAT H OCC
- Cherilea UK CAT H OCC sometimes small square hole under base
- Crescent UK CAT H YES
- Elastolin Germany CAT YES
- Herald UK CAT H YES
- Kentoy UK NO

Picture 100: Herald horses

The earliest Herald horse, for the Household Cavalry, was made out of a relatively brittle cellulose acetate plastic in two hollow halves. It is quite rare to find. I just have this one example with the tail missing, which often happened to it. The replacement horse was solid and much more enduring. The problem with early plastic was that it was difficult to get the paint to stick to the oily surface, so flaking has been a problem as here. The copy on foot is quite early, as it is marked 'Empire Made'. 'Made in Hong Kong' was required from around 1955.

- Lone Star UK CAT H YES
- Malleable Mouldings UK H grooved oblong base Made in England
- Marx US UK Yes
- Merten CAT Germany
- Nardi Italy YES
- Pfeiffer Germany CAT
- Preiser Germany CAT
- Speedwell UK NO
- Starlux France CAT YES
- Timpo UK CAT H YES on top of base
- Trojan UK CAT NO
- Unknown Hong Kong NO but often marked Empire or Hong Kong

Picture 101: Combat Infantry

When Herald brought out their superb British combat infantry in 1953 and 1954, all the other makers who rushed into plastic to emulate Herald's success wanted to issue similar figures. The result was a plethora of copies as never seen before or since. Benbros, F.G. Taylor, Johillco, Speedwell, Una, Lone Star and a Japanese firm under the initials AHI producing toy soldiers in metal for the U.S. market, as well as numbers of makers in Hong Kong, all produced figures looking remarkably like the Herald originals. Here is a selection of them. Try spotting which ones are direct copies and which are not. The four first figures from Herald are at the back centre left, with quite shiny smooth helmets. The whole row far left is of copies. The ones more to the front centre left are later versions of Herald. To the right are figures from John Hill and Co (Johillco), who at least had the grace to include some copies of Timpo and Starlux in their series.

Picture 102: Athena Greeks

Ancient Greeks as the Greeks see them. The foot and mounted figures on green bases are Greek Hoplites by Athena, the two with black bases by another Greek maker, all bought in Athens circa 1972 while I was on a Mediterranean cruise. Contrast with the brilliant Conte Spartan (front right, 2009) which although uncoloured, is about the same 60mm scale and rather more realistically muscular.

Plastic unpainted

- Airfix UK CAT NO
- Atlantic Italy
- Esci Italy
- Marx USA YES
- Matchbox UK CAT NO
- Timpo UK CAT H YES

Plastic unpainted for collectors

- Conte USA
- Replicants UK
- Armies in Plastic US
- Toyway UK

Die-cast

- Britains UK CAT early NO post 1973 H YES
- Unknown Russian NO

Aluminium

- Quiralu France CAT H NO
- Mignalu France NO
- Wend-Al UK CAT H NO sometimes had labels under base

Other materials

- Auburn USA rubber
- Chad Valley thick card UK OCC
- Dunwood White pressed tin UK NO
- Sonnenburg wood, Germany NO
- Gerbeau plaster, France NO
- Unknown wood, plaster etc NO
- Unknown Chinese, plaster NO
- Unknown Russian, plaster NO

New Toy Soldiers

See Appendix.

Picture 103: Chad Valley card figures

These were printed on thick card and put into small slotted wooden blocks as bases. Occasionally a short description of the regiment appeared on the back. The three Gordons marching as one vignette at the front are on much thicker card and probably by another maker. Chad Valley at the back, left to right, Cameron, Scots Grey and two Gordons.

Picture 104: Indian and Chinese plaster figures

Traditional style figures made out of plaster in India and China are a common souvenir of visits, and sometimes make their way around the world as exports. The Chinese ones in front are probably much the same as they have been made for centuries, the boxed set of an Indian Army band is a modern regiment in an ancient style.

Models

- Andrea Spain CAT YES
- Berdou France YES Signed
- Des Fontaines France OCC
- Hinchcliffe UK YES
- Julia Spain OCC
- Kiersley UK H YES
- Labayen Spain YES
- Rose UK CAT H YES
- Stadden UK CAT H YES studio paintings signed
- Willie UK CAT H NO, but usually in 30mm scale

Collector models
(Virtually all ranges of collector models include highlanders)
- All the Queen's Men CAT UK
- Almirall Spain NO
- Alymer Spain CAT YES

Picture 105: Collector models: Britains, Sudan

One of my grandfathers worked for much of the 1920s and 1930s in the Sudan. The current political turmoil there reflects more closely the war torn years of the 1880s and 1890s than the eradication of disease that he was trying to bring. For historians of the British Empire, the campaigns depicted by the figures shown here were a necessary pre-requisite to any kind of progress such as that my grandfather was engaged in.

The models by Britains are a step further towards realism, and in earlier years would have turned heads at modeling shows. Now in 2010 they are taken for granted as the sort of thing that Britains collectors can expect.

70

- Britains USA CAT YES
- Bussler USA NO
- Carman UK NO
- Casadevall Spain NO
- Conte USA CAT YES
- Courtenay UK OCC signed
- Courtenay-Greenwood UK YES
- De Agostini Italy NO
- Del Prado Spain YES
- Greenwood and Ball UK YES
- H & M UK YES
- Imrie-Risley USA OCC
- King and Country Hong Kong CAT YES
- Metayer France NO
- Ping UK NO
- Rose UK YES
- Scheid USA NO
- St Petersburg Collection Russia YES
- Vertunni France NO

Picture 106: Collector models: King and Country, The Streets of Old Hong Kong

On the docks, perhaps in the 1930s in Hong Kong, American sailors are much in evidence in this diorama, befitting the trading nature of the island. As a company founded in Hong Kong, King and Country have had somewhat of an inside track to the craftsmanship of the Chinese that has become all pervading in recent model production. Specialising in dioramas that can be assembled from ready finished modules, as well as individual figures, King and Country provide spectacle on a grand scale. There is even a display of this series in my local Chinese restaurant!

Toy soldier identification

When were they made?

In establishing the date of manufacture, another important consideration is where the figures came from. Did they belong to a family member, and if so, when would they have played with them? If acquired more recently, was it from someone who originally owned them, or from a dealer or auction? Always find out as much about the provenance of the figures as possible. Can you rule out the last forty years? As a rule of thumb, if they existed before 1973, they are probably toys – if made later, they are more likely to have been made for collectors.

It is helpful to know when you bought them, particularly if you had them from a toyshop when you were young. If you bought them before 1950, they are probably old toy soldiers. If they were bought after 1973, they may well be modern toy soldiers made for collectors. If they are solid in 25mm scale or less, they could be wargaming figures.

Recognising paint style and design

At the start of the twentieth century, the style in which toy soldiers were painted was conventionalised as follows. Best quality painted figures comprised headgear with ornaments and sometimes chinstrap, a face with eyes and mouth or moustache, pink cheeks, hair painted at the nape of the neck, uniform jacket with correctly contrasting coloured collar and cuffs, buttons and possibly some piping, hands or gloves, correctly coloured weapons, trousers with stripes, boots and a grass green base. Any falling short on this was not best quality, and was sometimes entitled second quality, and represented a saving to the manufacturer, being sold for less.

Researching which figure was made by which maker is often a matter of having your eye in for a particular style or design. Remember that some commercial designers worked freelance and made models for various different makers. For example, Wilfred Cherrington worked for Britains on occasion, and reputedly for Courtenay, before going into his own firm as the Cheri part of Cherilea. Once a mould was made, it could well change hands and be in use for various successor companies. This has been true throughout the commercial history of toy soldiers, although thankfully more with just the smaller makers than the larger more successful manufacturers.

The classic method of research is first by manufacturer's list or catalogue, to try and establish whether the manufacturer you suspect made something has it listed. Lists also appear in adverts in trade magazines. By and large, the more a manufacturer advertises, the more successful they are. Unfortunately, many manufacturers did not advertise and didn't issue lists, and certainly did not issue illustrated lists useful for marrying figures with maker. To complicate matters further, many wholesalers, importers and distributors advertised their wares as if they were their own manufacture.

To find out who made what, it is important to find original

Picture 107: Beiser moustache

Matching moustaches can be a useful way of checking if a set is in the same style. This is certainly the most magnificent moustache I have ever seen on a Britains figure, which is one of those shipped to the U.S. around 1908 to be included in a Beiser American Soldier Company game set. My thanks to Harry Kemp for allowing me to take a picture of this one, which he acquired from the world's foremost collector of Beiser sets in the U.S. (See also picture 220.)

Picture 108: Renvoize

These fourteen early British hollowcast figures are thought to have been made by Renvoize, with the possible exceptions of figures two and the last three on the right. Figures four to ten have a certain breadth of shoulder that hints at the same designer, who could well also have made the rather shorter sailors. He seems to favour full equipment. The infantryman, fusilier and guardsman five to seven appear at a first glance all to be the same body with different heads, but actually, although the best quality painting is the same style, the infantryman has designed in crossbelts that are rather wider than those on the fusilier, and the guardsman has none at all. It took me forty years to find the beautiful complete Highlander, who is in the uniform of the Black Watch. The armless one next to him is a Cameron. These figures are so much rarer than most Britains that they are well worth buying even in the poor condition of the fusilier figure six. One can get lucky and find them in junk boxes. The three sailors are shown with three different arms, shoulder, carry and slope. The arm at the carry on the colonial figure four appears identical to that on the sailor behind him, but rather different to the fusilier figure twelve. The rifle at the slope of figure two is very different to that of figure ten. Bases are all oval, but the paint colour compared shows a rather darker green for figure two than for the rest. These details add up to making a decision as to which figures belong with which, in the absence of any maker's marks.

figures in original boxes, and having established that the name on the box, if any, is not just a wholesaler, to extrapolate from the figures known to belong to a particular maker to figures where the make was previously unknown. This is done by design and painting style. I will illustrate this from my favourite period, before the First World War, when Britains was competing with Abel, Hanks, Reka and Renvoize, among many others.

Particularly helpful are movable arms, often fitted to the best quality range. Reka, for instance, sometimes used a shoulder stud that they pinched like the end of an axle on a toy car to make sure the arm stayed in place. Any toy soldier with an arm fixing like that is almost sure to be Reka, although occasionally an early Hill will look somewhat similar. The best quality infantry tended to be a little shorter than Britains and to have rather large heads for their bodies. The Hanks arms have a very distinctive style of rifle.

Renvoize specialised in producing very nicely designed figures once they had been warned off from copying Britains, but their output appears to have been limited. Abel figures can have very oddly shaped bases with metal blocks or sockets in them, used to fit them to patented drill trays so that they can be moved around in formation.

Apart from looking at the paint itself, comparing painting styles from figure to figure is useful. How the bases are painted is important. The shade of green used is often distinctive for a particular maker, and how much paint gets underneath the base can also be indicative. The colour of the metal is often unique to particular makers. Hanks, for instance, used a rather bright, light metal that was a bit too shiny to take the paint very well, so that they tend to be somewhat more flaked than other makes.

The finish of each manufacturer has its own patina, and can be a great aid to identification. Just as an art critic can instinctively feel which painter crated a particular picture, so are toy soldier manufacturers identifiable from the overall look and feel of their work.

Uniforms

Picture 109: London's soldiers – uniforms

London's soldiers, many of whom are prominently featured in the capital as souvenirs, can include Territorial regiments such as the Middlesex Yeomanry by Hanks in green. The Chelsea pensioner (back left by Heyde) and Yeoman Warder at the Tower of London (back right by Wend-Al) are usually well known. The Britains die-cast models of dismounted Household Cavalry are simply distinguished by the Life Guards having red jackets and the Royal Horse Guards having blue. The five regiments of Foot Guards are a little more subtle, the most obvious differences, shown here in Britains hollowcast, are the plumes in the bearskin head-dress, white on the left for the Grenadiers, red on the right for the Coldstreams, no plume for the Scots, blue on the right for the Irish and white and green on the left for the Welsh. The mounted officer for the Grenadier Guards shown here is an extremely rare figure from a Parade set.

Some uniforms like the British Foot Guards, Highlanders or Life Guards are usually instantly recognizable. After that, things become harder. Uniform identification is a large subject, so do not worry about getting this correct. There are useful books on uniforms, and the books by myself or Joe Wallis will give you the correct colours for each regiment depicted by Britains. Other toy soldier makers would have used the same conventions. Many regiments, for instance, of British infantry of the line in full dress would be indistinguishable from each other at the level of detail conventionally used for best quality toy soldier paintwork.

What people call toy soldiers and models

There are many names that people use to describe toy soldiers, and these sometimes get in the way of finding the best information on the Web to do with identification. You can try putting the following terms into search engines: toy soldiers, lead soldiers, tin soldiers, metal soldiers, model soldiers, antique soldiers, plastic soldiers, toy figures, little soldiers. All of these and the various manufacturer's names are often mis-spelled.

When was a Britains hollowcast figure made?

Britains toy soldiers are the ones most frequently collected, bought and sold. The following clues should enable you to decide within a range of a few years when a Britains hollowcast figure was issued from the factory. Here is what to look for, the dates given applying to Britains production. The terms are in common use among collectors, and are a useful part of the collector's vocabulary.

- **Set numbering**. From 1893 to 1961, Britains' standard size best quality sets were, with a few exceptions, very simply numbered in sequence from 1 to 2190. For any set, therefore, there is a year in which it first came out before which it could not have been made. Thus nothing with a set number higher than 103 could have been made before 1900, and nothing higher than 197 before 1917. 198 to 490 first saw the light of day between 1917 and 1932. The numbers from 500 to 1200 were reserved for individual civilian items. Sets numbered between 1200 and 1920 were first produced between 1932 and 1940. Many sets were discontinued from 1941, and new sets started from 1948 above 2000, reaching set 2190 in 1961.

- **Plug shoulder cavalry** (lancers or Scots Greys). The movable arm is on a long plug that passes through both shoulders. RARE 1893-1897.
- **Plug handed infantry** (highlanders or fusiliers). The hand grasping the weapon, rifle or sword, plugs into the wrist. RARE 1893-1903.
- **Oval bases**. Most new figures on foot produced with oval bases 1893-1906.
- **Officers on rearing horse**. First made in 1894 to go with sets 1-3, 12 and 13. If these sets have no rearing horse officer, they were made in 1893.
- **Gaitered infantry – firing or on guard**. The trouser bottoms above the boots are visibly tightened with gaiters. 1894-1934.
- **Bemedalled officer**. Early fixed arm marching officer figure with medal moulded onto chest. Included in some infantry sets. 1894-1900.
- **Drummers and buglers**. Infantry on guard sets 16-18 without drummers or buglers date from 1894.
- **Slotted arm musicians**. Method of fixing arms with instruments into slots in the shoulder rather than pivoting on studs. 1896-1911.
- **Movable arms**. Normally done with shoulder stud and arm loop which fits over it. 1896-1966.
- **2nd Version Life Guard horse with tin sword**. New larger fixed arm figure than the Germanic 1st version. 1897-1902.
- **Wasp-waisted officer**. Early movable arm marching officer figure with markedly narrow waist. 1897-1905.
- **Catalogue numbers on boxes**. Britains included these in box labels from 1898. Un-numbered boxes pre-date 1898.
- **Dated figures**. Figures initially designed between 1.6.1900 and 9.9.1912 have the design date embossed under the base. **Caution**: figures designed prior to this but still in use 1900 to 1912 will have no embossing at all, but can still have been produced during this period or later. Dated figures from 1912 were gradually replaced with undated proprietory embossing, a process which was probably complete by 1924.
- **Paper labels**. Dated figures were sometimes issued without the embossing having been completed at all. Many of these would have paper labels with the design date stuck underneath the base, presumably as an interim measure. The paper labels often dropped off after some time, and sometimes one can see a difference in the underside of the base where a paper label was once glued. 1900-1905 approximately.
- **Matt painted rifles**. In a major change to the way their rifles were painted, Britains switched from matt brown, to a metallic reddish brown about 1901.
- **Tie-in cards**. Internal box packaging changed around 1901 from partitioned boxes for cavalry and slotted box sides for infantry to the insertion of a card punched with holes through which the figures could be tied in. This was the preferred method of packing until 1966.
- **Slot-in strips**. These were used for boxed sets of suitable infantry models 1932-1940. The base and legs of the figures slid into an angled slot in a double strip of card and the set went into the box over a coloured corrugated card backing strip.
- **Dated second version small size cavalry**. All small size cavalry sets were converted to better models in 1904.
- **Gaitered officer, oval base dated 16.11.1905**. Sets with this officer would be 1906-1908.

- **Rectangular based figures**. From 1906, newly designed figures were made with rectangular (often also called square) bases. Very few of Britains rectangular bases are actually square, but they are certainly squared off as opposed to the oval ones.
- **Previously designed figures remade with rectangular bases**. From 1906, most oval based figures were given rectangular bases. Where there was no actual redesign, the figures retained their original oval based date. A few oval based figures, e.g. Japanese infantry and others with the same body, retained their oval base throughout production.
- **Whisstock labels**. From around 1908, Fred Whisstock, a commercial artist, was employed by Britains to design their box labels. Boxes signed by him will not pre-date 1908, but were in use until at least 1948, after which they were replaced as they ran out by Regiments of All Nations labels.
- **Movable arm bass drummer**. From 1909 this figure was introduced. Bands with this figure date from 1909 or later.
- **Dated second version small size infantry**. RARE. All small size infantry sets were converted to slightly larger models in 1912.
- **Movable wrist drum major**. From 1913 this figure was introduced. Bands with this figure date from 1913 or later.
- **Undated figures**. New figures designed from 1913 do not have a date embossed underneath. By about 1924, possibly as late as 1930, as moulds wore out, all the older figures were changed to embossing without a date.
- **Tight sling rifle, rifle with bayonet**. From around 1914, the arm with the old drooping sling rifle at the slope was changed to a different design with the sling drawn in to the rifle barrel, giving a rather flat appearance for the rifle. Later, about 1927, a new rifle with

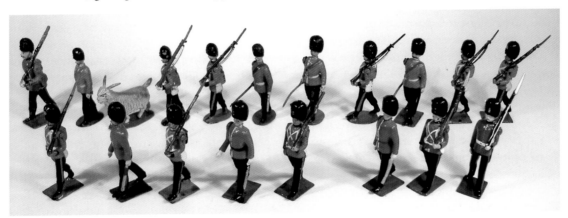

Picture 110: Types of the Royal Welch Fusiliers

The picture here shows the evolution of Britains fusiliers. The Germanic fusilier (left of the back row) was produced in a larger scale as one of Britains first trial models in 1893, and is exceedingly rare. All other figures except the last front right are Royal Welch Fusiliers. Back row, left to right. Bemedalled officer, goat mascot and valise pack figure with matt brown rifle from set 74 in 1897, valise pack figure with metallic rifle around 1900, wasp waisted officer from around 1898, oval based officer dated 16.11.1905, oval based box pack fusilier with drooping sling rifle dated 1.8.1905, officer and man with square base from about 1908, man with new flat tight sling rifle from about 1920, the sling ceased to be painted white when this arm started to be used. Front row, from the left, 1930s square section rifle from about 1930, officer with full trousers rather than gaiters as worn by all the previous versions, man with full trousers both from 1933, officer and man without moustaches from mid-1938, the man having the rifle without bayonet used in set 73, post-war figures in 1957 paint style with the new rifle with bayonet fixed to the side rather than the end of the rifle from 1949, and the last figure, the New Hollowcast series figure without a pack from 2004, with a noticeably glossier, darker red finish, and a rifle sling painted in once more.

the sling very close in to the outside edge was introduced, giving a square looking cross section. A new rifle with a large bayonet distinctively attached to the outside edge of the rifle came in about 1948.

- **Tight sling rifle, rifle without bayonet**. For the rifle without bayonet fixed the drooping sling version was replaced by the equivalent of the rifle with the sling very close in to the outside edge about 1920.
- **Short and long carbines**. Around 1916, possibly even a little earlier, the original movable arm with the short carbine, with a double barrelled look to it, was replaced for those cavalry so equipped with a longer, slimmer version.
- **Cavalry swords**. These were relatively thick and blunt until about 1908, after which a much thinner and sharper version was introduced. Before 1954, swords were carried at right angles to the forearm. After 1953, a new gauntleted arm was introduced with a more realistic carrying pose, closer in to the body.
- **Webbing equipment**. Britains introduced this for their new set 195 British Infantry in steel helmets in 1916, and previous sets 109, 110 and 160 were updated to the webbing equipment from the previous Slade-Wallace equipment with which they were at first provided.
- **Fumed metal finish**. Britains had until 1917 painted their toy guns and vehicles in a light grey. Possibly as a result of techniques learned during war work, they introduced a fumed metal finish which involved no paint, which they used until 1931, after which they went to a khaki paint finish.
- **Breast harness team horses**. These were introduced for all horse-drawn vehicles from 1920, replacing the old collar harness models.
- **Registered Trademark**. Britains registered a new trademark 459993 in 1926, which appeared on box labels or stamped inside on the insert card from that date onwards.
- **Rear opening limber**. This replaced the old top opening limber for gun teams from 1931.
- **Moustaches**. British army troops were depicted with moustaches (with the exception of boy musicians) until 1939, after which they were clean shaven. Most European armies followed this, but the US was always clean shaven from the start of the models issued in 1926.
- **Dating by association**. Most collections of toy soldiers for young boys were accumulated from the ages of three to twelve. If these come as a collection, it is often possible to infer the date of some of the less obvious sets from the ones where the clues above apply.

Advanced identification

The following example of the Chasseur gives a taste of the depth to which identification of figures can be taken. The correspondence follows on from having established perfectly happily that the figure is by Britains.

The Chasseur

Dear Mr Opie

I have two sets and spares of Set 139 Chasseurs à Cheval, post 1925 undated, and I recently bought a single figure which looks right in every way but some differences are puzzling me. My references books (your own included) show several variations but not this one. It is an earlier figure, dated 1902, and it appears different in that it has no blanket roll behind the rider and has a carbine holster.

Picture 111: Chasseur

This is the chasseur picture sent to me by John West to ask me why it had British style horse furniture rather than the continental style one might expect. Sending pictures over the internet has now become second nature to most collectors, and is one of the best blessings of the computer age.

Also the blue of the uniform is slightly darker than those I already have, although I am aware that this colour can vary. I attach a photograph.

Are you aware of this variation and can I be sure it is a correct figure? I hope you can help.

Kind regards,
John West

Further to my previous email, I have now looked more closely at the underside of the horse and find that there is a Depose mark. The actual underside reads in full: Copyright Wm Britain Depose 12.12.1902. It is not marked Made in England or Great Britain so it would appear to be a Paris office figure. Is it possible that this one was made in France, hence the differences in the moulding? Your help in this matter is much appreciated.

Kind regards,
John West

Hi John,
Thanks for your very interesting enquiry – sorry it has taken me until now to reply.

The difference in the moulding is that between the standard British cavalry figure and the one created for the Chasseurs based on the same figure but with the continental style blanket roll behind the saddle.

One might make the assumption that the figure you are showing me pre-dated the normal double dated figure, and was by way of being a first run of figures with a chasseur head before the conversion of the figure had been completed. Militating against that, however, is the fact that the figure is marked depose, a practice which, as far as I am aware, only started in 1912 when the Paris factory for Britains was opened.

Once that factory had started production, the standardisation of figures produced there seems to have been taken relatively lightly as compared with in London, so all sorts of anomolies such as this figure are known to exist.

Hence on balance, I think you have a Paris Office produced figure not earlier than 1912, made on the original British horse furniture pattern figure (used by the Paris factory for various productions), and hence with just the one date.

With best wishes,
James Opie

(Example from my emails included with permission.)

CHAPTER 5
THE IMPORTANCE OF CONDITION

As with most collectables, condition is important, particularly in terms of re-sale value. The current codes with which I categorise condition when describing lots for sale at Bonhams are given below, with their explanations. Everyone has to decide for themselves what is acceptable condition for them, and it will make a big difference to the quantities of figures they will be able to get for their money. Some collectors will just be interested in obtaining perfect pieces, preferably in their original packaging. Others, interested in the variety to be collected, will not mind less good condition in order to have an example to look at closely. Those interested purely in spectacle and history will be able, if so inclined, to buy broken figures and restore them, at a small fraction of the cost of unbroken originals with good paintwork.

The current value of nicely made Britains musicians, for instance, restored to a nice finish in the Britains style or somewhat enhanced with additional detail is about £3 to £5 per figure, depending on the quality of the paintwork.

I would not tamper with anything that already looks reasonably good on the shelves, but anything that is already broken or repainted would sell for much the same or less than a restored figure unless it was an example of something rare. You should therefore feel free to carry on with your projects to your own taste, which can either be restoration to fit in with existing Britains, or wholly changed for an even better look. Much of the value to you of this is in the enjoyment of producing a great looking result for not too much money.

The most valuable toy soldiers, and the ones most likely to hold their value (see also Chapter 12) tend to be original figures Mint in their original boxes. Some sets hardly ever turn up in this condition, so, for instance, virtually any set of Britains of a vintage before the First World War may well be worth having even in Fair condition with a Fair or Poor box, but a Mint boxed set worth £1,000 may well only be worth a quarter of that as Fair, even if undamaged in any way.

Terms to describe the condition of the paintwork and boxes of toy figures

- **M = Mint – apparently never taken out of mint original boxes**. This term, of course, derives from the perfect state of a newly minted coin. Nothing that exists in this imperfect world ever achieves a Platonic state of absolutely mint, but the letter M against toy soldiers should mean that it is extremely hard to tell that it is not. I examine boxed sets carefully to try and tell if the figures have ever left their packaging, and if there is a suspicion that they have, I will put them into the next category down. Some packaging is of a type where one can easily remove and replace the figures.
- **E = Excellent – no apparent paint chipping or defects**. This is the best state that unpackaged toy soldiers can aspire to, and is less common than is generally declared. New Toy Soldiers that have been well looked after, as one would expect, are the most likely to be E, but anything that has actually been played with, no matter how carefully, is not likely to make the grade. Equally E boxes should look immaculate. The only thing that should be wrong with E box E is that the soldiers may have left the box and been put back.

- **VG = Very Good – with minimum paint defects**. I only started using this grade relatively recently, but decided that it was unfair to downgrade toy soldiers that were not quite E to just G. VG boxes may have some nicks or writing on them, but are otherwise in very good condition.
- **G = Good – with very few paint defects**. This grade covers soldiers which on first glance do not seem to have any paint missing, but one can see a little wear when examined more closely. Boxes may have rubbing at the edges.
- **F = Fair – with an acceptable amount of damage to the paint**. Most collectors would feel it was a pity to repaint this grade, but they are obviously not as good as G. Boxes down to F grade will probably have tears or splits which may or may not be described.
- **P = Poor**. Anything goes, may well have lost a large proportion of their paint, probably ripe for restoration, conversion or repainting. Boxes in the P category may not have much left of them at all.

Any of these terms can be used in conjunction to give an intermediate grade, i.e. VG-G means slightly better than G but not quite VG. VG some G is used to show that some of the figures in a group are not of VG standard.

With all these grades, it is the paintwork that is being described, and any damage to the castings should be mentioned as well. If there is a lot of damage in a group, the description is likely to say simply 'damaged', in which case you would have to rely on what you could see in the photograph.

It is always quite difficult to see condition in all but the most close-up or zoomed in images, which usually don't show you the back of the figure, either. Thus you need either to be able to trust the stated condition, or to go see for yourself. The picture of doughboys above (picture 13) is quite good to get a flavour of various damage and conditions.

All other deviations from an original matched set in good condition should be in the auction description, e.g. damaged or mismatched figures.

Fakes and fix-ups

Most collectors enjoy refurbishing battered old toy soldiers and repainting them to a pleasant approximation of original condition. If they are good at this restoration, it can be quite hard to detect which are original and which have been re-done, when they subsequently come onto the market.

Unfortunately, as with virtually everything of a certain value, there are also people anxious to sell you things that are not as they seem, and prepared to doctor original figures to make them look like rarer sets.

Anything that comes through a reputable auction house will have been under the eye of someone more or less expert at spotting this, and if a set has not been viewed at the auction house, and the defects not described, it is perfectly in order to ask for a refund. At shows, however, and especially online, where you are looking and buying, it is as well to be on guard, *caveat emptor*, against anything that may not be correct. Unfortunately it is impossible to be certain from an Internet photograph, so sometimes one just has to take a chance.

Certain sets have become notorious for the ease with which they can be reproduced from less expensive materials.I would cite in particular the horse-drawn items in steel helmets of 1940-41 vintage, and set 2171 Colour Party of the Royal Air Force, of which there certainly more dodgy examples in circulation than there are originals. Naturally the more expensive something is, the more likely it is that someone will have tried to fake it, so Paris office

Britains are now perhaps the top target for the faker. This is particularly good for the faker, because there are so few Paris office in existence that checking out figures by comparison to known real figures is not often feasible.

It is possible to become so worried by the existence of fakes that one gives up buying figures of more than a certain value on the basis that too high a proportion of them may turn out to be fakes. Trying to weigh the significance of every flaw or inconsistency can cause untold anxiety. As one often reads in the art world, some paintings remain uncertain as to their genuine status for many decades. In the world of stamps, collections of forgeries can be more valuable than originals. In toy soldiers, there are fakes so good that they may never ever be detected, and these will give just as much pleasure as the real thing. Equally, however, blithely buying everything without thinking in terms of possible problems can result in expensive mistakes. If in doubt, leave it out is not a bad principle as long as you are prepared to lose some perfectly good items from time to time.

To my mind the answer is to acquire a reasonable knowledge and make up your own mind on a case by case basis, using the following checks, and certainly not relying on any remarks you may overhear from anyone else who may be anxious that you undervalue something so that they themselves may acquire it for a lower price at auction.

Picture 112: Paris Office Britains fakes

The front row are all genuine, and are in various conditions. Early oval based officer for Zouaves set 142 (Good to Fair), Paris office French colour bearer (Fair to Poor, arm glued on), French Foreign Legion Picture Pack officer (Excellent), the same officer casting as an original Paris Office officer for the group of Infanterie a grande tenue at the back (Fair, arm missing, neck broken and mended with tape), Paris office officer with blanket roll, horizon blue jacket (Good) and the same casting as officer for early French Infanterie set 141 in dark blue coats (Good to Fair). The eight men at the back, which look like Excellent condition Paris office figures are in fact expertly repainted, which cannot be seen in the photograph, where they appear absolutely genuine. They are in any case extremely rare original castings, never used in the London list. They appear to have been nicely stripped of whatever paint remained, mended of any breakages and then finished by someone who most certainly knew how to do it.

Paint style checks, spot the difference

Sometimes a so-called set may be made up of mismatched figures. Under normal circumstances, the paint style for a single row set of Britains will be consistent across the same figures, i.e. if there are seven marching infantry and an officer, one painter would have painted each feature of the infantry, but there might be differences for the officer, which would have been done as a batch of officers, either by the same painter or by another.

Running your eye along the row of troops, there should be minimal style differences in details such as face colour, cheeks, eyebrows if any, moustache or mouth, hair, uniform details e.g. thickness of cuffs, lines of piping, buttons, plumes or stripes. The colour of the base should fall within the range of Britains usage, normally a rich grass green with plenty of yellow in it. The colour of the rifles is particularly difficult to reproduce. Looking at many original reddish brown, slightly translucent and therefore metallic seeming rifles will prepare your eye for the rather different look of paint with metallic flecks in it or the non-translucent browns often used by re-painters.

Overpainting check

Examine the surface of the paint to see if there is any overpainting, using a magnifying glass if required. I use a fold out pattern photographer's magnifier, but everyone has their favourites. If the surface is at all pitted or uneven, suspect that old paint underneath has not been removed, in which case new paint over the top may have run unevenly into any chips from the old paint underneath.

Often the difference between one regiment and another is just a matter of collar and cuff differences. Check that there are not tiny portions of another colour peeping out from behind what is on top.

Vehicles and guns

For horse-drawn vehicles, check that the team horses match the vehicle and that the vehicle finish is correct for the version of horse. Where there are towed guns or limbered wagons, these should match the limber paint finish exactly, and all the wheels should be the same size. Seated men should be of the right version, and these and bucket seats should be carefully checked for reproductions.

Box check

If there is an original box, does it match the apparent date of the soldiers (see clues to dating Britains in Chapter 4), and does the insert card match the box? Does the set specific label on the end of the box match a known Britains style? This is particularly important for generic boxes with unspecific labels such as Armies of the World and Regiments of All Nations.

Detection devices

Ultra-violet (black) light can be useful in detecting inconsistently painted retouching. Certain lead free paints will fluoresce under UV, but you should be aware that Britains themselves were using lead free paints from the mid-1950s. 'Professional' fakers will use the correct paints to avoid this check.

Dental X-rays can be used to detect re-glued and soldered heads.

CHAPTER 6
WHAT SORT OF COLLECTION?

Some collecting highs

Finding Britains' Paris office in Paris

When I decided to stop going after the complete eighty year collection of British Toy Soldiers 1893-1973, there were still a few soldier collecting highs that I had not yet experienced, like going to Paris and finding a Britains' Paris office figure. Luckily, Mary, my wife, is very fond of going to France, and speaks good French. When we were given the opportunity to go to Paris together for me to attend a Book Club conference, she found some lovely old CBG Mignot *matelots* and what turned out to be Lucotte British First World War Infantry in a Rue Saint-Honore antique shop. When eventually we made our way to the Clignancourt flea market, my excitement really grew. There had been so many stories of people finding Britains' Paris office figures in Paris, I thought that by now the whole French metropolis must have been swept clean. If I did find any, obviously they were going to be at an extortionate price.

After a wearisome time wandering the aisles (that flea market is a lot bigger than any London equivalent), we found a shop that almost exclusively sold toy soldiers. Very neatly laid out, row after row of CBG Mignot, with the occasional Lucotte or French hollowcast.

Picture 113: Prussian Cameo

A little cameo like this can pack a lot of interest into a few figures. Having sold my normal Britains set 153, the Prussian Hussars, I was left with the two centre back, which are unusual variations with swords rather than lances. One has a tail missing and the other is missing the horse's left foreleg, but they are still splendid. The mounted officer on the right and the trooper on the left are examples of two of the many different paint schemes of this figure issued by Britains Paris factory, again, both are damaged, but nice enough to show.

The two Prussian infantry in field grey to the left are both Paris factory figures found in Paris in the flea market, the infantryman on the left, which is in near perfect condition, was my great first find in Paris with Mary (see text). The rest of the infantry are from set 154, the next two the rare first version early variation that has an unique arm with the rifle without a sling. Then come the normal first version figures of the men and officer, and finally the man most often found between 1919 and 1941 on the squarer base.

After viewing all the shelves and cabinets, asking at random about prices, I established that foot figures throughout the shop were about £10 each, with the exception of Lucottes, which were five times more than that. Those seemed to be the only variation in price. At length I was reduced to looking in the rummage boxes at the back of the shop, and there, finally, I struck gold. It was a perfect Prussian infantryman at the trail in field grey, a great iconic Paris Office figure which has been numbered among my absolute favourites ever since, both for its almost pristine appearance and for the great buzz it gave me to find.

'And how much is this one?' I said nonchalantly to the proprietor. '£10' says he, with a Gallic shrug. After some evident hesitation, I made the purchase, and retired with Mary, quivering with excitement, for a celebratory cup of coffee.

The temptation at this point was to come over to Paris every month and try and repeat this experience, and it is true that we have made a few further trips, but actually only as we needed to with other purposes in mind. A couple of these trips bore further Paris office fruit, but generally speaking French antique toy shops are by now well acquainted with the likely eagerness of Anglo-Saxons to buy these somewhat expatriate figures. Prices both for these and any other Britains (which have all in the Gallic mind now become Paris office) have risen accordingly.

Paris office Britains nevertheless remain one of the three major special interest areas for Britains hollowcast collectors which provides an almost inexhaustible supply of good 'fishing' stories and actual concrete proof every year of yet more previously unknown productions. Although there are disadvantages to the search for Paris office (see previous chapter – Fakes) those who are brave enough to collect them systematically are repaid by the envy of less fortunate collectors and the ultimate charm that they represent. The craftsmen at the Paris factory from 1912 to 1923 seem to have combined flair and imagination with a disregard for the mass-produced sets of their London parent in favour of trying out anything and everything that could be made with the existing moulds, arms and heads, plus trying modifications, and, towards the end of production, brand new figures.

Finding a previously unknown figure

A second highlight of my collecting career since 1986 came rather more recently and also has to do with the Paris office, when visiting a French friend of ours in the south of France. He is straightforwardly a Lucotte and CBG Mignot collector, and was looking to rid himself of the few Britains that he possessed at whatever they might fetch at auction. After several hours of admiring his magnificent collection of French masterpieces, he was giving me standard coronation procession type Britains to sell when he asked me whether I knew these other figures. Seeing something I did not recognise at all, I turned them over and was astounded to find a regulation Britains embossing under the base, complete with the depose wording normally employed by the Paris factory. They were a figure previously completely unknown, evidently designed for and produced only by the Paris factory.

'Are they interesting for you to sell?' asked my friend. I told him yes, and entered all thirteen of them for him in the Phillips sale of 27th June 1995, calling them, for want of any other title and in view of the French connection with Algeria, Paris office Barbary Coast Corsairs. They were sold for £4,485. A few years later, the mould number for this figure turned up in some Britains archive material, and I hope I am right in remembering that the description given with this was that the figure represented a Cochinese pirate, from the different French colony of Indochina.

Such are the occasions to which one can return time and time again with real joy in the remembering.

Reducing my collection

Those who have read my previous collecting book will remember that in 1986 I had already taken the decision to change direction and reduce its numbers to fit into our new accommodation. Make no mistake, I have enjoyed the decline of my collection just as much as the acquisition of it. From age 4 to age 40, I was adding rather than subtracting, although there were many figures that passed through as I got rid of duplicates or traded up in quality. My collection was at its peak in the period 1983 to 1987, with a total of about 65,000 figures. I had not then counted them – that only became possible as I numbered them passing out of the collection, so that around the year 2000 I was able to count the residue.

In 1985, in retrospect almost to mark the occasion of the collection's most swollen years, I put on the *On Guard* exhibition of about 5,000 figures at the London Toy and Model Museum, the only time when that venue, so well endowed with toy trains and die-cast vehicles, had a good selection of toy soldiers on show.

Sell-off from the collection then commenced in earnest, until by 2006 the collection numbered about 16,000, leaving aside pieces awaiting conversion and wargaming figures. During this decline there was no point at which, if I found figures that I liked and could afford, I would not collect them, although I was on a tight budget. With presents and holiday souvenirs, I have no doubt that figures I acquired from 1985 to 2006 amount to a couple of thousand or so (i.e. only about an average of a hundred a year), but the running total was always going down, even if some of my most treasured remaining pieces date from this period.

At its peak, and as described in my book *Collecting Toy Soldiers*, the collection had a number of themes, and I tended to part with each theme as a whole. In the meantime, if any of the themes I kept seemed to need additions, then I would try to acquire them. At that time, when I wrote that book, I had listed thirty Britains themes, and another thirty-eight non-Britains themes (re-listed below), and it is fascinating to see now which are the ones that have lasted.

One of the other things that has happened is that I have managed to keep a souvenir of all of them, so in reducing a collection it is possible to have a lot of fun choosing what is to be the icon (or, as so often, icons), of each theme as it is disposed of.

And of course, no-one can take away the memories, so as people proudly show you their latest acquisition, it is possible to say 'Yes, I once had one of those' which, it is true, is a little dismissive in a 'been there done that' sort of way. Do I wish I could have kept them all? Yes, of course I do, but given that I couldn't, I have come to feel that my life has been far richer for disposing of them, in many, many ways.

The motives for adding to or pruning the collection (apart from the economics of resources) may be historical or commercial interest, nostalgia or artistic merit. The organisational elements of collecting can be summarised as reference, display, iconic or cameo. Most collections will probably include all four, but a short discussion of these terms may well help in deciding how to organise.

Types of collection

The reference collection

Doing this is putting together a definitive series of something, perhaps collecting by types of figure, country of origin, manufacturer, catalogue number, period of production, style of figure, designer, scale, subject or taste. Any of these, or subsets of these, done thoroughly, will result in a reference collection. Beautifully shown mint reference collections with original boxes take up a lot of room, as well as often costing more than most of us can afford. In not such good condition, not necessarily with packaging and perhaps not even out on display, a very satisfying choice of subject matter can be devised on which you can be a world expert.

One collection which occurred to me recently was the idea of just collecting Britains sets in boxes with labels bearing the artwork of Frederick Whisstock. I wonder if anyone out there is consciously doing this?

The display collection

A huge part of the satisfaction of toy soldiers is in the spectacle of them, particularly in large quantities. It is the same thrill that comes from an epic movie, or viewing a major military parade. The displays represent past and present military glory and traditions, patriotism and the sweep of history in a way particularly poignant for those of us with forefathers who took part in these adventures, even if, or perhaps because, lives were lost.

The true display collector is interested in depicting units and occasions. The three most usual campaigns to cover from a British perspective, seen as the apex of empire, are the Zulu War, the Sudan campaigns and the Boer Wars, all of which took place in Africa. There are of course, many other heroic occasions and ceremonies that can be depicted, such as coronation processions.

The iconic collection

Iconic collections are formed from the best or most representative figures or sets to demonstrate a point. Sometimes these icons can be declared simply from the amount of money needed to buy them. Sometimes it is a question of settling on favourite figures, and saying simply that these, for me, are the epitome. At all times, the icon needs to tell a fascinating story. Since every figure in every collection has its own story, it is simply a matter of knowing what the story is, and why each figure has its stature as an icon.

In its simplest form, an iconic collection can be formed of single examples of things that interest the collector. These examples may in themselves have their part of the story to tell, or they may be in waiting to form a cameo when arranged or more along the theme have been collected.

Cameo collecting

Cameos are often formed around icons, amplifying and rounding out the iconic theme. I have been an advocate of cameo collections for many years now. Cameos can tell a better, more in depth story than just an icon, although naturally a collection of icons will take less room to tell a wider story. See Chapter 8 for examples of cameos.

Shaping the overall collection

The conclusion must be that each collector should decide which part of the story to tell, and in what form. Trying to have a reference collection of everything seems hardly possible, as there would be literally millions of figures to collect, even if one was able to know what they were. Most collectors will want to have some element of display, simply from the artistic pleasures and sense of occasion that it brings. Icons form the highlights of a collection, bringing out points and stories which the visitor will enjoy considering, and cameos build from the icons, while limiting collecting ambitions to readily achievable goals. (That is assuming that these goals are consciously set to be achievable, since one good way of limiting acquisitions and to have fun doing a great deal of searching is by setting a goal which is not so easy.)

As an example of how this works in my own collection, I now have a reference collection of just a few subjects: in Britains, Highlanders, small size, sequences of Life Guard, Royal Scots Grey and Royal Welch Fusilier boxed sets, and a fairly definitive collection of the different individual types of Foot Guard figures. This means that following on from 1986, when I was planning to keep intact nine subjects out of the thirty themes of hollowcast Britains (1, 8, 17, 23, 24, 25, 28, 29 and 30) only 28 remains complete.

To help you in your own organisational endeavours, the following list gives the thirty subject areas of Britains and twenty-four non-Britains areas into which I divided my original reference collection. Entitled *British made or distributed toy soldiers from 1893 to 1973*, at one point it contained some fifty thousand figures. In addition there were ten display collection subject areas, and eight of toys and related activity, which brought the total of figures up to sixty-five thousand.

Today, after reduction to a quarter of the size, sixteen thousand, this is what my collection looks like.

The 30 Subjects of Britains

1. Royalty – cameos: mounted queens, robed figures and thrones, iconic state coach.
2. Household Cavalry – Life Guards sequence and additional icons.
3. Foot Guards – Grenadier Guards Band icon, icons of most Britains Foot Guards issued.
4. Dragoon Guards and Dragoons – Royal Scots Greys sequence, small 1st King's Dragoon Guard cameo.
5. Hussars – 11th Hussar cameo, icons of most hussars issued.
6. Lancers – icons only – until recently no example of a cross-legged lancer.
7. Infantry of the Line – iconic set of Royal Sussex Regiment and a few other examples.
8. Highlanders – Reference collection of about 900 Britains, all types.
9. Other British Infantry in Full Dress – Royal Welch Fusiliers sequence.
10. Royal Artillery – the walking gun team from my box 73 (see page 185) is the last 54mm Britains gun team in my collection.
11. Royal Navy and Marines – some picture pack figures.
12. Auxiliary Services and Royal Air Force – display cameo of RAMC, which includes many repaints and conversions, and a few icons of RAF.
13. Boer War – single figure icons only.
14. Troops in khaki (from both world wars) – icons only.
15. Motor vehicles and guns – Centurion tank and Staff Car.
16. Indian Empire – some icon figures only.
17. Canada – a few icons.
18. Rest of the British Empire – a few icons.
19. France – French Foreign Legion cameo, early French figure and Paris office cameo.
20. Rest of Europe – small Carabinieri cameo, small Prussian cameo, various icons.
21. Asia and Africa – Arab and Zulu cameos.
22. United States of America – some icons.
23. Latin America – one Uruguayan cadet, as an icon.
24. Historical – Waterloo cameo, Knights of Agincourt cameo.
25. American Civil War, Cowboys and Indians – small cameo of each.
26. Buildings – not even a rabbit hutch.
27. Civilians – a few icons – I never had a reference collection of these anyway.
28. Picture Packs – only enough to form a cameo.

29. Small Size – Reference collection of about 1,500 of all types, with 63 original boxes.
30. Second Grade – icon collection amounting to a historical cameo sequence of the subject.

The 38 other subjects, 1893 to 1973 with extras

Displays
31. Royal Welch Fusiliers – about 700, mostly Britains.
32. Royal Scots Greys – about 400, mostly Britains.
33. Boer War – a small cameo display, including Lancer figures.
34. Boxer Rebellion – about 550, mostly New Toy Soldiers.
35. Sudan Campaigns – iconic group of 45, including a broken Britains Camel Corps.
36. Boyhood Armies – once 2,000 strong, now in assorted icons, about 200.
37. Field Manoeuvres – various little displays and icons, plus unfinished projects.
38. Castles – the troops to go with this are mostly in section 37.
39. Coronation Procession – nothing specific, but could be done by lending from other subject areas.
40. Indian Empire – various New Toy Soldiers as a cameo.

The other subjects within what used to be my reference collection, which I used to store by manufacturer, are now mostly distributed along my shelves by subject, so that I can compare and contrast them and Britains by what is depicted. The top subject for doing this

Picture 114: Superheroes

Character figures of superheroes have been made for almost as long as the comic book heroes have existed themselves. Timpo made hollowcast models of the original Captain Marvel about 1952, left to right at the front, Icky, Captain Marvel, Mary Marvel and Captain Midnight. I am missing the fifth model, Captain Marvel Junior. DC are represented by Cherilea plastic figures of Batman and Robin, interestingly in the sort of scale associated with Star Wars action figures (see page 36), which they pre-date by fifteen years. Superman, Dr Doom and Spiderman represent the most usual types of figures found today, metal ones sometimes sold with magazines (Dr Doom), smallish soft plastic ones (this Spiderman, crawling up Dr Doom's backing card, came from a key ring found in Tokyo) and 90mm scale flexible plastic ones similar to the last decade of toy soldiers most played with by children (Superman).

Picture 115: Armoured cars

Vehicles have always played an important part in toy armies, and no collection is really complete without some. I started out with the great series of military Dinky Toys (see also page 28) and then went on to Lone Star as suiting my paratroops better, before cutting back to a representative selection such as these armoured cars. Front to back, left to right, a very nicely detailed hard plastic Kleeware from about 1949 (my brother had one of the lorries that were so similar to the Lone Star die-cast lorries), Dinky, Italian made Micromodel, early and late Charbens, U.S. made in flexible plastic and Tri-ang, with its box (one of my brothers other military toys, of which he had very few). The box at the back is Kleeware, but I seem to have mislaid the contents, which is as illustrated.

Picture 116: Australian hollowcasts

I found these in one of Sydney's few old toy soldier shops (maybe Sydney's ONLY toy soldier shop at that time). They are based on a standard Reka then Crescent horse, but the detail is different from any others I have seen, and I suspect they were re-made locally.

is Highlanders, where I have in excess of two thousand, but I suspect that even here, as a reference collection, I probably have examples of less than half of the various figures that have been made over the last hundred and fifty years.

Metal British Toy Soldiers other than Britains Hollowcast
41. Pre-World War I
42. John Hill & Co.
43. Between the Wars
44. Timpo
45. Crescent
46. Post-World War II
47. Unknowns
48. Wend-Al and Aluminium
49. Die-casts
50. Artillery

Plastic British Toy Soldiers
51. Britains and Herald
52. Timpo
53. Charbens
54. Cherilea
55. Airfix
56. Marx
57. Hong Kong
58. Lone Star
59. Others
60. Vehicles and Guns

Other subjects types and toys
61. Blenheim and Nostalgia
62. New Toy Soldiers
63. Soldiers of the World
64. Fire engines
65. Toys
66. Lego
67. Souvenirs
68. Wargaming

Arranging my toy soldiers according to the historical subjects depicted has also been a favourite of mine since my shelves were ready, so that of the sixty shelves I have available, three are laid out in what is effectively a short military history of the world to 1860 AD. Then, skipping the late 19th century that is the subject of so many shelves, six shelves are devoted to a military history of the 20th century. Apart from this, three shelves are filled with personal souvenirs and other souvenir soldiers, one shelf with civilian icons, seven with soldiers of the world, guns and vehicles, and five with heroic subjects such as Robin Hood, Wild West, Superheroes, Comic and Children's characters, Science Fiction and Fantasy. These latter parts often form the most fascinating bits of the collection for 'outsiders', who have never had an interest in toy soldiers in their lives. Here are some pictures from the Robin Hood shelves.

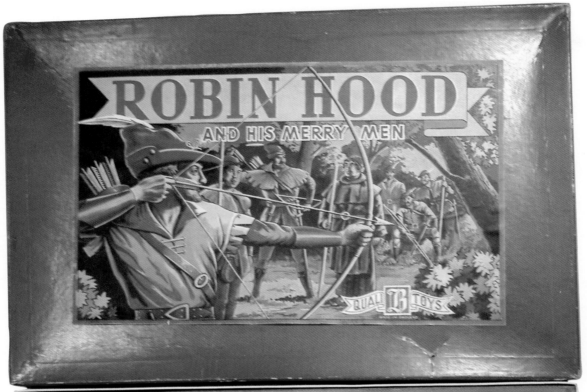

Picture 117: Benbros Robin Hood

This was a wonderful series in hollowcast, which in cameo terms adds to the Ivanhoe series made by Timpo, though it may well predate it.

Picture 118: Sheriff of Nottingham

The sheriff and his men come from the Benbros Robin Hood series and are one of the few reliable medieval infantry squads to emerge from the hollowcasting scene. Very businesslike with their poleaxes.

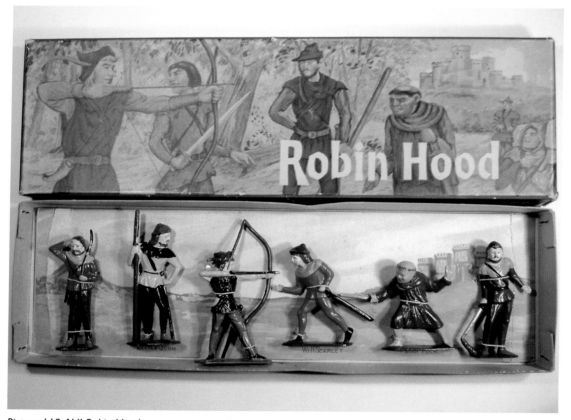

Picture 119: AHI Robin Hood

The only AHI series I have come across which is not a copy of Herald, but then it could pre-date the Herald Robin Hood series. The figures are definitely not as good as the Herald ones, but at least have their own originality.

Picture 120: Herald Robin Hood

The issue of this set in 1957 prompted a rush of competitive series from other makers in plastic. The 1950s had seen a large number of film and television productions featuring Robin Hood, and as the characters were not copyright, the subject was ideal. So enduring is the romance of Robin Hood that Britains re-visited the subject when they moved to Nottingham.

Picture 121: Cherilea Crusaders

These were produced in both metal and plastic, opposed to the Saracens which look so much like Assyrians that many collectors name them as such. The mounted figure is evidently Richard I, and so the whole series works well with the plastic Robin Hood set brought out in 1957 by Cherilea of which the crossbowman is part.

Picture 122: Marx Robin Hood and others

These bags of copies of the original Marx Robin Hood figures were on sale in W.H.Smith around 1990. The Marx originals were in green plastic, unpainted, to the left and part of the plastic figure collection given to me in 1963 by Len Richards. For some reason the Robin Hood had had his bowstring cut away, and my own original I had painted. Not right as a collector, but he looked much better! They were certainly one of the series issued around 1955 through Woolworths. The two figures in grey are similar Marx men at arms. I think that the small Friar Tuck in front of the green one is from the standard size Marx set, converted and repainted. Plastic Robin Hood sets were issued by Cherilea, Crescent, and Lone Star in the U.K., and to complete this picture I have put in one from each series, Lone Star Robin Hood, Kelloggs by Crescent Friar Tuck, and Cherilea Sheriff of Nottingham (base repainted) as well as a Hong Kong copy of the original Herald Robin Hood, the Robin Hood from the later Deetail style series, two other unpainted Robin Hood figures back right, and a Graham Farish model of King John, reputedly designed for them by John Niblett around 1953.

Picture 123:
Krolyn and Papo
Robin Hood

The mystique of Robin Hood translates well into other languages. Here are larger scale versions from Krolyn (Sweden, 1950s) in aluminium on the left and Papo (France) in plastic. Note how the recent Papo

kneeling Robin Hood, bought this year, is a great deal more elaborate than the early mounted version from around ten years earlier, testifying to the ongoing design competition between manufacturers of this style of toy. For comparison of scale, I have included on the right a Star Wars action figure of Luke Skywalker.

How to finish collecting

In my role as cataloguer of toy soldiers and figures for Bonhams, the auctioneers, and previously at Christies and Phillips, I have described literally millions of figures for sale. I have sold nearly fifty thousand figures of my own collection at auction, and I would contend that returning them to other collectors in this way is the most convenient, exciting and satisfying method of ceasing to collect or reducing a collection.

I aim to present in each lot a value of £200 or more which provides a particular set, sets or group of figures that will fit right in with a collector's plan, and so be the most attractive to the largest number of potential purchasers. Because it is an auction, and every lot is illustrated on the auction website, the lot will find the right current market price. Lots will all be fully vetted and properly described, and the purchasers will have the confidence to bid to the value they can afford.

The catalogues form a permanent record of everything sold – some of the major collections that have come to auction provide valuable reference material in themselves thereafter, and are a superb souvenir for the former owner.

Less valuable odds and bits can always be made into job lots, which are of great interest to dealers or starting collectors in their 'magpie' phase, or, if you have the time, it is perfectly possible that more money could be obtained for these by means other than auctions.

In disposing of toy soldiers to the best advantage, it is good to think about where collectors will expect to find what you have for sale. People expect to find and compete for rare and expensive things at auction, and it is likely that even with the commissions, the best net price can be obtained for such items there. People will only stumble upon them by chance on eBay or at the shows, because not everyone is taking the time or trouble to examine everything, so you are cutting out the possibility of offering to everyone who might be interested.

For regular or less valuable things, on the other hand, shows and the Internet may be the better answer, assuming you have the time to spend (see also *Time is money* in chapter 3). This is because you will be able to offer each individual item, down to £1 or less, individually, and therefore cumulatively achieve the greatest value. Do be prepared to lower your prices and haggle, otherwise it is no fun for the buyer.

CHAPTER 7
CONCENTRATING ON SPECIFICS

Looking for something specific: the joy of the hunt

As we journey hopefully to shows or examine the latest auction offerings, we have in the back of our minds the sort of thing we might want to get next, rather than just anything that takes our fancy. The honeymoon that a toy soldier collector in the first flush of acquisition experiences with his early purchases is a real rush. I have been through this on a number of occasions, in fact on every occasion when I have made the decision to collect something in particular, and form a new reference, display, cameo or icon group within my collection, or indeed to hunt for an iconic figure of some kind to make a particular point.

For this show (March 2010), I thought I would try and hunt for iconic Romans. I think the best ones I found were from the Spartacus series by Conte on the Maison Militaire stand, but these were display models only; the series has pretty much been and gone, and they certainly couldn't sell me any of those actually on display. Other than that, the show was remarkably short on nice looking models of Romans. But while I was engaged in the hunt, all the adrenaline, hope and anxiety returned to give me a great buzz. As it turned out, I didn't buy anything, and consoled myself with one Fusilier Miniature, four Crescent Highlanders, and an early Timpo composition figure. Aha, you didn't know there were Timpo composition figures, did you? More later (page 129).

On returning home, I had a quick glance through the two hundred or so Romans I already have on my shelves. Not nearly enough.

The Roman Empire

As this most famous of empires played such a large part in the origins of today's civilisation, its military might is a favourite subject for historians and modellers. One of my favourite photographs is in *The Art of the Toy Soldier* (page 82) where forty or so CBG Mignot Gauls battle it out with a sixty strong legion of Romans. As a picture, this is hard to beat, and I was able to include it in the catalogue for my *On Guard* exhibition. I have been trying to bring my CBG Gauls and Romans up to this level ever since – I have so far reached fifty-six out of a hundred.

In old toy soldiers, the best known Romans are the Heyde sets that form the Triumph of Germanicus, the plastic figures by Elastolin and Starlux in 40mm, 62mm and 70mm scale, as well as the models made by CBG Mignot already mentioned. All three of these series are excellent toys, and as is the way of toys, look well *en masse*. Another attractive series of Roman models in 60mm is that of Emmanuel Steinback with his Maximus in Minimus (MIM) range made in Belgium and now much sought after.

When models became the vogue in the 1950s, most of the leading manufacturers brought out series of Romans, but those of Russell Gammage in his Rose Miniatures range (the marching legionary actually measures 52mm) were to me the outstanding example of portraying the soul of the legions. For no matter how good are the individual models, and those of Conte, for instance, really are very good, it is as a group display that Romans shine most, supporting each other in the way that legionaries had to do to survive in the line of battle. The Rose designs are sufficiently economical, slender and unobtrusive that they do

Picture 124: CBG Romans

Masses of CBG Romans look very businesslike, and much more part of a Legionary team than most models.

Picture 125: Elastolin 40mm Romans.

These quite small figures are exactly the same design as the larger 70mm range, but take up a lot less room, so are better for displaying in quantity. Although each individual piece is a masterpiece of animation, especially the wild looking Huns, the team spirit evident in the CBG Mignot legionaries above seems to have been somewhat lost. The individual marching legionary is still a satisfying model, just not so formidable in ranks (of course I only have two here).

Picture 126: What figure is the best Roman of them all?

Left to right Elastolin 40mm, Timpo repainted by me, Courtenay, New Toy Soldier, Rose, Argentine plastic figure based on Deetail, Elite Blue Box die-cast, Starlux and Elastolin 70mm. CBG Mignot above and Niblett designed Airfix (picture 207) are also in contention. Which ones do it for you, let me know.

Picture 127: Julius Caesar

The brooding personality of Julius is captured by seated figures left, Japanese plastic, and right, rather battered CBG Mignot.
Egyptians by Courtenay, guards by CBG Mignot.

Picture 128: Elite Blue Box Romans

I was surprised and delighted when the old Blue Box brand was resurrected a few years back with the die-cast Elite series. This looked like a real revival of toy soldiers, with Napoleonics and three sets of really nice looking Romans, including a Testudo, for very little money. Shame they stopped adding to the Romans after three sets, but nice try. I suppose it would only have worked if it had gone over big with the general public, and evidently it didn't.

Picture 129: Marx Romans

The hard plastic painted versions of the larger size Marx Romans to the right, made and painted in Hong Kong, were being distributed from Swansea in the late 1960s. I liked these simple sentries who built up into nice looking ranks, and kept a squad of them. They had also been through Woolworths unpainted in white flexible plastic in 1955. Three I painted then, as well as the signifer, are to the left. Front left is a Hong Kong copy in a slightly smaller scale.

Picture 130: Unknown Romans

I have no idea who made these, but they are quite evocative – maybe they are Spanish

Picture 131: Roman chariots

Another icon of Rome was the Roman chariot, as publicized in Ben Hur. Left to right, Johillco, Taylor and Benbros, in their individual 1952 boxes. (Courtesy Bonhams)

not fight each other when they are massed for battle, and the whole array is many times better than the individuals. Since the Rose designs passed on to Fusilier, the wonderful Roman figures seem to have dropped out of sight, but I may be behind the times in knowing where they have ended up.

Of the true model makers, Andrea has a wonderful range of Roman figures, but here, in the model tradition, they are really each stand-alone pieces. The model making ethos would here require that I put together a fifty man Roman maniple from scratch, but this would cost me £15 apiece unpainted (or a mere £110 per figure if I wanted the job done properly) and once I had mounted them on a scenic baseboard and had my fill of admiring them, the second hand value would be perhaps about £250, or a third of what I paid for the castings. The value here is deemed to be in the undertaking of the work and the satisfaction of the finished article. Few people seem to be ready to pay out big money for second hand models, but if that is true on the one hand, then the more spectacular of the new ready-made models to be seen on the Conte website, such as the amazing Roman galley, will I have no doubt be the collector's pieces of the future. Also, the East of India Company seems to be making a fourteenth Legion series that looks promising.

Although the recent (since 1950) tradition in toys and models has generally been to produce series of figures that work best as individuals, I would advocate the production of sets that would suggest their deployment as squads rather than a mixture of models and poses. Maybe I have in this been suborned by my love of the old parade ground Britains, yet I would see no harm in someone trying out some boxes of marching legionaries. It was always a problem assembling all the marching figures one wanted from the Airfix 20mm scale boxes (see picture 200).

Making a plan: a hierarchy of collecting

First in the hierarchy of collecting specifics comes the Universal collection, the sort of collection you rush out and put together at the very start. It's just a huge bunch of toy soldiers, of every sort. Initially, the hierarchy looks very similar to the identification questions posed in chapter four for sorting a heap of toy soldiers. A large part of my task at the auctioneers is just this, starting with a child's universal collection that has lurked in an attic for decades, and ending up with lots that will fit neatly with someone's speciality lower down the hierarchy.

The specialist hierarchy

At the second level of the hierarchy, specialisation is in methods or styles of toy soldier manufacturing, including selecting a scale or scales. You may like, as I do, to have a few of each of these to demonstrate to people what they are, but you will in all likelihood choose one or more types and scales of manufacture to concentrate on, mostly discarding the rest. It is perfectly possible to construct very interesting cameos of the commercial history from mixing and contrasting manufacturing methods. Chapter 2 shows where this could be interesting.

Three periods that intrigue me particularly are the mid-nineteenth century when flats, semi-flats and solids compete with each other for dominance in Germany, the end of the same century when hollowcasting competes with solids and the technological surge after the second world war when solids, composition, aluminium, die-cast and plastic go head to head before plastic comes out as the winner for toys.

- Flat
- Semi-flat
- Solid
- Hollowcast
- Composition
- Aluminium
- Die-cast
- Plastic
- New Toy Soldiers
- Models
- Everything else

Each type of manufacturing can be usefully subdivided by the country of origin, and then by individual manufacturers. Already, as we drill down we are arriving at more of a grid than a hierarchy, since many manufacturers have produced in more than one method or style, and today brand names and moulds change ownership and nationality, so that today Britains are owned by Americans and produced in various styles in China.

A list of the most interesting manufacturers in my view is given in Chapter 4, and of New Toy Soldiers with a style and significance guide in the Appendix (page 195).

With the major manufacturers, particularly Britains, one very popular way to collect is by acquiring all the catalogue numbered sets. This has the advantage of straightforward simplicity while being almost impossible to complete, depending on how large a chunk of the catalogues is aimed for. Some collectors enjoy having a goal they are not going to achieve anytime soon.

Continuing the hierarchy to even deeper speciality, within a manufacturer one can concentrate on the subject matter of what is depicted, either by period of history, nationality or particular types or named units from the armed forces, e.g. artillery or medical services. The sections listed for my collection of British production in the previous chapter demonstrate this.

In addition to these are the cameos based on the commercial connections, demonstration of scale, design style, individual manufacturers and their compatibilities and rivalries, or the work of designers across various manufacturers, such as Roy Selwyn-Smith, Wilfred Cherrington or Holger Eriksson.

Historical highlights
I have at least an icon from most of these, a number of which are shown here and elsewhere in the book, picture numbers with a P after the entry.

- Ancient world P 132
- Egypt P 132
- Mesopotamia P 132
- Persia P 132
- Greece P 102
- Alexander's Empire P 132
- Rome and her enemies P 124
- Soldiers of the Bible P 84
- Byzantium
- Conquests of Islam P 121
- Charlemagne

- Vikings and Anglo-Saxons P 22
- Hastings P 30
- Crusades P 121
- 100 Years War P 155
- Wars of the Roses P 28
- Spanish Empire P 138
- Tudors P 133
- 30 Years War
- English Civil War P 89
- Marlborough's wars P 23
- The '45 P 87
- Seven Years War P 25
- American War of Independence
- Napoleonic Wars P 90
- War of 1812
- Crimean War P 206
- American Civil War P 76
- Franco-Prussian War P 2
- Zulu War P 208
- Sudan P 105
- Boer War
- World War I P 137
- World War II P 221
- Korean War
- Vietnam War
- Falklands War
- Middle East and Afghanistan P 70

Picture 132: Alexander

At the start of the history of the western world, a few iconic figures can remind us of our roots. Here are an Authenticast Egyptian, a CBG Mignot Assyrian, a Courtenay Persian Immortal, a Japanese plastic model of Alexander with an escort of two CBG Mignot Greeks and a Pixyland Greek.

Picture 133: Tudors

The Tudor period has not been well served with models, possibly because most of the action as far as England was concerned took place at sea, during a period of relative domestic calm between the Wars of the Roses and the English Civil War. There were, however, several iconic personalities. This version of the many models of Henry VIII is by Bill Carman about 1938. The Executioner, Mary Queen of Scots and Queen Elizabeth I are by Courtenay from roughly the same date. The plastic priest and Tudor yeoman are from an unusually ambitious (and rare) Tudor series by Charbens.

Picture 134: Richelieu

The Vertunni personality figure looks on impassively as a French hollowcast figure spars with a French plastic by Guilbert.

103

Picture 135: Britains second grade American Civil War

After the Second World War, interest in the American Civil War increased markedly, and during the 1950s most toy and model soldier manufacturers produced series of figures. Britains alone have produced seven series, Best Quality and second grade hollowcast, Herald, Eyes Right, Deetail, Toy soldier and a huge ongoing output of model quality. Here are just a few of the Britains hollowcast Union second grade figures. The charging figure was unique to the second grade series. The firing figure is in Best Quality paint to compare. The Zouave at the front is the Union Picture Pack 1362B, distinguished from the French one by the gold stripe down the pantaloons. The Zouave to the right is from the New Hollowcast set 40198, New York Zouaves, which was the only figure in this series from the American Civil War.

Picture 136: Herald copies, American Civil War

At first glance you might be forgiven for thinking Oh no, not more illustrations of Herald's famous ACW figures, but then a closer look reveals that they are copies made in metal, one of the few examples of plastic being copied in metal. The Japanese maker known by the initials AHI seems to have specialized in doing this for the U.S. market during the mid-1950s, with one or two notable exceptions such as their original Robin Hood figures (see picture 119). Maybe by the time Britains Robin Hood came out, Britains had had a quiet word with them. Mixed in with these metal copies on the right are the Timpo first series plastic Union troops which went so well with the Herald ones. I always thought that the Timpo figures lost realism when they changed to Swoppet style figures.

104

Picture 137: BMC First World War

To the right are BMC figures from eight different sets in the flat caps and khaki of the British Expeditionary Force. There could well be eight different scales as well, from the lovely slightly semi-flat marching men many of whom are smoking pipes, through the lying firing men, the beautiful bicyclist, the marching men behind the pipe smokers, and three sizes of mounted to the small figures poking bayonets towards the German prisoners of war. The prisoners are not BMC. Allied toymakers such as Fry and CBG Mignot were somewhat wishfully keen on producing German soldiers with their hands in the air, so I show a mixture here with a guard of five Fry Highlanders.

Heroic highlights
- Trojan War P 58
- Thermopylae P 102
- Spartacus
- Anthony and Cleopatra
- Robin Hood P 120
- Agincourt P 155
- Three musketeers P 134
- Pirates
- Waterloo P 66
- Alamo
- Charge of the Light Brigade P 92
- Siege of Lucknow P 194
- Wild West P 166
- Rorke's Drift P 205
- 55 Days at Peking P 185
- French Foreign Legion and Arabs P 32
- SAS P 70
- Science Fiction and Fantasy P 33

The national possibilities are self-evident. Particularly in terms of world uniforms at the end of the nineteenth century, with Britains, Heyde and CBG Mignot all producing troops of many nations over the ensuing decades, the opportunities of putting together display or iconic collections of national troops, which can then be extended to the present day or back in time are quite obvious, yet most interestingly compelling. One such collection for Spain was that of Don Dario Loraque Perez, which comprised some 12,000 figures depicting the

Picture 138: Spanish Tercio

This magnificent representation of the Tercio of Flanders in 1525 shows the Spanish Imperial military machine at its apex, a system of warfare that, with some modification, was the way battles were fought until the disappearance of the pikeman 150 years later. At this stage, the tercio was made up of a core of pikemen who kept cavalry at bay while the arquebusiers killed them off and the light swordsmen prevented the formation being penetrated by enemy infantry. The models are by Castellana, one of the Spanish makers who continued in the tradition of Heyde in the 1950s and produced a beautiful and extensive series of Spanish historical subjects. To the right, for comparison, are two of the figures made by Heyde to represent this period.

Picture 139: Turkish Detachment revisited

The Turks hold on the left flank, with supporting artillery, while the main infantry attack goes in on the right, supported by cavalry. Compared to twenty-five years ago, the detachment has slowly but surely acquired some weight of numbers. It would, of course, look even better spread out a bit, so here are some pictures of some of the components as well. In my opinion, this is what a compatible group of old and new toy soldiers should look like. Although it includes originals, repaints, recasts, conversions and New Toy Soldiers, the overall effect is homogenous and unless you look carefully, none stand out as not belonging.

history of Spain from the earliest times to the present, including many superb models as well as in the toy style. Cataloguing this collection for sale at Phillips in 1998 was one of the most instructive of my auction house career.

My own favourite nationality for something a little different has been Turkey. Starting out as the spearhead of Islam, the Turkish Empire eventually transfigured into one of the 19th century Great Powers, before becoming essentially part of the European scene during the 20th century. In *Collecting Toy Soldiers*, I showed 64 troops in my Turkish detachment of Turkish troops c.1900. I have continued to add to this, and it is now 113 strong. That is adding an average of two figures a year! In my view, this detachment is a good example of a small display collection, which could easily be expanded by the inclusion, for instance, of the armies of Turkey's opponents in the Balkan Wars. In a few reserve boxes are battered and broken Turkish Britains waiting to be mended and repainted to add to the Turkish detachment. I have about ten of these projects left out of forty or fifty I was collecting bad condition figures for when I was younger.

Picture 140: Turkish Artillery

One Steadfast Krupp gun with crew, and three Mark Time cannon with a few 'Artillerymen'. These are, after all toy style soldiers. The CBG Mignot figure right front looks ready to give up, but the Turks were on the wrong side in the First World War.

Picture 141: Turks by Alex Riches

These converted recast Britains figures by Alex Riches are very good examples of what can be achieved by imaginative extensions of what Britains might have made had they had the inclination. For every standard Britains set there are probably a dozen other possible sets Britains could have made by a combination of heads and bodies that would have added to the subject. Anyway, when I first saw these, I thought they were so evocative that I had to add them to my regular Britains Turkish sets (see picture 44) and they formed the core of the Turkish detachment that I have been adding to ever since. Even the Freddie Green figures (see below) do not overshadow them.

Picture 142: Turks by Freddie Green
The Turkish cavalry here are superb, and some have the Green trademark soldered on moustache.

From each period of history, region or nation, there may well be particular occasions or ceremonies that will form the subject around which to build a collection. The most frequently used of large-scale events are the Coronation processions and the Delhi durbars, or there are the other London ceremonies such as the Changing of the Guard or the Trooping of the Colour. The histories of a national army or individual regiments can also be brought into play.

Personalise your collection by association with your own family or forefathers, and with souvenirs of your travels or collecting opportunities. Do not forget to collect in support of lost childhood playthings or unfulfilled longings from that period, which can then be pleasant memories rather than nagging feelings of loss or deprivation.

The full hierarchy
So an overall hierarchy for defining specific collecting can be summarised as:
- **Level 1**   The universal collection – a bit of everything
- **Level 2**   Method, type, style and scale of production
- **Level 3**   Country of origin
- **Level 4**   Manufacturer or designer
- **Level 5**   Subject depicted: historical and heroic
- **Level 6**   Subject depicted: geographical
- **Level 7**   Specific events, individuals or units
- **Level 8**   Personal association or nostalgia
- **Level 9**   Icons or cameos

The following famous collections all, with the exception of that of Barrie Blood, have come to auction as a whole or in part, and the catalogues for these sales form an excellent reference library in their own right.

- **Famous universal collections**: Malcolm Forbes, John Hanington.
- **Famous reference collections**: Len Richards, Ruby family, Bill McDade, Barrie Blood, Bill Miele.
- **Famous iconic collections**: Burtt Ehrlich, Lenore Josey, Arnold Rolak, Dmitri Ilyinsky.
- **Famous display collections**: Henry Harris, Colonel Bath, Terry Hanly, Kemble Widmer, Brian Hornick, Don Dario Loraque Perez.

By well-planned selection from or across the hierarchy, a logical or indeed famous collection can be built up. Display collections such as that of Major Henry Harris, planned at 5,000 figures representing the British Army of 1900, or Brian Hornick, showing Britain and the Empire at four stages of the last 150 years and comprising over 100,000 figures, were compulsively spectacular and satisfying.

Highlights at any level of the collection as it is formed may include rare variants, points of interest to be discussed among expert friends or contacts, readily recognisable figures that will amuse guests and neighbours, or collecting stories to enthuse possible recruits. As various interesting things come your way, serendipity will often suggest new subjects and associations from which to form new cameos. This may lead to more research, acquisitions and articles for *Plastic Warrior* or the *Old Toy Soldier Newsletter*. In the next chapter we will look at examples of such cameos.

At the end of the hierarchy comes the Joker. No well-planned scheme should ever prevent you acquiring something you are drawn to. Get it anyway, if you can afford it, and you will very seldom regret it, because if you like it, it is odds on others will also, so you are playing to the WOW! factor, the valuable asset of attractiveness in the model.

CHAPTER 8
DEFINING A SPECIALISED COLLECTION: HIGHLANDERS

Now let's look at an example of a specialised collection. Highlanders are a favourite of mine, and I would like to demonstrate a relatively small but hopefully instructive cameo of fifty pieces as a core. This would be a reference collection of all the individual castings of Britains hollowcast Highlanders 1893 to 1966. As we follow their introduction, the suggestions for extensions or limitations will easily occur. These will enable you to examine in detail the thought processes in putting collections of this nature together, and what considerations may, or may not, according to your taste, be included. Then we can consider the ramifications of extending such a collection into other makers, countries or connections.

To my mind, one can go overboard with single subject collections, and I didn't want the Highlanders in my collection to overwhelm everything else. Over one in seven of my remaining toy soldiers are Highlanders, and I would get worried if the proportion ever rose above one in five. I think that like me, many collectors would risk getting bored with a collection that had too little variety, even if the number one subject was their favourite.

The reference collection of Britains Highlanders

As my mother is Scottish, and her grandfather was chaplain to the Gordon Highlanders before the First World War, I have a strong association with the highland regiments. These, in order of seniority in the army list of 1893 were, The Black Watch, the Seaforth Highlanders, the Gordon Highlanders, the Cameron Highlanders and the Argyll and Sutherland Highlanders. In the full dress of 1893, they appear in red jackets, tartan kilts and tall black bonnets with a large hackle on the left hand side.

The Gordon Highlanders are the most often depicted as toys of all the highland regiments, probably because the Gordon tartan is easily represented by thin vertical and horizontal stripes of yellow on a dark green cloth. The Black Watch are the dullest of the five regiments, as their tartan can be shown simply as dark green alone. They do, however, have a red hackle to their bonnets, and Britains in their best quality paint before 1946 painted their tartan with black horizontal and vertical stripes that give a better representation of it. All four other regiments had white hackles. Britains showed the other regimental tartans as follows:

- **Seaforths** – red horizontal stripes, overpainted with white vertical stripes, on blue cloth.
- **Camerons** – yellow vertical stripes, overpainted with red horizontal stripes, on dark green cloth.
- **Argylls** – light green horizontal and vertical stripes, on dark green cloth.

N.B. The order of painting and overpainting of the tartan stripes can differ according to the whim of the painter – I simply give the order that I have seen most often. One early version of the Argyll tartan showed it as white horizontal and vertical stripes on black cloth. For a full discussion of British Army uniforms of the late 19th century as depicted by Britains, see my book *Britains Toy Soldiers 1893-1932*, chapter 13. See if you can spot the different paintings of tartans in the accompanying photographs for this chapter.

As part of my *Eighty years of British Production* collection, I already had an extensive selection of Highlanders. From my personal association, and to form a relatively small collection, I

might have been tempted to limit myself simply to Gordon Highlanders. However, I decided to include all of them. Already my collection of Gordons, where I might have had a target of 1,000 figures, assuming I was not looking to include any large unit displays, has the potential to expand to maybe three times that.

Given that I want a reference collection and not just icons or cameos, in terms of Britains alone, I have to decide the scope of my Highlander collection. Will it perhaps include just one example of each different version and position? Within hollowcasts will it feature small size and second grade figures, as well as best quality? Will it go on outside hollowcast to plastic, diecast, new toy soldier and model styles? Should it feature sets and packaging?

In the following account of Britains Highlanders, the figures in brackets show the number of different figures offered as Highlanders by Britains, which I would need to build my 'one example of each' cameo. You will see from the illustrated examples that I only have forty-eight out of the necessary fifty-four models, so I still need another six, one of which will be near impossible, and two very difficult, as I will mention below.

In terms just of individual single sets, the Highlanders form one of the strongest and most numerous sections of Britains output, not to say also one of the most picturesque. Starting at the very beginning in 1893 with one of the 'Germanic' figures, the famous 'plug-handed Highlander' (1), Britains issued set 11 Black Watch and set 15 Argyle and Sutherland Highlanders. In 1897, Britains added a nice little figure of a piper with befeathered Glengarry (2) and issued set 77 Gordon Highlanders and in the next set 88, a double row set of Seaforth Highlanders. The very next set number, 89, completed all five regiments with a set of firing Cameron Highlanders in foreign service helmets with pugarees, which included a standing officer (3) and kneeling officer (4) as well as figures standing (5) kneeling (6) and lying (7) firing. The standing figures had an oval base, while the kneeling and lying ones had none. Initially for a very short period, the standing and kneeling officers had helmets modelled without the pugaree, so when the pugaree was also included for them, shortly afterwards, we have standing officer (8) and kneeling officer (9). This set of Camerons was not issued until 1901, and all the figures bear the design date 1.7.1901. The earliest figures have paper labels stuck to the bases rather than embossed lettering in the mould, so there is a case for saying that there are three more different figures to collect because of this. The kneeling figure had nowhere to put any label or embossing, so did not change. Cutting off at this point would make an interesting cameo in itself, the first Britains sets of the five highland regiments.

According to my game plan here, I would have to decide whether to include in my Highlander collection all Britains sets containing Highlanders, all sets containing differently

Picture 143: Britains Highlanders 1893 to 1901
Left to right, Highlanders 1 to 9 as described in the text.

painted Highlanders or simply all sets containing different figures of Highlanders. The widest interpretation here would include set 73, the largest early set of Britains, that had at its inception a row of plug-handed Gordons included in it.

In the meantime, Britains had embarked on a major programme of re-making earlier poses, in part to gain the benefit of new designs that they could emboss with the date of design and their copyright, to help prevent their figures being pirated. In Highlanders, the Gordons of set 77 were the first to benefit, with an oval base box pack marching figure dated 20.1.1901 (10). In itself this figure was remarkable for being the first Britains model with a box pack. Other British infantry marching with box packs only appeared four years later in 1905. The new figure was also used to launch a new set of Seaforth Highlanders marching, numbered set 112.

The next highland figure to appear was the marching Cameron Highlander in foreign service helmet, the same figure as the Gordon, but with a different head (11) which was used to make up set 114. Both the Gordon and the Cameron at first appeared with paper labels. As with the firing officers, the very early men had smooth helmets, but rapidly the heads were changed to show a pugaree (12). The smooth helmeted Camerons, officers and men, are among the most rare of all the Britains Highlander figures.

During this period Britains were also producing small size troops. The first Highlander among these, for set 23b, was another figure with foreign service helmet with pugaree, of a Cameron at the trail (13). The officer for this set comprised the same figure with the rifle removed (14). An alternative figure with a spiked infantry helmet was occasionally used, but this version was much rarer (15) and (16). Occasionally, both versions could be found painted in red jackets rather than the normal khaki.

Set 118 was a single row set of Gordons lying firing, and set 122, a single row of Black Watch standing firing. Both used the same figures as the Camerons of set 89, and were in fact issued in 1901 at the same time as set 89, which may have been substituted in the list for something else that was never issued at an earlier date. The Gordons had a kneeling officer and the Black Watch a standing one, and at the very beginning, as with the Camerons, these had smooth helmets.

In 1903, Britains finally replaced the plug-handed Highlander in sets 11, 15 and 88 with a new oval based fixed arm charging figure (17) dated 17.12.1903 that was also used, with gold facings, as the officer. As a result the content count in these sets went up to eight to a row, rather than seven.

Set 157, issued in 1908, a new single row set with a variety of Gordons firing and no officer included, could almost be seen as an add-on set to 118.

During the course of the next few years, most Britains figures were changed to a distinctively

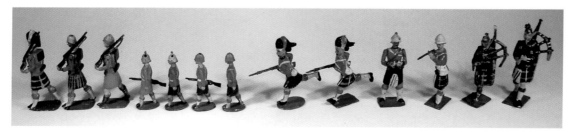

Picture 144: Britains Highlanders 1901 to 1912

Left to right, Highlanders 10 to 22 as described in the text.

Figure 12 is an extremely rare Paris office version painted all in khaki. Note that the rectangular based charging Seaforth is the officer figure from set 88, with gold facings.

112

rectangular base. Once the rectangular base for the charging Highlander was made (18), no more changes were made to this pose, but it would be possible to collect four or five further changes to the embossing underneath the base up until the end of production in 1966. The standing officer (19) and standing firing figure (20) also received a rectangular base at this time. As part of this programme a rectangular base version of the early piper (21) was also made, but this is rare, as it was only for a short time, and a new larger piper (22) was designed, dated 6.3.1912. Immediately adjoining this, came a second version small size Highlander (23), this time in full dress and dated 8.4.1912. This figure was used after the First World War in the second grade W series which replaced most of the B series best quality sets.

The final Highlander created before the First World War was the definitive marching Highlander in full dress without a pack (24), probably created in 1913, following on the similar standard British infantry figure dated 24.2.1910. Early variations of this figure were fitted with the pre-war rifle with the drooping sling, as normal for the marching Highlander sets 77 and 112. They must have changed to the next moulding of a rifle arm at the slope fairly promptly thereafter since I only ever remember seeing the packless figure with this arm in one set of Gordon Highlanders. Probably also at about this time the foreign service helmeted marching Cameron figure used in set 114 was changed to a packless version (25).

At what date the second grade Highlander marching was made is something of a mystery. Judging from the paintwork, I would say not until the 1920s. This would mean that it was the second grade Highlanders in khaki created for the First World War which came first, but once more there is no certain dating available, and they were evidently created after 1912, when Britains ceased to need dates to appear on their figures. Whatever the dating actually was, we should include these Highlanders here, so there were four depicting the First World War, possibly inspired by the exploits of the London Scottish at Messines in 1914, where they were the first Territorial regiment in action. There were two poses, charging (26) and stabbing downwards (27), both with fixed bayonets, and at first painted with a ferocious moustache.

It could be that both these figures, created at first in Glengarry caps, were produced in riposte to other makers, since a number of figures in similar poses exist by Britains competitors (a cue for a small but very interesting cameo). It was recently pointed out to me that the figure stabbing downwards has Depose embossed under the base, so the possibility is that these figures, which are of a design very different to the normal Britains figure, were designed in Paris, since the Paris factory was at this time open and doing design work. At some point thereafter came the rather more common charging (28) and stabbing (29) figures with the headgear changed to steel helmets, which are usually painted without moustaches in the normal second grade manner. All four figures were a little larger than the normal Britains figure.

The second grade fixed arm Highlander at the slope (30), by contrast, was rather annoyingly smaller than 54mm, actually standing about 50mm tall not counting the bonnet. Generations of collectors would have been grateful to Britains had they made this ubiquitous highland marching figure the same size as the standard best quality figure. Inherent Commercial Probability, however, would suggest that not only was the smaller figure surprisingly economical of metal to make, but also demonstrated a good difference when shown in a shop alongside the more expensive model that fully justified the higher price. Against this consideration, in later times firing Highlander castings identical to the best quality were widely used in second quality paint. Perhaps the fixed arm was the over-riding consideration here.

Before leaving second grade highland figures, there were two larger sizes to include, the 70mm scale H series Highlander (31) which is reasonably rare and was available in gilt

Picture 145: Britains Highlanders 1912 to 1930

Left to right, Highlanders 23 to 32 as described in the text.

The second version small size Highlander is the paint variation issued by the Paris factory. I have no example of figure 25 to show.

or second grade finish and the 83mm scale HH series Highlander (32), which is about as rare as things get, and seems to have only been available in second grade finish. The only commercial explanation for these that I can think of was that they were meant to counter the influx of Elastolin and Lineol 70mm and 100mm highlanders between the wars. They remained in the catalogue until 1941.

For some considerable time after 1908, Britains appeared happy with the number of single row highlander sets in their best quality range. In 1932, however, they added a magnificent set, number 437, of Officers of the Gordon Highlanders that, short of bands and colours, really completed the look of the marching Highlanders in full dress. The officer on foot (33), of which there four in the set, was totally splendid, matched only by the superb mounted officer (34) that accompanied them. These are well in the running for the best Britains hollowcast models of all time, and knock the socks off most other makers' highland officers. While Britains were remarkably reluctant to use them in other regular sets, they appear to have been happy to sell them individually, as they turn up from time to time in various regimental uniforms, both in standard best quality paint and as special paintings with additional detail.

Customers were able to ask Britains for specially painted highland sets during the late 1930s, and although they are very rare, suggesting that the number of customers taking advantage of this service was small, when discovered they are some of the most artistic toy soldiers ever created.

In 1931 Britains introduced their Parade series, sets that were packaged to stand up inside the box, and both the Black Watch and the Gordons participated in this venture. The sets were evidently not too popular, as very few survive, but they gave rise to a second mounted highland officer (35). The problem with using the just created new mounted officer was that it was a little tall for the new packaging, and also Britains had made a mounted officer for the whole series from a second grade figure, by putting a base between the rear legs of the horse, which enabled it to fit inside the slotted baseboard of the Parade series box. I have examples of this mounted officer for Fusiliers and Middlesex Regiment, but until recently had never seen the one used for the Black Watch, which was revealed in an *Old Toy Soldier Newsletter* article and is probably the rarest regularly catalogued highland figure ever made by Britains.

Also in about 1931, when Britains were improving some figures, they created a highland piper in bonnet (36) which they used to replace the piper in glengarry just for the Scots Guards set 69, retaining the old figure for the Gordons, Argylls and Camerons. The article mentioned above also suggests that seven of this figure formed part of the Black Watch Parade set 480. The only element of doubt is that this would bring the total content for this set to twenty, two more than the stated content of eighteen.

Around 1934, Britains made a new lying firing figure (37) to replace the rather unsteady old one with his feet rather too close together to make a good shot. The new one had the feet spread apart in the approved steadying position. Around 1935, the figure of the marching Cameron in set 114 was changed by substituting a Wolseley helmet (38) for the old foreign service helmet with pugaree.

In 1937, Britains joined in a venture with the British Model Soldier Society to make British troops from the battle of Waterloo, and as part of this a new Highlander was made with two movable arms, and fitted out with musket (39), half pike (40) or sword (41) to represent private, sergeant or officer.

Around 1937, all the highland pipers were revised with a wider plaid and somewhat sturdier figure, so there were new pipers in Glengarry (42) and in bonnet (43). In 1940, the figure used for set 114 was repainted and brought out as the Cape Town Highlanders, set 1901. An officer (44) was provided for this set by replacing the arm with the rifle with an empty handed arm. This completed all the Highlanders made between the wars.

Picture 146: Britains Highlanders 1932 to 1941

Left to right, Highlanders 33 to 44 as described in the text.

I would certainly like to have shown here a Parade series Black Watch officer, but I have never seen, let alone owned, one. There is always something more to try and find. The piper in the bonnet is a Scots Guard, as this figure was not, although it could well have been, used for highland regiments. The marching figure in the Wolseley helmet is a Cape Town Highlander, and I currently do not have the officer (figure 44) to go with this.

Post-war Britains Highlanders in themselves make up an interesting cameo, including as they do a new row of marching Black Watch with officer which was now included in the final version of display box 73. Of the pre-war sets, at first only set 11 Black Watch and set 77 Gordon Highlanders were revived. A little later set 11 was, for the first time, given a piper in bonnet. In 1952, new additional sets were created, and set 1519, the Waterloo Highlanders (painted as Gordons) was revived. Set 2025 was an eighteen piece replacement for the old Camerons firing set 89. Set 2062 replaced the old Seaforth set 88, and included a mounted officer. Set 2063 presented Argylls firing for the first time. There was also a row of Seaforths marching in set 1323, painted either with buff facings or no facings at all rather than the pre-war yellow. Occasionally, an officer was included with these.

In the second grade, the ever-popular Highlanders standing, kneeling and lying

115

in red jackets and foreign service helmets were re-issued, and to enliven these, a new mounted officer figure (54) was created by using a mounted second grade figure with the foreign service helmet and painting it as a second grade highland officer. The effect was very similar to the mounted West India Regiment officer. I am pretty sure I had one of these when I was young and repainted it, but I can't find it now, so I have to count this as another missing figure to find.

In 1953 Herald came out with their superb Highlanders in plastic, and as a direct result of this Britains responded with set 2109, a 21 piece Highland Pipe Band of the Black Watch in bonnets, which is another of the all time hollowcast greats. This was available from 1956 for ten years, and proved very popular, so it is not rare, but as a great favourite among collectors the price has been high. A smaller nine piece set of the same figures was issued in 1959 only as set 2179, and is one of the most difficult numbered sets to get hold of in its original box. The colour party which followed as set 2111 was equally popular, and as it was only around for five years, there are less of them to find. These sets were generally already bought just by adults, since the toy market had moved on to plastic, and the equivalent Herald figures were probably produced in more than a hundred times the quantity.

In terms of new figures this completed the tally, and these were some of the best ever done. The drum major (45), side drummer (46) tenor drummer (47) and bass drummer (48) were small masterpieces. They are still much sought after as castings for repainting and converting to grace any full dress highland band. The colour party was also based on new figures, the colour bearer (49) and the colour sergeant (50).

Just four more additions to the Highlander scene of the Britains hollowcast range remain to describe. In 1954 Britains brought out its range of individually boxed figures, the Picture Packs. In this series, Britains used Gordon Highlanders, and here a standing Gordons officer with binoculars and a charging Gordons figure were available for the first time. As part of another valedictory series, the half row sets, issued in 1957, set 2126 contained three figures, one of which was a mounted officer of the Black Watch. Around then also, there was a revival of interest in the Waterloo series, and a new highland figure with just a single movable arm appeared. This is extremely rare, as the set was discontinued in 1959, and the quantity of sets

Picture 147: Britains Highlanders 1956 to 1959

Left to right, Highlanders 45 to 54 as described in the text. The mounted second-grade officer (54) I cannot show. The revised version of the Waterloo Highlander with only one movable arm is hard to find. I just have the one man with musket, as shown here. For comparison, I show to the right the New Hollowcast series version of the private and sergeant, which were painted as Camerons. As you can see the paint style is totally different, even to the extent of painting in shadow lines behind some of the crossbelts.

issued with the new figure must have been relatively small. It does, of course, involve three more figures, with musket (51), half pike (52) and sword (53). Finally, the mounted officer of the Gordons was available in an individual souvenir box, with an illustrated interior backdrop of Edinburgh castle, as set 2168.

A cameo of the Britains postwar hollowcast highland sets and rows would contain 130 figures even if only the first post-war packaging was incorporated. One might add the attempted revival of hollowcast figures or the even more recent Archive series Highlanders.

Having come to the end, for the time being, of Britains hollowcast production, now came the era of plastic and die-cast. Britains soon took over Herald, and the Herald plastic ranges of Gordons and Black Watch, started in 1953, remained a staple of the list until 1976. To begin with the painting was of best quality standard, but this was later reduced, and when production was moved to Hong Kong, the painting became much less intricate.

In 1983, Britains produced their first die-cast highland figures for their Metal Models series, with men marching at the slope and an officer figure. The rifle shown was the old short Lee-Enfield, giving the appearance of men in full dress from the early part of the 20th century rather than the contemporary feel of the Foot Guards with their SLRs, changed to SA80 rifles in 1990. The sets first issued were the old favourites, Black Watch and Gordons, but a special Limited Edition of Cameron Highlanders with fixed bayonets was issued for the American market in a quantity of 3,000 sets.

In 1984 I commissioned 2,000 Argylls with 500 officers as souvenirs of my *On Guard* exhibition at the London Toy and Model Museum. These had enhanced paint details, and were done on the understanding that Britains would not otherwise produce Argylls with the new figures. In 1985 the Seaforths were produced as a limited edition to complete the tally of the five regiments, and by this time pipers had also been added, both in Glengarry for the Gordons and Seaforths, and in bonnets for the Black Watch. In 1988, the Seaforths re-appeared in a limited edition, this time in Wolseley helmets and with a colour party.

In 1996, a limited edition of the Pipes and Drums of the Black Watch appeared, which needed side drummers, bass drummer and drum major to be created to complete it. In 1997, the Black Watch was added to with a contemporary full dress colour party limited edition, with Kilmarnock bonnets and SA80 rifles. This set also had two buglers in bonnets. In 1999, side drummers were made available singly for both Black Watch and Gordons, and finally in 2004 a full Black Watch regimental band was issued as a limited edition. Hamleys commissioned pipes, drums and regimental band of the Gordons sold in two limited edition sets (see picture 218 for Britains die-cast Highlanders).

These Metal Model or Ceremonial Series figures form a nice cameo of their own, as they all present with a very uniform appearance. It is instructive, though, to put one of these marching and an old hollowcast figure alongside each other. They are in fact both exactly 54mm scale, but because of the differences in their design and paintwork, they look completely different, and do not blend in with each other at all. Partially the 3mm thick base on the more recent figures are to blame, particularly for the feeling that the newer figures must surely be larger than 54mm, but it is not so.

When Britains decided in 2001 to see if they could revive proper hollowcasting with Chinese production, the Cameron Highlanders were nominated to lead the way. In the old hollowcast days, Camerons had never appeared in the regular sets in full dress bonnets, so this 'revival' was most welcome. The new figures had fixed bayonets, another difference to the old highland marching figure, and were available with officer, colour party and a 79th foot Waterloo version with sergeant. The new figures on first glance looked superb and very true to the old style, but then close up the paint style was very different, and made them look out of place with old figures even if the castings were identical. Such are the difficulties of attaining compatibility even with the best of intentions.

In 2003 a pipe and drum band came out to accompany the regiment. This was in three sets of five figures, and one of six, but unfortunately the sets were wrongly configured to make up a full band. If you bought all four sets, you ended up with four too many pipers, two too few side drummers and one too few tenor drummers to make a standard small pipe and drum band of twenty figures like the old Black Watch set 2109. The sets should have contained three pipers each, with drum major and bass drummer, two side drummers or two tenor drummers, then by buying the three sets and an extra set with the side drummers, the right band would be formed. As it was, things ended up very lopsided, and you have to display the band coming round a corner so that the missing drummers are hidden behind something.

Picture 148: New hollowcast Camerons – also see text

The curious make up of the sets of pipe band figures is reflected here with a full tally of one of each set, with the colour party and two sets of marching figures to the left. The figures are based on the Britains castings 24, 33, 42 and 45 to 50 (see pictures above). These were then painted up as full dress Camerons, which had never previously been done by Britains except as specials. Although they are very splendid, the paint finish is considerably different and glossier, with the colours varying from how the earlier models would have looked in the 1930s, thus allaying collectors fears that the new hollowcast venture might be clever enough to be indistinguishable from priceless originals.

Britains have brought out various other highland items over the recent period, for instance the 2003 William Britains Collector's Club Special of the Black Watch preparing for Hogmanay. There were the Gordons officer, colour party and escort for the Queen's Golden Jubilee procession, with the Black Watch at present arms, and a Gordons pipe and drum band in five sets, still not making up to a complete band, whatever combination one used. There were Black Watch infantry in the Premier series. A Black Watch piper was included in a paint and collect set. The archive collection started in 2008 began with Cameron Highlanders and has since added Gordons.

In 2007 a 79th Regiment Highlander 1815 was brought out for the History of the British Army 'Redcoats' series, and six other highland figures have since been added to the series. In the same year a 42nd Highlander (Black Watch) was added to the French and Indian Wars range. The Victoria Cross series included a Sutherland Highlander from the Thin Red Line, and the Collector's Club was treated to a matching piper and the same regiment featured in four sets from the Indian Mutiny. 71st Highlanders appear in the American Revolution series, and the Napoleonic series featured 42nd Highlanders from 2009 as does the World War I series from 2007. The Museum collection from 2008 is almost entirely composed of Black Watch (see picture 25). One might even include the Highlander who sat in Queen Victoria's Barouche. In all, far more highland figures have been created by Britains since 1966 than were ever done before that date.

Smaller collections or cameos with Britains Highlanders

If resources or room do not permit of a collection as above, it can easily be limited by sticking to a certain period or type of figure. Here are some possibilities with Highlanders, of collections or cameos in the Reference (R), Display (D), Icon (I) or Cameo (C) style.

- Example of each of the different Britains hollowcast fifty-four figures (see bracketed numbered figures above). (R)
- Example for each figure of each different painting of the different regiments or officers. (R)
- Cameos presenting any one or more of the five regiments. (D or I)
- Iconic groups of your favourite Highlanders. (D or I)
- Plug-handed Highlanders (R) WOW! factor 7. A tough cameo to collect, especially in original boxes. 35 figures.
- First Britains sets of the five highland regiments (R) WOW! factor 7. The plug-handeds with set 89. 65 figures.
- Britains Highlanders with smooth foreign service helmets (R) WOW! factor 8. Officers with binoculars and set 114. 12 figures.
- Dated Britains Highlanders. (R)
- Interwar Britains Highlanders. (R)
- Highlander specials by Britains. (C) WOW! factor 8. My cameo has 30 figures.
- Highland square. (D) WOW! factor 7. My 'square' is set out as a wavy row along one shelf, and comprises 345 figures. The 'highland square' first came into prominence when it was used as the cover illustration for the paperback first edition of Len Richards book *Old British Model Soldiers*. His 'square' passed on to the Forbes Museum. I formed a similar square to illustrate in *Britains Toy Soldiers 1893-1932* that was then made into a poster on sale at my *On Guard* London Toy and Model Museum exhibition. This cameo is exceedingly popular among collectors, containing as a minimum the 18 piece set 2025 or 30 piece set 89, usually with additions and often with conversions. Almost entirely due to the high WOW! factor of this concept, firing Highlanders in foreign service helmets attract over twice the price of firing Infantry of the Line or three times that of firing Foot Guards at auction.
- Waterloo Highlanders. (R)
- Post-war Britains hollowcast Highlanders. (R) 121 figures.
- Herald Highlanders. (R) My display cameo of these has 76 figures, with a further 10 in boxes and 72 awaiting repainting as a project. As first series in immaculate paintwork, these figures are rare, but including the Hong Kong versions (which suffer from warped weapons), it is easy to pick up quantities of them inexpensively in poor condition for re-conditioning, repainting and conversion to bring out the strengths of the beautifully balanced design.

- Hollowcast style Highlander revival. (R) My Camerons are 42 strong (see above).
- The Black Watch Museum collection series (see picture 25). (R)

Additional collections or cameos to fit with the Britains Highlanders

The temptation is always to edge the boundaries of the collection outwards a little. How would it be, for instance, if I included all the Scottish regiments, not just the Highlanders? This would bring into play my favourite cavalry regiment, the Royal Scots Greys, and also a regiment of Foot Guards, the Scots Guards, together with a number of other famous regiments, the Royal Scots, the King's Own Scottish Borderers, the Cameronian Rifles, the Highland Light Infantry and the Royal Scots Fusiliers. One must not neglect, either, the Queen's bodyguard for Scotland, the Royal Archers, or the many territorial units. Then one can go on to the linked highland regiments in the dominions of Canada, South Africa, Australia and New Zealand.

Unless you have limited yourself purposely to original paint, you can add repainted or converted figures. It is perfectly in order to fill out all the things that Britains never made by this means, now that you can no longer order such things from Britains themselves as you could in the 1930s or 1950s. I have, for instance, a full military band, pipes and drums of the Argylls.

A collection of pipe and drum bands either in highland dress or other pipes and drums e.g. Scots Guards, Irish Guards, Gurkhas, Indian Army regiments, Parachute Regiment, Royal Navy and Royal Air Force. I have a lovely pipe and drum band of the French navy by Starlux that I have enjoyed for many years (see picture 62). The Bonhams sale of 13th April 2010, for instance, had on offer nineteen pipe bands other than the five highland regiments, which sold for around £4 per figure.

In addition to the Britains hollowcast reference collection above (964 figures) and the few post-hollowcast Britains (145 figures) I have a series of cameos making up a reference collection of hollowcast Highlanders by British makers (about 564 figures). Then there are

Picture 149: Cherilea late series Highlanders

This boxed set of the six larger scale Cherilea plastic Highlanders is relatively uncommon. Virtually all the British manufacturers of any note made Highlanders. Notice the bass drum, which was made of two halves which plugged together, sometimes, as here, not too successfully.

iconic cameos of the production of these famous troops by makers around the world (about 235 figures). Plastic, diecast, aluminium, New Toy Soldiers and a few other items account for a further 470 figures, for a total Highlander collection, excluding conversions, other Scottish regiments, territorials or colonials, of 2,377 pieces.

Anything else but Highlanders

After this, you may well ask, do I care for anything else but Highlanders? It is true that in subject terms I have made Highlanders the strongest theme of this book, and used Highlanders to demonstrate or include in many of the chapters. The next chapter, however will offer a multitude of other subjects as cameos, and as a taster, perhaps, for a future publication, I would like to show here a – to me – WOW! picture of my earliest Britains small size figures, the fixed arm mounted cavalryman in Best Quality with continental horse furniture, which is usually quite difficult to find in any variant.

Picture 150: Minikin Highlanders
A lovely little boxed set of historical Highlanders, commissioned in the US and made in Japan for the American market around 1947.

Picture 151 (inset): Composition Highlanders
Elastolin and Lineol exported large numbers of Highlanders into the UK during the 1920s and 1930s, in three main scales, Elastolin, with oval bases, used 100mm at the back, 70mm in the middle row and 60mm centre front. The Lineol Highlanders on rectangular bases are a little larger than the smallest of the Elastolins. The spectacularly detailed 70mm scale figures were some of the nicest ever made by Hausser-Elastolin, and each figure cost 4/6d, as can be seen on the labels attached. This was over twice as much for each figure as a whole boxed set of Britains at the time! Maybe they were intended for the Scottish tourist trade.

Picture 152: Britains small size fixed arm cavalryman

From their inception in 1896, Britains used this small size fixed arm mounted figure in many of its small size sets, but after a very few years phased it out in favour of the movable arm version. For this reason, any of these are difficult to find, although they were still in use in the Paris factory in 1912. Centre back is a standard 1897 tin sword second version Life Guard for size comparison. The four turned back figures to the left are Hanks very similar figures to the Britains, but these have English horse furniture as opposed to the Britains, which have blanket rolls behind the saddle. The Hanks figures shown are Life Guard, Royal Horse Guard, 6th Dragoon Guard and 1st Dragoon. The Britains figures, from right back, then coming forward along each rank, are 1st Dragoon Guard trumpeter (grey horse) and officer (brown horse) from set 57, Scots Grey officer or trumpeter from sets 58, 85 or 6b, mounted infantry trumpeter from set 58 or 15b, 11th Hussar officer from set 10b, 13th Hussar trumpeter from set 87, 5th Dragoon Guard trumpeter from set 85, 1st Life Guard officer from set 1b or 2nd Life Guard trumpeter from set 84 (there was no difference in the painting), 17th Lancer officer from set 13b, gilt finish Life Guard, and French Chasseur troopers on black and brown horses from the Paris factory.

I still definitely have three to find, the officer for set 87, the officer or trumpeter of the Royal Horse Guards from set 58, and the 16th Lancer officer from set 12b. Then it is always possible that grey horses can turn up where I only have a brown one, or brown ones where I only have a grey. Usually, the greys denote a trumpeter. There may also be any number more variants from the Paris factory in as yet undiscovered further sets of cavalry.

CHAPTER 9
COLLECTIONS FOR SMALL SPACES
AND BUDGETS: THE CAMEO

The nature of a Cameo

How big might a cameo collection be?

A cameo collection can be as big as you want it to be, but what it means as an adjective is miniature, small and perfect of its kind. The small aspect can be small in numbers or small in subject breadth, and the perfect of its kind aspect suggests that it is probably a complete collection of a well-defined proposition. A complete collection of a manufacturer's output would normally be too large to be a cameo, unless it was a maker such as Faudel Phillips or Reynolds where the known output or availability is strictly limited. To my mind, a comfortable cameo, a little jewel on the shelves, is a space of about one to three feet wide, which is more than just one set, perhaps of between ten and a hundred and fifty figures, and tells a particular story. This could be a defined grouping that is hard to collect, or a familiar subject presented in an interesting and freshly angled way.

Forming a cameo

Cameos can be acquired ready made, when an interesting group presents itself, but more often and more interestingly they can grow gradually from browsing round shows and auctions, or swopping between friends. It is fun to have a few things that one looks out for which are hardly ever likely to turn up. My Turkish detachment, which is shown in the previous chapter, comes under this heading, as Turkish troops are not the most popular of subjects. I got enthused when Alex Riches made some really beautiful Britains look-alikes of Turkish infantry lying firing and charging, to complement the on guard figures which were the only pose provided by Britains themselves.

What a contrast in France, where CBG Mignot usually took the trouble to provide a full range of poses for any uniform that was ordered. I have just three CBG Mignot Turks, all different, but if I ever came across any more I would certainly be very tempted. Interestingly, the Britains Paris Office tended to try to compete with CBG Mignot in providing many different poses, which is one of the major reasons why it's output is so varied and interesting. In London, Britains concentrated on selling a lot of each numbered set, while keeping the possible variety relatively low. This doubtless worked well to help keep prices down. Only in the modern era when there are so many gifted amateur producers has it been possible to emulate Mignot's variety in Britain.

Cameos can be formed whenever two or more items are linked in your collection, maybe when you serendipitously come across something at a show or on a stall that you know would add to what you have in an interesting way, as with my Hill 'Monarch' Highlanders.

Cameo possibilities

Given the many different themes and subjects to be collected discussed at the start of Chapter 7, the possible cameos are virtually limitless. I mention some hundreds of them in this book, and I am certain that you will be able to devise many more. The cameo collections that I suggested in *Collecting Toy Soldiers*, and what I have done with them since, are given below,

followed by a dozen additional examples in detail of the favourite ones that have occurred to me over the last twenty-five years, and a hundred and one (or more) further cameo titles to whet your appetite and get you thinking about the many thousands of possibilities to come up with something new and unique to your own collection.

Revisiting the cameos in 'Collecting Toy Soldiers'

Page numbers preceded by *CTS* refer to *Collecting Toy Soldiers*. Exhib = on display at my *On Guard* exhibition at the London Toy & Model Museum, 1985.

- Britains Waterloo hollowcasts: *CTS* frontespiece. (I have added the hollowcast revival versions to this.)
- Holger Eriksson: *CTS* page 24. (I am a great admirer of this designer's distinctive style, see page 28.)
- Unknown Hollowcasts: *CTS* page 25. (I still have plenty to include here, although I have solved the identities of some.)
- Britains plastic English Civil War: *CTS* page 33. (This one has diminished in size, as the figures are too valuable, but I have added a few figures as well, see picture 89.)
- German and British made soldiers compared, c1900: *CTS* page 40. (A favourite.)
- Turkish Detachment: *CTS* page 70. Picture 139 shows the detachment as it now looks.
- Larger than standard scale figures: *CTS* page 76. (This remains as a contrast to my favourite small size collection. See also Wild West picture 163.)
- Boyhood soldiers: *CTS* page 84. Exhib. (I doubt I will ever part with my first soldiers, see also pictures 6 to 9.)
- Britains Picture Packs: *CTS* page 88. Exhib. (The splendid cases have departed, individual figures distributed to other cameos.)
- Monarch Highlanders – three presentations: *CTS* page 89. (No change, still one of my favourites, but I could add in the box in picture 211.)
- Britains Colour Parties: *CTS* page 94. (Disposed of all but the Black Watch.)
- Britains Half Boxes. (Just three examples remain as a mini-cameo for demonstration.)
- Balkan Wars, Britains, Heyde, CBG Mignot or all three contrasted: *CTS* page 95. (Mine sold long since, except for the Turks.)
- Britains drum and fife bands: *CTS* page 96. (I now have just the Royal Welch Fusilier special, see jacket picture for this book.)
- Boer War: *CTS* page 97. Exhib. (Much reduced, to 124 figures.)
- Britains Canada: *CTS* page 99. Exhib. (Reduced to 27 around a nucleus of Fort Henry Guards.)
- Italy: *CTS* page 99. (I still have 37 figures, some interesting Carabinieri and a few individuals.)
- Britains Latin America: *CTS* page 99. (Sold long since – one iconic Uruguayan cadet retained.)
- Royal Welch Fusiliers: *CTS* page 100. Exhib. (Now down from 1,100 to 688.)
- Royal Scots Greys: *CTS* page 101. Exhib. (Now reduced to a mere 387.)
- Britains X Series: *CTS* page 101. (See Cheap Britains, chapter 12.)
- Britains Royal Engineers: *CTS* page 102. (Sadly, this beautiful cameo of standard and special figures have nearly all departed, with the exception of the mounted officer on the black horse at the halt and the standing officer in front of him which I kept as icons.)
- WWII Air Raid Precautions: *CTS* page 103. (Reduced, but still prominent – can also feature in Churchill, see below and picture 153.)
- Post-WWI Paris Office Figures: *CTS* page 104. (I proposed this as a deeply specialised

cameo – not that I ever had more than one or two of them, which are painted in a distinctively different style to the earlier ones.)

- Britains germanic figures: *CTS* page 104. Exhib. (Down from a set of each to individual examples only.)
- Souvenir figures: *CTS* page 104. (I still collect souvenir figures – see picture 82 re. Westair, and Chapter 3.)
- Britains Territorials and Yeomanry: *CTS* page 105.
- Britains figures not in standard scale: *CTS* page 105. (I WAS able to complete this, as by a fabulous stroke of good fortune I acquired the only other complete set of the Doll's House figures, see *The Great Book of Britains* page 196. This set has the highest WOW! factor of anything that I have ever had in my collection.)
- Sudan Campaign: *CTS* page 114. (My Sudan campaign display collection is now down to a cameo of just 45 figures.)
- Britains steel-helmeted horsedrawn vehicles: *CTS* page 131. (I have never possessed any of these.)
- Britains aircraft: *CTS* page 133. (I have just one left out of three, but it is the rarest – the Bristol Beaufighter Dennis Britain flew in the Second World War.)
- South Australian Lancers: *CTS* page 138. (Sold, sadly.)

Additional proposals for Cameo Collections – a dozen in detail

The Churchill collection

Picture 153: Churchill and A.R.P.

Churchill's finest hour was during the darkest days of the Second World War, when it seemed that nothing could stop the onslaught unleashed by Hitler. His dogged determination ensured that Britain fought on. None of his many mistakes and shortcomings could outweigh the worth of his will to victory. At the back of this picture are four representations of Churchill, by Alymer, Wend-Al, a very nice if a bit battered contemporary model engraved underneath James 1941, and finally a New Toy Soldier style figure that came with figures of Queen Elizabeth, King George VI and a steel helmeted soldier with a pick, having a cup of tea during a rest from rescue work. At the end of that row is a Hill figure in an anti-gas cape, leggings and respirator, with a litmus paper gas detector stuck on his bayonet. The next row forward includes Hill policeman in steel helmet, Crescent policewoman and W.R.A.F., Taylor and Barrett A.T.S. girl and Hill policewoman. In front are contemporary Britains, the air raid warden (careful examination would reveal a loose head) rare stretcher party in khaki with peak caps, and khaki versions of the earlier wounded figures from the R.A.M.C. sets.

Winston Churchill (30th November 1874 - 24th January 1965) embodied the essence of being British during the 20th century. A great and varied collection of toy soldiers could be built up using him as a central theme. Any of the following episodes in his life would form the core of an interesting cameo.

He played with toy soldiers as a boy (likely to have been with German flats, semi-flats or small scale solids).

1. Sandhurst.
2. On service in India with the 4th Hussars.
3. North West Frontier.
4. Sudan.
5. Boer War.
6. May well have played with H.G.Wells at *Little Wars*.
7. In charge of the Navy.
8. Served on the Western Front, First World War.
9. Advocated re-armament.
10. Once more in charge of the Navy.
11. British leader for most of the Second World War (to include the ARP cameo above).
12. Prime Minister during 1950s.
13. State Funeral.

Collectors of anything to do with Churchill would have a real interest in this collection of linked cameos, and of course everyone has heard of Churchill, so it makes a good exhibit for the uninitiated toy soldier spectator.

Historical hero and villain cameos

Picture 154: Napoleons

There must be hundreds of figurines, models and toy soldier style representations of Napoleon to collect. Napoleon seems glamourous today in ways that Hitler could never be, and so the French remain inordinately proud of him. Here are just a few. Left to right, in his coronation robes, by Vertunni (the hand with his imperial staff is missing), 40mm scale hard plastic model by M.D.M. sold in Paris hotel gift shops in the late 1950s, recent die-cast model, French hollowcast vignette with kneeling staff officer holding map, made around 1935, Mokarex large scale unpainted plastic figure available free with jars of coffee and foot and mounted aluminium figures.

126

Personality figures are usually readily available in model form, and there has been a trend towards producing them recently. The obvious one for the toy soldier collector is the group produced by Lineol and Elastolin in the late 1930s depicting Hitler and his henchmen. There would also be some hundreds of Napoleon to collect. As with Churchill, these are names that will mostly strike chords with the uninitiated viewer.

Combining Heroes with Big Battalions

Picture 155: Joan of Arc
Always ready to give a new view of the superb Knights of Agincourt, here they are attacking a group of CBG Mignot French archers led by Joan of Arc. The Britains Collector's Club model of Henry V in the right foreground (slightly anachronistically) urges on his troops. The Knights of Agincourt are generally held to be Roy Selwyn-Smith's best work.

Picture 156: Australian heroes
Every nation makes figures of its heroes and icons. Here for the Australians are Ned Kelly, a South Australian Lancer, and an early Militiaman, by DB Figurines of Australia, with a Swagman and a Duck-billed Platypus

I enjoy using personality figures as a focus for cameos on historical periods. Some of the names I would conjure with are Rameses II, **Alexander**, Hannibal, **Julius Caesar**, Boudicca, Attilla, Charlemagne, Alfred, Harold, William I, **Richard I**, the Black Prince, **Henry V**, **Joan of Arc**, Ghengis Khan, Tamerlaine, William Tell, **Henry VIII**, **Elizabeth I**, Francis Drake, **Richelieu**, **Cromwell**, Louis XIV, **Marlborough**, **Bonnie Prince Charlie**, Clive, Wolfe, Frederick the Great, Washington, Nelson, **Wellington**, **Robert E. Lee**, Gordon of Khartoum, Churchill, Lawrence of Arabia, Wingate and **Montgomery**. Pictures of the heroes from this list in bold are shown in the following pictures: 19, 23, 75, 87, 90, 121, 127, 132-3, 153, 155 and 204.

Brigader-Statuette

Some of the makers who produced in a style to fit in with Heyde no.2 size achieved some very pleasing results, and one of these was Brigader-Statuette. The boy cadet battalions of the Danish Life Guards are probably their most charming product, actually a rather more intricate improvement on Heyde, and a couple of millimetres larger than Heyde No.2 size. They also did a fair number of Highlanders, the ones in bonnets being, to my mind, more successful than the ones in foreign service helmets.

Picture 157: Brigader Livgard

Brigader-Statuette probably produced more of these Danish Livgard than any other subject, since even though they were expensive in Copenhagen souvenir shops, their charm justified their purchase by many tourists.

Picture 158: Brigader Highlanders FSO

These Brigader Highlanders can be contrasted with the ones in full dress in picture 90.

Picture 159: Zang and Selwyn Smith

See text for this cameo demonstrating toy soldier production history. On show, as a small part of the huge number of items to which this cameo could be extended: Boxed set of miniature composition Highlanders from the moulding press of Zang's Modern Packages company. Left to right, Skybird figure, showing where the tradition for miniature figures came from, two metal (make not known to me) infantry at attention, similar to the next, made in composition, possibly by Modern Packages, as are the infantryman in field cap and more certainly the airman, followed by an example of the first Herald infantryman who may well have followed in the tradition of figures to the left.

Zang and Selwyn Smith

These two men had a profound influence on the first three decades of the post-war era in Britain as far as toy soldiers were concerned. Myer Zang was an entrepreneur who for a time owned Skybird. Because he had a company which boasted moulding expertise, he was involved in the toy moulding business, at first using a composition material. These items were mostly sold to Timpo.

Roy Selwyn-Smith was taken on by Zang in 1947 as a trainee modelmaker, and his extraordinary career encompasses much of the most exciting hollowcast output of Timpo as well as the amazing early models comprising the groundbreaking Herald range. One group of metal Britains for which he was responsible is the famous Knights of Agincourt series, originally developed by him as a venture backed by Otto Gottstein. This cameo demonstrates the products for which Zang and Selwyn Smith were responsible.

For a highly detailed account of this fascinating story, there is no better publication than *Suspended Animation* by Peter Cole, which I enjoy re-reading as often as possible. There is always something else in it that I cannot remember registering the previous time around.

The Timpo Story

Illustrates the toy figure output of Timpo. There is considerable scope for a long, linked collection of cameos which would make a whole collection here. My cameo would just include an example of each of the stages in the company history. Collecting Timpo has become very popular, especially in Germany, where the products of the Lanarkshire factory were extensively distributed. Alfred Plath was kind enough to send me his excellent book on this Scottish output, and has another one in preparation which tells the whole Timpo story. Michael Maughan is the acknowledged expert in the UK. The following headings might make a framework:
- Ally Gee, getting it together, Timpolene composition figures, Stoddart and other people's moulds.
- Willmore, Roy Selwyn-Smith and excellence in metal hollowcast.
- Starting up in plastic.
- Second only to Britains.
- Overmoulding.
- Action packs.
- Toyway.

Timpo Quentin Durward

Within the Timpo output are opportunities for many individual cameos, some based simply on single series. As an example, I give you Quentin Durward.

Picture 160: Quentin Durward

These figures made as character merchandise for the 1955 film Quentin Durward were the last series made in hollowcast metal by Timpo. All Timpo hollowcast production from its own designs took place in just six years, from 1950 to 1955. This swansong is one of the best series of all, with its provision of men at arms both for the French royal guard and for the Burgundian Duke, who even has a mounted version, plus the Landsknechts with their crossbows and arquebuses. All of these look good in some numbers around the central caste of characters. Quentin Durward himself, in the uniform of the French royal guard, and Philip de Creville, the Burgundian noble are given both mounted and foot models. William de La Marck, the principal villain, and the Gluckmeister lead the Landskneckts. With today's access to the internet, looking up the original Walter Scott novel and the film in Wikipedia is easy enough, but finding the actual models is difficult, time consuming and/or expensive.

Reynolds

This small manufacturer may have done nothing more than commission Timpo or Willmore, the people who produced most of Timpo's hollowcast moulds for them.

Known output is limited to a Treasure Island pirates set, Vikings, Romans and policemen and Michael Bentine's TV characters, the Bumblies. Design style and painting is extremely similar to that of Timpo, as Norman Tooth designed for both firms. Finding nice examples of their complete known output makes for a small but satisfying cameo, quite difficult to achieve, particularly if the aim is also original boxes. See picture 22 for the Vikings and Romans.

Picture 161: The Bumblies

Very few examples of these television characters created by Michael Bentine survive, particularly in as good condition as these. They were the only T.V. character figures made by Reynolds, designed by Norman Tooth. Wow! factor 8.

MSR

An even smaller but also hard to complete cameo would be the output of MSR, which amounted to just three figures. These could be added to the Bullock range of guns made by the same company.

Picture 162: Three figures from MSR

I only realised the other day that although I knew I had the Foot Guard and the Highlander from MSR, I also had a Royal Horse Guard to represent the household cavalry figure. Only in Fair condition, and missing a sword, it had been languishing in a box of unknown maker figures, but now can make a triumphant appearance. Wow! factor 5 once the MSR story has sunk in.

The British square

The term the British square came to represent the formation of choice used by Imperial troops in the late 19th Century when dealing with irregular native troops not possessed of much firepower. This was most useful in the wide-open spaces of the Sudan, as at the battle of Abu Klea. The predecessors of this formation included the square formation adopted in the Napoleonic Wars for infantry protecting themselves against cavalry, and before then every closely ranged defensive arrangement of infantry in the open seeking protection against a surrounding enemy. The pre-requisite for success in this formation was that the enemy was not able to deploy artillery or other long-range weaponry against the masses of the square. The so-called Highland square (see also page 119) is simply a British square made up of highland regiments. To see the on guard toy soldiers often used to form British squares, go to picture 95.

The Wild West

Toy soldiers often reflect contemporary adventure literature (pulp fiction). The romantic adventure story of the North American frontier, with its cowboys, bandits, gold and red indians, was particularly popular among readers (mainly boys) of all ages during the period 1880 to 1980. Cinema and television westerns cemented the genre during the twentieth century, but later, as the Wild West belonged more and more to history rather than near contemporary life, thrillers became generally more to do with science fiction (e.g. James Bond, *Avatar*).

The Wild West, during its period of major popularity, and particularly from 1908 when Britains produced their first North American Indians, probably inspired more toy figures than any other individual subject. From the 1920s through the 1970s, when Cowboys and Indians were a very acceptable substitute for wargames, the output was prolific. Any boy's collection of toy soldiers was likely to contain an element of frontiersmen, particularly as this subject would readily spring to mind as a good and non-controversial present. I was given a box of Wend-Al Red Indians in 1952, and the Wild West section formed a major part of my collection of plastic figures, as virtually every manufacturer of any size produced them.

The Wild West is not primarily classifiable as a military subject, more as a way of life, but its folklore encompasses so much violence that if I had to add it to either military or civilian, I have always myself included it with the military, under the heading of the Indian Wars. Nevertheless, it forms perhaps the largest of all standalone subjects to collect. Its many attractions include the very large variety of poses and activities, the animals, accessories, vehicles and buildings with which scenes can be made up. Interesting add-ons to the genre include the American Civil War and the Royal Canadian Mounted Police, while the later nineteenth century US military, particularly, of course, the cavalry, are *de rigueur.*

The major manufacturers of toy soldiers, Britains and CBG Mignot, were not particularly imaginative when it came to cowboys and Indians, Elastolin being the exception. Many of the so-called lesser manufacturers, on the other hand, let their imaginations run riot, which resulted in many beautiful models. The French hollowcast makers sometimes produced outstanding results in this subject.

Picture 163: Wild West in large scales

There are two reasons for having a total mixture of toys such as these. Firstly, you might want to see how various types of figure look before going on to specialize in something. Secondly, as I have done here, you might want examples of all sorts to show people what they are like. Hence in my latter days I have to a large degree gone back to being a magpie. Back left is a large scale Heyde, then come two large Johillco figures, followed by a tinplate bucking bronco toy and a wonderful WOW! 6 French hollowcast rodeo rider. The indian in the centre is a typical U.S. Barclay dime-store product, and the two seated Indians to the left are German Elastolin, an early 100mm scale and a 70mm drummer.

Picture 164: Reka Red Indians

This box (about 1920) has loads of period charm, especially the interior label featuring the seated boy in the toy soldier playsuit.
Some of the figures inside continued into the Crescent era.

133

Picture 165: Marx redskins

Marx produced some brilliant redskins in white or red plastic, the latter being the reddest redskins I ever came across. The Pioneer woman will have her work cut out. To the right are some of the 1/32 scale figures that were not on offer in the UK. The others, to the left, were in UK Woolworths in the late 50s. I have had a go at painting the chest of the kneeling bowman. I like the plentiful supply of squaws with the red series, making for good camp scenes. The modeling is, as usual, superb, a fine foundation for the current generation of designers in plastic to build on and perhaps (but only with difficulty) surpass.

Picture 166: Starlux redskins

A book I recently purchased on Starlux reveals that there are over 500 different Wild West models to collect issued by this French company, and indeed, the cult of Far West is deeply entrenched in Europe. I bought these figures on a boyhood trip to Paris, about 1958, and they include one non-Starlux French made figure, the bowman on the extreme left, and two Italian made rubber figures in the foreground. For contrast, I placed the Hill cowboy and indian shooting from behind their horses in front.

London

Picture 167: Dismounted Life Guards

Representing London. The best toy and souvenir figures are not far off even well regarded models, as can be seen in this comparison. Left to right: Timpo hollowcast, John Greenwood model, Herald trumpeter, Stadden design for Cavendish Miniatures, Blenheim and Britains die-cast.

I have lived and worked in London for by far the majority of my life. I love London. Mary and I have lived for the past twenty-four years within a mile or two of Lambton Road, where one of the Britains family properties became their first factory. As Londoners themselves, it was natural that their first toy soldier products would be the Household Cavalry. Their first set of infantry, the Royal Fusiliers, was also a London regiment. They seemed curiously reticent about introducing Foot Guards, which first followed in 1895, two years later.

After the first ten years of production there were fifteen out of 129 sets of standard size figures featuring Foot Guards, rather more than eleven per cent, with an additional fourteen sets containing Household Cavalry for a total of twenty-nine, or twenty-two per cent. Only one set, 93, had Household Cavalry and Foot Guards together in the same box, which is strange given the likely souvenir market for a box of Royal Guards, mounted and foot, together in a box. The only box in which Life Guards, Royal Horse Guards and Foot Guards come together on their own is in the miniaturised Queen's Dolls House set, of which it seems likely only two examples were ever produced. Why this set was not produced in full size, I don't know, since I am sure it would have been a winner.

Only after the Second World War did Britains produce combined Life Guard and Foot Guard sets in the second grade ranges. Herald and other competitors may have had a hand in that, as post-war London became more and more a tourist destination for the world in a way that was not so before. Certainly the German manufacturers who had supplied the U.K. prior to 1893 had produced plenty of guardsmen, and the history of toy soldiers can be amply told, from the 19th century onwards, just in terms of London's soldiers and the depiction of them world wide.

Various collections and cameos can be assembled within the confines of this subject. The Foot Guard is the archetype of the image of the British ceremonial soldier, and more have been made by British manufacturers than any other type. The only other British soldiers of perhaps equal renown are the Highlanders, who I have already used in the previous chapter to demonstrate specialist collecting in a full scale reference collection scenario. London is, of course, larger than Scotland in terms of population, so one might expect the two collections to be comparable in size.

The London collection can include all the ceremonial occasions on the London scene,

135

Picture 168: Garde Republicaine

Appropriately representing Paris, French Gardes Republicaines at the salute in aluminium by Quiralu, with mounted figures behind.

Picture 169: Papal Swiss Guards

From the back, a wooden figure held together by strings, which collapses when the button under the base is pushed. The other figures at the back are mostly Brevetti, composition figures made in Italy with a very high propensity for the paint to flake off. Front left are two Eriksson figures, the next to the right are by Italian makers Figir, with a Britains souvenir figure far right. In front are two Quiralu aluminium souvenir figures. The figures not in the uniform of the Swiss Guard are Noble Guards.

136

as well as be expanded by adding all the London territorial units, and one should not forget the Chelsea Pensioners. I was thrilled to be given a Heyde Chelsea pensioner by friends, to mark my retirement! Examples of the uniforms of some of London's soldiers are shown in picture 109.

Collecting London's military could form the start or centrepiece of a Cities of the World ceremonial military collection. Here are pictures to represent London, Paris and Rome, and the Brigader Livgard above in picture157 would represent Copenhagen.

Britains Set 73 cameo

What with acquiring a set 73 on my 21st birthday (see page 185) I have always had a good feeling about this set. Each set contained artillery, three regiments of cavalry and three of infantry. It was the first of the large Britains display boxes with more than one layer of figures in the box. It contained, except in it's final version, both Royal Scots Greys and Royal Welch Fusiliers. With the various changes to its content over the sixty-eight years of its inclusion in the catalogue, it has around thirty possible versions and many more variations, should one be wishing to go the whole hog. Twenty-five of these versions are during the years 1897 to 1912.

A set 73 is pretty much a cameo in its own right. I had three of them, a set dating from about 1901, a set from 1940 and my original set dating from 1961. Had I had a fourth set from around 1905, a fifth set from 1912 and a sixth set from 1928, I would have covered much of the story of the changing style of Britains production in just six sets. For those particularly interested, my analysis of my 1901 set of set 73 is on page 95 of my book *Britains Toy Soldiers 1893-1932*.

Additional Cameo Collections – 101 or more ideas
From my 'On Guard' exhibition of 1985 not already listed above
- Massed bands of the Royal Marines
- Cavalry regiments of the British Army (see picture 152)
- Britains Specials and New Toy Soldiers contrasted
- Britains before toy soldiers (mechanical toys and novelties)
- Copies and piracies of Britains
- Britains pre-1916 British Horse and Foot Guards
- Britains horsedrawn vehicles and guns
- Britains WWI trench warfare
- Britains WWI artillery and aircraft
- Britains French and the Paris office (see picture 112)
- Britains 1920s export lines for the USA
- Britains military motor vehicles
- Britains and re-armament 1938-41
- Britains post-war highland pipers
- Britains American Civil War (since I wrote this, there is now much more to collect from Britains on this subject) (see picture 135)
- Britains Herald and Eyes Right contrasted
- Britains current range, 1985
- Britains depict colonial regiments
- The Zulu War (see picture 205)
- Conversions, what are they, how do they work?
- Freddie Green, a tribute (see picture 142)

- Lancer (tribute to David Bracey, one of my closest collecting friends, now sadly deceased)
- British hollowcasting 1946-66
- Media commemoratives (see pictures 14 to 16)
- Dan Dare (see picture 10)
- Figures used for advertising or as premiums (see picture 201)
- Blenheim USA bi-centennial set
- Royal personality figures
- Officers with binoculars
- State Coaches
-

From my display shelves (in no particular order)
- Soldiers that will shoot
- Camp fire scenes (see picture 165)
- Early machine guns (see picture 216)
- Wellington Toy Company
- Malleable Mouldings
- Wild West Indians painted with metallic copper flesh
- West Point Cadets
- BMC (see pictures 97-9)
- Indian Army
- Islamic troops (see picture 121)
- Territorials
- Marines
- Royal Navy Landing Party (see pictures 216-7)
- Toytown figures (see picture 68)
- Papal guards (see picture 169)
- Danish Life Guards (see picture 157)
- Today's armies and Desert Storm (see picture 70)
- Paratroops in red berets (see pictures 9, 55 and 221)
- Gilt figures
- Copies and pirated figures early Herald (see pictures 58, 101 and 136)
- Large Britains box cameo
- Britains fakes (see picture 112)
- Royal Marines drill squad (picture packs and others)
- The first Blenheim figures (see picture 66)
- Royal Army Medical Corps (see picture 192)
- Beiser game trays and figures by Britains and others (see picture 220)
- Moustaches, a military fashion (see picture 107)
- Kleeware and Lone Star vehicles (see pictures 115 and 9)
- Khaki figures in red jackets
- Contrasting Lineol and Elastolin (see picture 44)
- Wend-Al and Quiralu
- The Chad Valley story
- Toy soldiers of unknown manufacture
- Early action figures
- Fashion and modelling
- Salvation Army
- The origin of die-cast Britains

- The Courtenay story
- Taylor and Barrett toy soldiers
- Britains individual best quality infantry c.1900
- Britains Paris office Prussians (see picture 113)
- French Foreign Legion v Arabs (see picture 32)
- Robin Hood (see pictures 117-123)
- *Lord of the Rings*
- Characters from comics (Asterix, Captain Marvel, Spiderman etc – see picture 114)
- The English Longbow (see picture 28)
- The '45 (see picture 87)
- Blenheim Sikhs and the origins of Nostalgia
- Hill Abyssinian War
- The Boer War in small size
- Checkpoint Charlie

Picture 170: Checkpoint Charlie

As someone who grew up with the Cold War, Berlin's Checkpoint Charlie was a well known spot. I made up this small cameo to represent it, with some die-cast Red Army troops at attention made in the USSR, two Authenticast and one Britains advancing, a tinplate sentry box, some Timpo plastic West Germans, Britains British troops on guard with the later more rounded helmet, and a couple of officers to show the difference, two Asset and one Britains Military Policemen, a very rare Britains special Irish Fusilier and a batch of what I now think are Crescent U.S. Military Police, which appear to be hollow but made of a very brittle metal, and all of their batons are missing. These came from Len Richards collection, and I have never seen any others.

- Herald British Infantry at attention (see picture 57)
- Wooden tanks from the Richards and Hanington collections with charging Britains infantry in gas masks
- WWI Highlanders in khaki
- Germans surrendering (see picture 137)
- WWI The British Army goes to war, in peak caps
- French hollowcasts (see picture 42)

- The Beatles (see picture 16)
- Plastic civilians
- Children's stories and fairy tales
- Religious and nativity figures (see pictures 35 and 84)
- Folk figures (see picture 85)
- Charity figures
- Science Fiction figures
- Band of the Grenadier Guards (see picture 11)
- 1956 Britains band series (see pictures 11 and 147)
- Fusiliers by various makers (see picture 17)
- Heinrich charging cavalry
- Rifle Brigade and KRRC
- Souvenir figures, contrasting styles (see picture 82)
- Figures in different materials (see picture 204)
- The same figure design made in metal and in plastic (see pictures 9 and 101)
- Knights of Agincourt (see picture 155)
- Spanish Tercio (see picture 138)
- The British armed forces by French manufacturers and the Britains Paris office

CHAPTER 10
HAVING FUN WITH TOY SOLDIERS

I t's no fun having toy soldiers if they can't be played with. OK, you don't have to cut the string on all your priceless boxed sets, but usually there will be some need in you to get them out on a table and move them around. If you start to put aside troops that you regularly bring out for their spectacle and the thrill that they give you on parade or on campaign, this is your display collection.

During my first trip to New York, one of the highlights of my visit was to go and see the Kemble Widmer display collection in New Jersey. This contained about 17,000 pieces spread around a large basement that measured perhaps forty by thirty feet. Everything was laid out in displays on tables at waist height, with corridors around which one could walk, and this mass of figures stretching into the distance made an unforgettable impression, quite different to having them on shelves or in cabinets. I think that was my favourite of all the collections I have visited.

He had parades, regiments, British squares and campaigns (and some railways) arrayed around the room in rivers of troops. Had I been put on the spot to guess how many there were, I would have said there were far more than the actual number, and it was only when I came (much later) to catalogue them for sale at Christies that I discovered how this extravagant display had been achieved with not that many figures.

Even five hundred toy soldiers can put on a brave show, and I would now like to give you an example.

The Boxer Rebellion

When I started to put together a few display collections, I naturally thought in the first instance of the big three trouble spots of the late British Empire, famous for heroics, incompetence and tragedy of various sorts. These are the Zulu Wars, the Sudan campaigns and the Boer Wars. These are all in Africa, as that is where much of the colonial action was at the time, the European nations all taking part in the scramble for Africa.

All three of these subjects have received a good deal of attention from New Toy Soldier makers over the last three decades, and Britains as well as other contemporary toy soldier makers produced a number of sets for the Boer Wars. In my previous book, I showed part of my own display for the Sudan campaigns, and Britains themselves have made these the subject of their big new series for 2010 (see picture 105).

The Boxer Rebellion, however, with the siege of the Peking legations in 1900, is less well covered by models, and to my mind is more intriguing as an event. This is partially a personal interest, in that while at university I studied International Relations of the Great Powers in the Far East under Dr Jones, a genuine Old China Hand. The Great Powers all agreed that in letting the legations be besieged, the Chinese Dowager Empress had gone too far. The diplomatic staff and their garrison contingents would have to be relieved, and the Empress punished.

Here then was a multi-national force tasked with sorting out a failed state, and such was the ability of the various participants that in fifty-five days, without a single helicopter, the job was done.

From the toy soldier point of view, it is a wonderful excuse to put together the forces of the Great Powers on the one hand, and glorious arrays of Chinese on the other. As when I started this display there were very few Chinese available, this was my cue to have a dabble in selling New Toy Soldiers on my own account, and I commissioned a small range of Chinese troops and British expeditionary force sailors from Jan and Frank Scroby of Blenheim.

As I was sending out toy soldier lists at that time, I was able to reach a number of collectors, and enough of them bought some that I was able to recoup the cost and keep a fair number for my own display. I am also happy to report that they have held their value well in subsequent auctions, and are probably among the rarest of Blenheim manufactured soldiers that exist.

They actually look quite well in among Great Powers troops by Britains. I tried to insist that Jan Scroby made them as slim as possible in contrast to many of the other Blenheim and nostalgia figures. Looking at the Boxer display, see how many of the figures shown do not fit in to the general look of the scene.

The major parts of the Boxer display (548 figures) are:

- **United States 58** – the main icon for the US is a beautiful set of US Infantry in Montana hats at the slope, with a band, solid cast in the Britains style by Derek Wailen. The rarest inclusion is six Reka fixed arm doughboys in khaki. A small reference cameo of nineteen individual Britains doughboys (see picture 13) finishes off the section.

Picture 171: Reka Doughboys

These doughboys marching, by Reka, dated 6.7.20, were a real find, in spite of being only in Fair condition. Not only do they pre-date the Britains marching doughboy by six years, but as dated figures (why Reka dated figures long after Britains had stopped is a mystery – of course now Britains have started again) they imply that they are earlier than the more common marching figure in steel helmet seen to the right. As I was writing this it suddenly clicked that the marching Crescent guardsman that was one of my first figures (see picture 6) is the same model, complete with puttees – no wonder I always felt they looked a little odd.

Picture 172: Wailen U.S. Infantry

Derek Wailen specialized for a time in reproducing toy soldiers in the early Britains style, often adding figures and poses that Britains never did. Here he added a colour bearer and a band to figures re-cast from Britains set 91, first version. As far as I know, only three of these U.S. sets were ever made by Derek.

Picture 173: Britains Russians

The Cossacks at the back, set 136, are early dated figures, so even if they are in Fair to Poor condition, they are worth showing for that reason. The officer on the grey horse is Paris office, where they liked to put all their officers on greys. Note that he has a gold top to his cap, and gold belts and collar, as opposed to the London version.

- **Russia 40** – this used to be a very interesting section including a lovely set of the Bertrand et Vertunni toy soldiers which used to fit so well with CBG Mignot. Sadly, they had to go. Still there are six beauties from the US, on guard, for which I discovered the manufacturer, William Feix, in a recent *Old Toy Soldier Newsletter* article, after not knowing for thirty years. Four other rarities among the Russians are Renvoize Russian infantry in greatcoats, and I actually possess the box for these, though not the other four figures. Ged Haley once showed me a wonderful Russian cavalryman Renvoize made to accompany these, but I have never been able to acquire any. There is

Picture 174: Renvoize Russians

The four marching here are marvelous models from Renvoize.. I wonder if they copied their uniforms from the CBG Mignot figure charging to the right. Kneeling figure also by Mignot.

a rather battered but early dated set of Britains Cossacks, and to go with that there is the unusual Paris Office officer which is the same figure, but on a grey horse, as all the Paris Officer mounted officers tend to be.

Picture 175: Feix Russians

After years of not knowing what these beautiful figures were, I found them in one of Richard O'Brian's books. Apparently they were made in New York by an Austrian émigré, William Feix, which explains why they look very similar to German made hollowcasts around 1900. I may even have acquired these at one of the Chicago shows, which would figure.

Picture 176: New Toy Soldier Russians
The lying firing Russians were made for me by David Bracey of Lancer, and the running figures in summer dress are by Joe Shimek.

- **Germany 21** – my Germans are made up of nine Britains Prussian infantry, all with something wrong with them or embellished, plus one mounted and four other conversions by Freddie Green. Two lovely marching Prussians by Bischoff and five New Toy Soldiers make up the tally.

Picture 177: Germany, Britains repainted
A sturdy squad of repainted Britains Prussian Infantry, second version is headed by a converted officer in a greatcoat and another converted figure to the right. You can easily see that there are a variety of painters at work here. Compare the ones in the front row and at the left of the second row, which may be Freddie Green, with the ones further back: the faces and the rifles are of a completely different quality. Have you noticed that the figure in the centre of the first row of marching men has full trousers, and so must have been converted to a Prussian with a head swap?

145

- **France 28** – twelve of the French figures are the set of *matelots* mentioned on page 83. Others include some designed by Holger Eriksson, who seemed particularly good at capturing the feel of the French military. I should mention here that I have a lot more assorted French troops that could reasonably be added to the section, but as they are mostly in full dress I prefer to keep them in a separate French full dress cameo. A series of CBG Mignot that I have always coveted is the French infantry in colonial dress with white foreign service helmets. I have a couple of examples included here. CBG Mignot always made available most of their poses in any uniform the customer desired, as did Heyde, by contrast with Britains, who stuck with specific standard sets.

Picture 178: CBG French

This set of CBG French sailors firing (the officer, colours and bugler complete the set) was spotted by Mary in the Rue St Honore while we were on a business trip to Paris. She couldn't wait for me to get back from the conference and go with me to see if we could buy them. There were also some Lucottes – lucky me. The two figures on the right are French colonial infantry, one of my favourites of all CBG Mignot figures.

- **British Empire 76** – the British were first in with an attempt to relieve the legations, mounted with a couple of thousand sailors and marines in the best Royal Navy traditions. It failed, and had to await international re-enforcements. Nevertheless, the British naval contingent remained large, and could be increased from my Naval Brigade cameo that was able to be used in virtually all the colonial expeditions of the late nineteenth century undertaken by the British. It is a most interesting reflection upon the building of empires that by and large, just as in a game of *Risk*, the more territory is controlled, the more local troops can be raised to help police the empire and extend its boundaries. The Romans were expert at this, and so were the British.

Many of the British units of this sort were depicted in the famous Nostalgia series masterminded by Shamus O D Wade, and for the greater part executed by Jan Scroby of Blenheim. The Wei-hai-wei regiment was raised by the British from local Chinese to protect their local concessions, and took part in the march on Peking. Their twenty-six piece drum and bugle band as depicted in the Nostalgia series, the largest set that the series spawned, forms a centre piece of the Boxer display collection. It is followed by sixteen light khaki Wei-hai-wei regiment soldiers from Bastion, who did an excellent series on the Boxer rebellion that fits in well with the Nostalgia style. In fact I used to have an eight man set of Bastion figures for each participating country, but since they didn't fit

146

too well with the mostly Britains' style troops in each national contingent, I just kept one example of each, with the exception of the very attractive Japanese and the Chinese themselves. Trophy also did very nice and compatible Boxer period troops.

Picture 179: British Sailors and Wei-Hai-Wei Regiment

The Wei-Hai-Wei (1st Chinese) Regiment was raised by the British from local Chinese in one of their treaty ports in China, and these troops were available to take part in the expedition to relieve the Peking legations. The drum and bugle band right back is one of the most splendid sets in Shamus Wade's Nostalgia range, executed to his commission by Jan and Frank Scroby of Blenheim. The ordinary rank and file to the left are by Andrew Rose in his Bastion Boxer rebellion series. The sailors at the front are my Imperialist figures, also commissioned from the Scrobys, and the charging Brit in khaki is a regular Blenheim figure.

Picture 180: British Indian Army

The British brought Indian troops to help out in China. Most of these these are original or repainted Britains Indian infantry. A recent acquisition is the three Britains first version Japanese that someone has simply re-headed with pillbox hats and repainted as Gurkhas. They even have Britains rare original paper labels underneath the bases.

147

- **Japan 68** – the Japanese provided the largest national contingent for the relief expedition, following their recent (1897) war with the Chinese and foreshadowing their coming struggle with Russia. My Japanese cameo contains virtually all the Japanese troops I have, including a rare set of Britains cavalry in dark blue jackets, which unfortunately has a couple of breakages, but is something I most likely would not otherwise have been able to afford.

The Japanese also have the Bastion contingent, and a number of other New Toy Soldiers, in addition to the charming marching CBG Mignot set which is only in fair condition. Hill was in the habit of painting up their standard British infantry in khaki as Russians or Japanese, so there are a few of these as well. In one of my projects boxes is a large unit of Fry British infantry waiting for me to give them similar treatment to fill out the Japanese ranks.

Picture 181: Britains Japanese

The cavalry at the back are full set 135, the rare final paint variation from 1940 with dark blue jackets. There are a couple of breakages there, but they still look great. Across the front, the back row is of three second grades, which use the same casting as the Best Quality. The next row has four normal infantry from set 134, the one on the right being the variation with dark blue jacket. In front of him is the first version with the smaller kepi rather than the cap. At the front are eight of the kepi version repainted in matt colours.

Picture 182: CBG Japanese

There is no doubt that the CBG Mignot practice of having a standard set of twelve infantry figures including officer, bugler and colour bearer made for a more interesting group of figures than those of Britains. Compared with the Britains grouping above, the CBG set wins in this instance. The single figure is unknown, but could possibly be attributed to Fry, while the lying firing figures look like French made hollowcasts from the 1920s.

148

Picture 183: Hill Japanese

Hill used a low cost method of depicting foreign troops. They took the most suitable existing casting, and painted them in the appropriate colours. The Hill marching figures here, originally British in khaki, were issued as Russians and Irish Infantry as well as Japanese. It may be that the two at the back are repainted, or at least a paint variation, as the black belts have disappeared.

Behind the Britains officer without the arm, centre front are two rather nice Japanese cavalry, possibly by Hanks or a successor, as they are copies of the Britains pony horse but with a fixed arm.

Picture 184: New Toy Soldier Japanese

The three firing and the kneeling officer on the right are Trophy, and the marching figures Bastion. The two in between are Authenticast. In front is a set sent to me by Joe Shimek, recast from old hollowcast figures in the same tradition as his more famous new pieces in the style of Heyde.

- **China 256** – as the opposing side, the Chinese almost outnumber the International Relief Force. Here are 112 of the figures I commissioned from Jan Scroby, with Bastion and Trophy figures which match well. A number of these New Toy Soldiers are of the Boxers in their white robes with red characters. There is a set of CBG Mignot that came from a well remembered and much appreciated visit to Steve Balkin's apartment on an early trip I made to New York. Eriksson did a very good figure of a charging Chinese, and I managed to find twelve of these as well as four of the advancing ones.

Britains figures are well outnumbered in the Boxer display, as Britains, as opposed to other leading European manufacturers, did not make Chinese figures at the time, and didn't bring out any Chinese at all until set 241 in 1926. Even this figure may well have been putting into use a figure originated by the Paris Office, since the design is highly unusual against the normal run of Britains. It is a rather ugly man with a long knife or short sword, evidently nothing to do with any regular Chinese unit on the European pattern. I also have five more Freddie Green conversions of this figure to add in. To depict Chinese Imperial regulars, I did a quick paint job on forty-four Britains American Civil War castings which seemed to fit quite well with the illustrations I had seen.

As the Chinese are clearly outclassed, I found them a few antique style brass cannon. Should the expeditionary force need them, there are plenty of guns and machine guns which could be pressed into service from other cameos. As a finishing touch, I have placed a Rose Chinese executioner ready to deal with any faint heart.

Altogether, the Boxer display makes an interesting place to park a number of cameos, and somehow the Britains and New Toy Soldier styles seem to blend in quite well. Have a look at the pictures and see what you think.

One of the main focuses of putting together a display collection is this blend of manufacturers, because unless you find one maker who makes all you need, you will usually want to use a blend to arrive at a completed collection. My Boxer display includes over twenty different makes.

Picture 185: Boxers and Foreigners

A crowd of Boxers, in their white robes, attack a mixture of New Toy Soldiers depicting the great powers. The line of figures angled right show the Bastion models of French Marines, Italian Bersagliere, U.S.Infantry, Russian in summer dress, Japanese, British Wei-Hai-Wei regiment and Austrian sailor, produced to depict the Boxer incident. The three Prussian figures at the back are Quality Model Soldiers produced by veteran dealer Ged Haley as part of his Franco-Prussian War series. The British Colonial figure charging in front of them is a Jones figure from the U.S. adapted from the Britains charging British Infantryman in gasmask. The neat running figure further forward is Imperial, and the two marching front right are an Australian maker. The Boxers are a mixture of one Trophy, two Dorset, three Bastion and ten Imperialist.

Picture 186: CBG Mignot Chinese

These beautiful French made Chinese, six marching with bannerman, came to me from Steve Balkin on my first ever visit to New York. Since then I have only managed to acquire three more, the marching man with the beige base (beige bases are after 1906) the man advancing, which is the same figure as the marching men but with the arms moved about, and the firing figure. The other figures in the picture came from a show junk box, and are not CBG although they look similar. The Chinese ship's captain leaning on a rail is one of the meticulous works of Lionel Gaurier.

Picture 187: Authenticast Chinese

All the running figures here, and the four advancing centre back, are the varieties of the two Eriksson designed Chinese figures. The metal they were made from was not of the highest quality, and sometimes can warp or crumble as visible in a few of these examples. At the back is a Poor condition headless solid German Chinese bowman, which when complete is spectacular, and spectacularly expensive. At the front are Best Quality and second grade Britains Chinese, which I have always found rather disappointing. I cannot work out why Britains would have brought these out in 1926, unless they were a figure designed in the Paris factory as Indochinese at the end of production and never issued, which was then used in London.

151

Picture 188: Boxer Guns

I forget where I found these antique looking brass cannon, but they seemed just right to give to the Trophy and other gun crews. The Chinese at the front on grey bases are also Trophy, with Dorset left rear and Bastion right rear. The Chinese executioner behind the rear gun is Rose, and the two Mongol bowmen left back are Fusilier Miniatures.

Picture 189: Imperialist Chinese

When I started to be serious about my Boxer display, around 1975, I knew I would need a lot more Chinese than were then available from New Toy Soldier manufacturers. Answer, commission some. Jan and Frank Scroby obliged with the series you see here, which I sold under the name Imperialist. As with many New Toy Soldier Chinese, the uniforms are loosely based on some of the illustrations in the Osprey Men at Arms volume, and a few contemporary old toy soldiers.

Picture 190: Bastion Chinese

The two Kansu braves front left are by Trophy, the rest of the Chinese shown, including the regular infantry in blue, are Bastion. The camp followers are modern copies of traditional Chinese figures that give an authentic eastern flavour to the scene.

Picture 191: Chinese painted from Britains castings

At the end of Britains hollowcast production, Bill Pierce and James Luck bought up all the remaining Britains castings, about a quarter million of them, and sold them off at their respective shops for a shilling each. I bought a fair quantity with the idea that at some point I would do something with them, and one of the few things I more or less finished was this array of regular Chinese infantry using the Britains American Civil War castings. The uniforms are probably not very accurate, but with three small brass cannon added they do well enough.

Royal Army Medical Corps

Many collections feel obliged to avail themselves of the services of the Royal Army Medical Corps. Without, I suspect, actually having any longer a complete set 137, I have 69 Britains mostly from that set, with two large field hospital tents of the sort, possibly made by Heyde, that Gamages appear to have included free in every purchase from them of set 137 (as illustrated in the Gamages catalogue). These are supplemented with conversions, other hollowcasts and New Toy Soldiers to make a total of 114 pieces. This is not as grand or nearly as valuable as the magnificent Heyde set from the Hanington collection illustrated in *Collecting Toy Soldiers* page 18, with its charming and intricate vignettes, but it gives something of the same feel. Both my grandparents were army medics, so I have some family connection to it too.

Picture 192: Reka R.A.M.C.

The Britains set 137 of the British Army Medical Service is one of the best known and most attractive of all Britains hollowcast sets. Not many of the competing hollowcast firms could stand comparison, but Reka and Hill came close with these stretcher parties and nurses. The Reka party at attention and especially the man standing with the rolled up stretcher are particularly well made.

Other activities to do with toy soldiers

The British Model Soldier Society website is a good starting point for great cyberspace journeys into the delights of all these ancillary pastimes.

Casting, conversion and restoration

If you are inclined towards the display collection, and most collectors have such feelings, the challenge is to have the most troops in the best condition for the least time and cost. This is where the auctions can come in, either for acquiring ready made recast, repainted or converted battalions at anything from £1 a figure or laying in stocks of broken or badly worn toys which can then be worked on at leisure. Shows, particularly those run by the BMSS, usually have rummage boxes from 50p a figure to supplement any job lots that may come your way.

I have in the past (the dim and distant past) engaged in doing up poor quality and broken Britains. Many collectors get good ideas for subjects to try. Probably favourite are all the things that Britains, restricted by their mass marketing strategy, never got around to doing. The one I most liked the idea of was British cavalry in foreign service dress at the halt, based on a Simkin picture I saw once. I also have all the raw materials for doing the thin red line at Balaclava (still feels like the dim and distant future).

Picture 193: The Legendary Freddie Green

Frederick Green was a prominent and much loved member of the British Model Soldier Society, and his forte was converting Britains into a rather more elaborate style, but keeping the spirit of the original model. While his work was not as meticulous as the similar but more restrained brilliance of Roy Dilley, the BMSS long time President, nevertheless his best conversions really are little works of art. His trademarks were beautifully executed flags, little extras like extremely sharp bayonets, and drum cords, and wonderfully executed faces, often including soldered on moustaches. What an improvement on the original rather boring Britains Chinese are these colourful enhancements, waving a variety of weapons. Look at the Prussian regimental colour and the caplines on the hussar. No wonder his prolific repaints and conversions often sell for more than the originals.

Picture 194: Mutiny

Messing around with plastics is easier than cutting and soldering with metal. It struck me that these Timpo French Foreign Legion figures could easily convert into British Infantry in India at the time of the Indian Mutiny, so here they are. Not too painstakingly finished, but I had great fun doing them, realizing my vision quite quickly.

Model making

In your endeavours to cast, convert and restore you will be using most of the skills necessary to engage in military modelling, so there is no harm in the occasional foray, particularly if you have started to collect figures at this end of the style spectrum. There are plenty of magazines, books and websites for this activity.

Picture 195: Barbarians

The mounted model is a Del Prado Alemanni, with another rather cruder model by an unknown maker in front of him. The rest of the figures are plastic Gauls by Starlux, which are made in a sufficiently tall scale that they fit well with the models. The figure on the right has been rather heavily repainted in the model style, and I am not sure whether I really like it, although it is quite striking.

Entering competitions

If you find that you are good at model making, you can spend much of your time trying to find out just how good you are. The best of the international exhibitions provide between them an arena for model makers that is just as tough as professional tennis. If you feel that you might not make the grade with models, there are competitions for toy style figures as well, which are judged not on realism, but on the charm of the figures and their imaginative presentation as well as artistic merit.

Campaigning

Campaigning is simply bringing out your largest and best cameos of a particular historical period (see Chapter 7 *Historical highlights* for a choice of possibilities). Bring the troops to the table and set them out in fighting scenes. Add toy or model scenery, buildings, trees (see *Display*, chapter 11) to taste and take pictures. Move around a bit and take more pictures. Get enthused and go on the hunt for twice or three times the troops, plus suitable opponents, move to the billiard table or the garage floor, you see where this leads. The best method of filling the ranks is to integrate your casting, conversion and restoration activities (see above) with your campaigning needs.

Picture 196: The guns H.G. Wells used

A wargamer's eye view of the famous Britains 4.7inch Naval gun endorsed by H.G. Wells for wargaming and shown in the drawings and photographs for Little Wars. Indeed, so pivotal was this weapon to the game that it appears in the book no less than thirty-six times, not counting occasions when there is more than one example in the picture. If you would like to have one these guns to show as that used by the great man, you will need the closed spring version on the right. The open spring one on the left was a later improvement in that you could more easily access the spring to replace it if there was a problem.

Wargaming

If it was good enough for H.G. Wells it will work for you. I was lucky enough to get to the finals of the National Championships, and received a runner-up prize at the hands of Brigadier Peter Young, no less. During the same period that Britains toy soldiers were gaining popularity, wargaming with toy soldiers was a craze that spawned a number of pamphlets, manuals and books, not least H.G. Wells *Little Wars*. If you read this, you will see that what is going on is campaigning, as above, but with rules for movement, casualties and morale. Wargamers are divided into three sorts of people: the competitive ones who like to win games; the ones who like to field magnificent armies; and the ones who spend their lives devising rules. Most wargamers do some of all three, as I did, and for two or three years I did little else.

In 1913, wargaming tended to be done with 54mm figures. Since the 1950s, the preferred scale for this has been 20-28mm, but if you keep up with *Plastic Warrior* magazine you will know that the 54mm war game has always been alive and kicking ass. Fantasy wargaming has enjoyed a vogue over the past thirty years, but now even Games Workshop is entertaining historical wargaming.

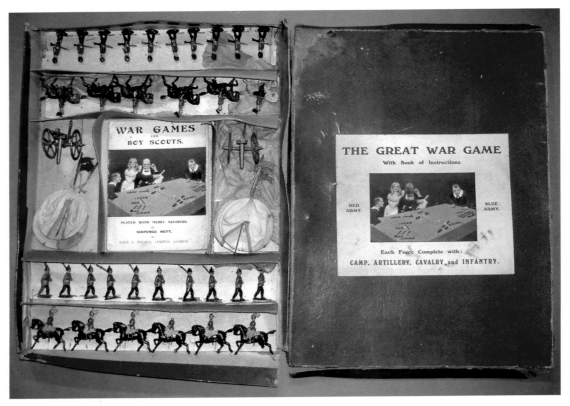

Picture 197: Hanks wargaming set

The figures I found inside this battered box when I got it were the very Britains-like small size ones made by Hanks. As the box was incomplete, I added everything I thought necessary, hoping that I have got the contents right. The book included is in a series done for Boy Scouts by Gale and Polden, the Aldershot based military publisher, and Hanks uses the cover art for the box label.

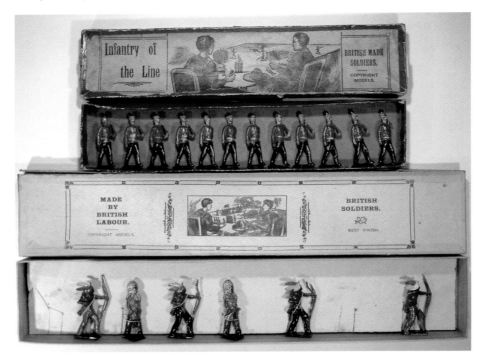

Picture 198: Labels with boys wargaming

In 1908 a craze for wargaming began. Makers cashed in with boxes like these. The top set is probably by Hanks, with twelve of their second grade game board figures in the box. The other unknown box's picture is different to the Hanks', although looking very similar.

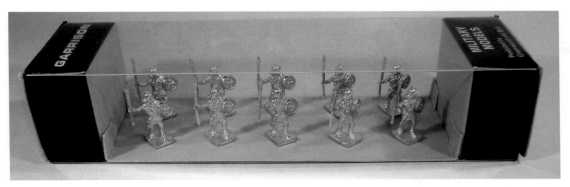

Picture 199: Garrison Romans

Once the model soldier business had become well established, it was a small step to starting to turn out smaller models for wargaming. They were expensive, but normally well made in 25mm scale. Then along came the Airfix 20mm figures for the mass market.

Picture 200: Airfix Romans in 20mm scale

One of my favourite figures, maybe because when I was building a Roman wargaming army I had a LOT of them (maybe a thousand of just this one pose). These two twelve man squads, which were the best ones I ever painted, say it all to me about the Roman Legion, no matter if the uniforms or formation are historically correct. Designed by John Niblett, this is a candidate for the best Roman figure of all time. Of course they are virtually worthless, but they carry a lot of WOW! for me on the nostalgia front, as well as being hard to beat as models.

Virtual war

There are now limitless possibilities for wargaming online, which is a wonderful way of saving space through not having to store any figures. All one has to beware of is being sucked in to endless effortless gaming as a way of life. I have certainly found it great fun to look over my stepson's shoulder while he manoeuvred immaculate squadrons of Tiger tanks somewhere on the eastern front.

Collecting other military related stuff

Many of my collecting friends have astonishing collections of militaria of various sorts, paintings, photographs, books, medals, uniforms, weapons and ephemera. Much of this stuff is highly atmospheric, and in addition I have family medals on the wall. I have succumbed to various books and pictures dating from the 1890s and 1900s, in particular the work of Harry Payne and Richard Simkin, who in my view capture the essence of empire in their paintings of British uniforms. My favourite objects are a series of presentation tins to contain whisky bottles decorated with Harry Payne pictures of Highlanders.

Picture 201: Advertising figures

This eclectic group of figures with a predominantly highland flavour are all advertising something or free gifts, with the exception of the highland pair on the left, which are souvenir items of the MacGregor clan. The boy eating the bar of chocolate is by Britains, although probably not an early attempt at Jonathan, the boy who features in the later Cococubs series. He seems more akin to the boy in Fry's Five Boys Chocolate to me. The tins at the back contained Whisky bottles, and are illustrated by Harry Payne. The large plastic Highlander, the smaller metal one in front of them and the row of small die-cast Highlanders in the middle are all advertising Whisky. The cow is the famous Britains cow with a world map on its flank advertising Nestle's Milk. Sir Kreemy Knut, the gent with the monocle, is a character advertising Sharp's Toffee and the archer is the Gibbs Dentifrice archer. The other four figures all come free with products. The plastic musketeer and the penguin come from Kinder eggs, the unpainted French dragoon is from Mokarex coffee and Donald Duck comes with a McDonalds Happy Meal.

CHAPTER 11
MOVING AND SHOWING
TOY SOLDIERS

Transportation

The most arduous part of possessing, acquiring or disposing of a collection is the physical effort required to take it from place to place. There may have been an Internet revolution so that transfer of words and images is instantaneous and cheap, but transport remains hideously expensive both of time and money.

Suggestions for packing toy soldiers

A straightforward house move is not too bad, and the same goes for taking soldiers to exhibitions or shows. All that is needed is boxes the right size for any original boxes you are taking, plus plenty of tissue or bubble wrap to cushion the soldiers during the move.

Hand carrying

Loose figures can be stacked in layers inside original or larger boxes, so that each layer is held down by another layer on top. It works best if the figures are placed with enough room between each that the next layer of figures goes in between the previous layer, like a stack of egg boxes. To a maximum of about ten layers, the soldiers will be fine as the weight of the soldiers will tend to keep them all in place. Transporting soldiers like this only works as long as the boxes can be transported upright, and there is no chance of anything tipping over. Remember to drive carefully!

Figures in original boxes can be interleaved with tissue or plastic inside the box, and then the boxes put in a suitably sized carton with a layer of newspaper or bubble wrap between each layer of boxes.

NB Many scratch built or assembled models, as opposed to finished models for collectors or old toy soldiers, are almost impossible to send by carrier without damage, and should be hand carried at all times, preferably without any packing other than to gently wedge them in place within an open container.

If they are to be hand carried in a suitcase or other luggage, for instance in an aircraft, then the best way is to find some shallow boxes similar to the original boxes if no original boxes are present. The soldiers are then individually wrapped in tissue and placed inside the shallow boxes, any remaining space being filled until the total contents cannot move. Underfilling will allow movement and hence damage. Overfilling will cause possible crushing of the contents. Once the box lids are back on, place paper or bubble wrap round the outside to protect any original labels, and put rubber bands round the outside. Ramming the lids shut may cause crushing. Within the suitcase, once more try to ensure that the case is full enough to prevent movement, but not so full as to crush the contents. Wadded newspaper is a good filler.

Packing for transport by carrier or post

If this is unavoidable, then here are two suggestions for reasonably secure packing.

Small box method

In shallow boxes, either original or of similar size, sew the soldiers onto a fairly stiff backing card. This is how Britains shipped their soldiers, but without their specialised sewing cards and machinery it is a fairly lengthy procedure. Make sure before sewing that the cards fit each corner of the box, so that there is no movement, and then that sufficient tissue or wadded paper is put in on top of the sewn card that there is no risk that with a major impact the card might crumple.

Slightly less secure, but almost as good, place a piece of bubblewrap in the bottom of the box – put in half the soldiers. Fold over the bubblewrap and put in the other half of the soldiers. Fold the remains of the bubblewrap over the top and replace the lid. Five layers of fairly thin bubblewrap will fill a Britains box with soldiers in it perfectly. Once the box lids are back on, place paper or bubble wrap round the outside to protect any original labels, and put a single piece of Scotch tape to secure each end. Ramming the lids shut may cause crushing.

Then pack the boxes inside a suitable size of three wall shipping carton. One that takes four Britains single row cavalry boxes across and four or five deep is good, for a total of twenty boxes to a carton. It will need to be big enough to allow for the wrapping around each box, and around the outside. Within the carton, once more try to ensure that the case is full enough to prevent movement, but not so full as to crush the contents. Wadded newspaper is a good filler.

'Swiss Roll' method

Taking a similar size of shipping carton, line it with several layers of thin bubble wrap. Take another sheet of bubble wrap, a bit wider than the carton. Lay it flat, and put a row of five infantry soldiers along the centre of one edge, about a hand's width in from the edge. The row should be spaced so that there is room for another soldier between each figure, and the whole row should be shorter than the width of the carton. Fold over the edge, and holding the ends of the row firmly, fold the enclosed row of soldiers over again. Place a further row of soldiers between the first row, on top of the bubble wrap, and fold the free end of the wrap across the top, not concertina style, but as a roll. For slim figures, a third or fourth layer can be added to the roll, but for bulky figures or cavalry, two rows is enough. For artillery or large pieces, one layer will be enough. Take care not to make the roll too tight, which might cause heads or rifles to bend or snap. If it is too loose, on the other hand, the figures will be able to move about. Once you have practised how to do this, it can be done quite quickly. Each bubble wrapped roll of soldiers is then placed lengthways inside the lined carton until the carton is filled. The ends of the roll can turn up to help cushion the sides of the carton. Do not secure with sticky tape which can cause damage. If empty space remains, fill with further bubble wrap. Overfill just a little, then press gently down to seal the carton with tape.

Put all heavy guns or vehicles into a separate carton individually bundled in bubble wrap. These pieces tend to be less fragile. Fill and seal as above, though with heavy items, firmer filling is better, and they are less likely to crush.

Put all the original gun and vehicle boxes into a separate carton. Once the box lids are on, place paper or bubble wrap round the outside to protect any original labels, and put rubber bands round the outside. Then pack the boxes inside a suitable size of shipping carton, and fill as before.

Displaying toy soldiers

This aspect of a collection has interested me much more since I stopped using boxes and Mary designed a beautiful display room for me.

Certainly the most spectacular display is a large flat surface which can be viewed at anything from waist height to eye level. An old billiard table looks very good, for instance. Not everyone has the room for this (see my description of Kemble Widmer's collection on page 141) and the more normal arrangement is ranks of cases or shelves around the walls of a room. Sometimes, for individual figures, a wall hanging case with narrow shelves is attractive. At least one case with good deep shelves to give some variety to displays and accommodate parades or campaigns would seem in order. It is the one shortcoming of my own display that I don't have a deep cabinet of this sort.

Shelves for 54mm figures need to be set at least nine inches (22.5cm) apart vertically to give the figures room to breath, and a minimum of nine inches deep to take a set of eight infantry or five cavalry. As a rule of thumb, one square inch per 54mm infantryman in toy style, and four square inches per cavalryman should work out about right. Very soon you will be able to work out exactly how much space will be needed for a given cameo or group of figures.

Picture 202: My shelves — revisited

This shows what I consider to be the ideal width and space between shelves, just right for displaying eight infantry or five cavalry abreast. See how each subject is given some space before going on to the next. Another shot of my shelves features in the introduction. Note that shelves will need dusting every so often, although the dust accumulation you can see here is probably about two years worth.

Display is an art, and everyone should please themselves. The main principles are not to overcrowd, and to mix makers only when they are reasonably compatible, leaving a decent space (a few inches is enough) between different cameos or styles of figure. If you are the sort of person, as I am, who enjoys having themes or rationalisations to explain on every shelf, then organisation and re-organisation will suggest itself at every turn.

Picture 203: Human wave

Britains second grade charging Red Army infantry represent the Russian Steam Roller, a term invented during the First World War as the hoped for effect of massive Russian manpower on the Central Powers. When the tide turned after Stalingrad in the Second World War, the Soviets concentrated huge numbers of men and equipment to crush the resistance of the Wehrmacht. The few Trojan plastic Germans shown here are quite historically accurate in proportion for the last days of the war. The odds were against them. A display like this can bring out the best features of the models and make an historical point at the same time.

Compatibility

Some manufacturers figures are consistently compatible with each other, and others are not. Most Britains hollowcasts will look good with each other, but the painting style change from the 1890s to the 1950s is quite startling. Most old paints that have survived from a hundred years ago will have dulled down considerably. Most modern gloss paint finishes are almost unbearably shiny.

In setting up display collections or cameos with soldiers either ancient or recently made, the look of the ensemble can be ruined if some of the figures stand out by being in a different style from the rest. Your eye is the best judge of this, but the main criteria are:

- All the figures have the same quality of paintwork, and the gloss or matt of the paint should be consistent.
- The scale is constant to within two or three millimetres of the mean.
- Toy soldier style or model style is followed throughout. If there are mixed styles, graduate them from one end of the group to the other, so that there is never a sharp break between two styles.

In terms of scenery, once more, continuity of style is what I concentrate on. For toy figures, using toy scenery or buildings seems to me to work best. With styles more towards the realistic model, then backgrounds and scenery more in keeping with fine scale modelling would be more appropriate. I am particularly fond of using toy castles for backgrounds.

Sometimes material other than toy soldiers can be incorporated in displays. Medals, models, pictures or militaria can all provide good highlights to a display, and provide variety. Another interesting idea is to frame groups of boxes or lids and hang them as if they were pictures.

Picture 204: Muddle

From one aspect, this picture is a cautionary tale of how not to display things if you want to make sense of them. I have deliberately muddled just about every possible type of figure to see how awful I can make them look. However, the result is a strangely compelling mixture that draws the mind in trying to understand it, like a puzzle, and so I am not ruling out the idea that shelves of oddities are great fun. See if you can find all the different materials and styles included here. Spot the fake. Where are Alexander Graham Bell, Field Marshal Montgomery, Oliver Cromwell and General Picton? Which figure is an aluminium copy of a hollowcast? Which figure was made in Poland? How many Britains figures are included? Which First World War staff officer was made by my friend Bill Connolly and given to me as a gift? Which two figures represent Camden Market, and which two the horrors of war? The large Royal Scot back left missing a hackle is made of plaster by R. Briton Riviere.

Picture 205: The Zulu War

New Toy Soldiers, but the tents are old. This group represents a camp in 1879, such as that at Isandlwana, where the Zulus overwhelmed a British column. I was once able to put a couple of hundred Zulus in the field. Now, the Zulu hordes have to be imagined in on the left of the picture. Most of these figures are Blenheim, with a sprinkling of Soldiers Soldiers, Steadfast and even one Britains. The two men firing from behind lying horses are converted from the Hill cowboys of the originals (see picture 166).

165

Exhibitions

Most collectors enjoy showing and discussing their collections, and there is no better way to do this than exhibiting. Local modelling clubs and the British Model Soldier Society often arrange shows, and space can be booked at these or local charity events. Sometimes the opportunity arises to put on displays in shop windows or museums.

Here is my checklist of points to cover when planning an exhibition, based on the OPIE acronym of getting things done:

O is for objective

1. What is the purpose of the exhibition, or what does it commemorate?
2. How will the success of the exhibition be judged? Numbers of visitors? Income generated? Interest expressed?

P is for plan

1. Is the exhibition to have a title?
2. Where is the exhibition to be held?
3. Under whose auspices does it take place
4. How long is there to get everything ready?
5. Who is to do what?
6. Is there sunlight that will need to be guarded against?
7. Will there be a method of preventing visitors from touching the exhibits?
8. How much room is available for display?
9. What figures can be used to fill the available space?
10. For how long is the exhibition open
11. How much time is available to set up?
12. Is access arranged?
13. Has a plan of the display been drawn up?
14. How firm are any bases on which the models are to stand?
15. Is the lighting adequate?
16. Is the venue cleared and ready, or will it need additional preparation time?
17. Has insurance been arranged and at whose cost?
18. How will the display be transported to the venue and at whose cost?
19. Is there to be associated written material – notices, handouts, catalogues, captions etc.? Who is to write the copy and who is to look after printing and lettering and at whose cost?
20. What are the arrangements for dismantling the exhibition? Is there a deadline?
21. Will help be needed with fetching and carrying, or with security?
22. Is any remuneration involved, or reimbursement of expenses?
23. Can the exhibition be photographed for posterity?
24. Are souvenirs to be sold? If so, what, and from where?

I is for implementation

If the items under plan are properly planned, implementation will be a doddle.

E is for evaluation

1. How well was the objective achieved?
2. Any implementation issues to plan for for next time?

Websites

Another means of bringing a collection into the public gaze is to put it on a website. After fifteen years of the Internet, it is now much easier to set these up, and every extra item posted there stays put, so it is a very satisfying cumulative venture. After vowing never to write another book, I found myself writing articles to post on my website (*www.james-opie.co.uk*), and I have to say I have been very flattered by some of the entries in my guest book.

When I started this website about six years ago, apart from the auction news I found myself posting much the same sort of things as I had included in *Collecting Toy Soldiers*, and that triggered me off to thinking that an updated version of that book should be done.

Websites are an incredible, almost miraculous, way of recording a collection so that everyone can enjoy it. The best part is that one can put up pictures of all the good bits, especially those spectacular campaigns and parades, without having to go through the business of tidying away all the stuff that gets spread around between people coming to see it.

There are currently just a couple of dozen good websites of people's collections out there. I would love to be able to visit more, and I am sure it is the future for toy soldier collecting. For sure it is a great deal easier than putting on exhibitions or going on actual physical tours of people's collections. Maybe we can get a site going where people could post photos of their displays or favourite pieces, if it is too much trouble for people to do their own sites.

Storage, cleaning and preservation

Until I released my remaining collection into my display room, I had preferred to store my soldiers in cardboard boxes of the right sort of size to fit either the original boxes with the soldiers in them or a single layer of figures. Boxes that are too shallow mean that fragile protrusions are at risk. Even though slightly deeper boxes take up more room, it is as well to allow a little more depth in case when stacked the bottoms of the box weigh downwards in the centre quite heavily and crush something.

Lead and lead alloys

Toy soldiers containing lead can be prone to oxidation, more or less according to the proportion of lead in the alloy. When this occurs, lead oxides form on the surface of the metal, a greyish-white powdery looking substance which ruins the paintwork and eats away at the metal so that hollowcast figures eventually collapse in upon themselves. In the early stages it will appear as a grey bloom on exposed metal surfaces such as bayonets, helmets and breastplates, but particularly underneath bases.

This is known among collectors as 'lead disease' or 'lead rot'. The good news is that it will not spread to other models, as it is the conditions that cause it which are the problem. Correct storage will prevent it or stop it. Various agents are known to increase the risk, particularly damp or high humidity, atmospheric impurities, domestic mothballs or organic acids from unseasoned wood. An absence of ventilation in concert with these can set off a fairly immediate deterioration, which to my chagrin I experienced twice before I was alert to the dangers.

Many collectors will not touch figures with lead disease, and so prices for them tend to be cheaper. Most people avoid items that have seriously deteriorated. However, there is further good news, in that models which just have a touch or so of it on the surface can be pretty much fully restored with the gentle application of one part medicinal grade mineral and one part artist's turpentine (NOT turpentine substitute). As with rusty iron, the oils prevent further oxidation, and also as a bonus revive the varnished appearance of the painted surfaces. Handling the toys frequently can have a similar effect just from the oil

secreted by the skin, an example of loving attention being physically beneficial.

In fifty years of storing figures, I have not yet detected any harmful effects from wrapping them in tissue paper (acid-free paper is probably preferable just to be on the safe side), or from keeping them in cardboard boxes. The main precaution is not to put the soldiers in too airtight an environment. Airtight cases are therefore a no-no. Equally, wrapping in plastic for any length of time should be avoided. Now that bubble wrap is almost universally used to pack things, owing to the huge benefits of its cushioning effect, the trick is to take the models out of the airtight wrap as soon as convenient. That old standby cotton wool, on the other hand, is actually harmful, as in common with other fibrous packing it can get into cracks in the paint and pull flakes of it off.

Cleaning lead soldiers is not recommended other than the restoration above. A light brushing to remove dust, sometimes just blowing will do it, is all that I ever try, sometimes with small stiff brushes, very gently, to get into corners. The peril with any cleaning is that if paint is flaky, it will inevitably come off.

High tin content figures

Tin is a much more stable metal than lead, and both flats and most of the better modern collector figures other than those which are die-cast are made with such a high proportion of tin in them that they are unlikely to come to harm from oxidation. The only problem with them is that they can break when bent, but then this is true of most metal toy soldiers. When buying new collector figures, it is a plus to know they are unlikely to suffer from oxidation.

Die-cast figures

Prior to the 1970s, die-casting was not often used for making toy soldiers themselves, but since the early 1930s it has been extensively used for vehicles and guns. The metal used is a zinc alloy, often known as Mazac after the name of one of the leading commercial suppliers. Early die-castings often suffered from impurities in the alloy, most problematically too much lead, which resulted in a phenomenon that has been dubbed 'metal fatigue' among collectors. The symptom is a maze of tiny cracks forming in the metal over a period of years until, finally, the model collapses into fragments. Once a figure shows these cracks, there is no known cure, although a dip in polyurethane can help keep the pieces together. Modern die-castings, made from the 1960s on, use perfected alloys and the problem doesn't occur.

A useful way of detecting fatigue in a die-cast gun barrel is to see if it is at all bent. If the barrel is cast in two halves, sometimes one half has 'metal fatigue', and the expansion caused by the cracks makes the barrel bend towards the unfatigued side.

Composition figures

Once more the chief enemy is damp, as the wire skeleton inside the figure can rust, and the composition itself crack if exposed to too much water. Cracks or breakages can be repaired with plastic wood or plaster filler, but the figures will never be the same again. Plaster figures are subject to much the same problems. Cleaning these is also very problematical, as if the figures are flaking, even touching them to pick them up can cause loss of paint. There is really no solution to this except spraying them with varnish, which inevitably means they no longer have their original appearance. Your choice.

Aluminium figures

These are truly virtually unbreakable as long as they have been designed without thin parts or sections. They are generally used in the way that any child treats unbreakable toys, i.e.

with frustration that they won't break, so there are large numbers of surviving toys with very little paint left on them.

Plastic figures

Contrary to the claims of many early manufacturers, plastic soldiers are not unbreakable. In normal play they become unpleasantly dirty, pitted, bent and paintless in a rather shorter time than hollowcast toys become scratched, headless, bent and crushed. As with aluminium, part of the fun of owning unbreakable plastic was to test it to destruction. Particularly in the early days, plastic was a highly experimental substance, and very little of it has yet had to stand the test of time for more than 70 years. The two main types of plastic from which toy soldiers have been made are the Alkathene/Polythene group, and the Polystyrene group.

Polythene

Polythene gives good 'bendability', but it is difficult to paint satisfactorily as it has a somewhat slick, oily surface. For some years Herald, Timpo and Lone Star experimented with mixing chalk in with Alkathene to give better paint adhesion. It didn't hurt that the accountants noted that the chalk filler was less expensive than the Alkathene, so sometimes the mix erred on the chalky side. If that happened, the oiliness in the plastic eventually dried out, making the plastic brittle and liable to snap. Britains Eyes Right models, for instance, can become very easily damaged, with heads snapping off necks if you try to twist them. Dropping a figure onto a hard surface can result in it shattering!

Some of the accessories for Swoppet infantry made out of a soft plastic have a disconcerting habit of melting rather messily, and the same can happen to some of the very early experimental acetate plastic figures, such as those made by Airfix or Malleable Mouldings in the late 1940s.

Polystyrene

The harder plastics such as Polystyrene are brittle enough to have easily breakable small parts. Malleable Mouldings made figures of this material, and the normal use for it is in plastic kits, as it is able to be cast into very fine detail. Most figures of this sort are made up Historex kits, which do need an incredible amount of care to transport safely. The plastic seems to be perfectly OK, however, so apart from allowing for the fragility, there should be no problems with it.

Undoubtedly most plastic figures are perfectly stable, and if they have lasted this long will probably endure for much longer, but it is advisable to treat them as fragile rather than robust.

Paintwork and printed materials

The main enemy of paintwork and printed packaging is sunlight, the ultraviolet radiation of which can fade the colours. Paintwork or boxes are best cleaned gently with a stiff sable brush to remove dust. Anything stronger could risk flaking paint off with the dust. If you feel moved to experiment, do it with badly chipped figures to get the feel of it without putting anything expensive at risk. My own inclination is to leave things alone.

Paintwork on polythene plastic figures is particularly liable to flake off. Minimum handling is the only solution. Even the act of wrapping flexible figures may result in paint loss.

Certain paints attract mould or fungal growths. I have noticed some of these on military Dinky Toys and some Starlux figures in my own collection. It is time consuming to remove the mould, but it seems that it can be done. I would like to try an anti-fungal spray to see if it helps, but so far the problem is not extensive enough to be classed as an emergency.

In summary, my plan is that anything not on display in well ventilated cases or shelves is stored on cupboards or covered cardboard boxes, with or without tissue paper. Keep everything dry and ventilated and inspect them regularly. Never expose them to sunlight, and keep them at normal domestic room temperature (between 40° and 80°F or 4° – 27°C). Do not drop anything, especially plastic; carpeted floors are a safeguard.

CHAPTER 12
VALUES, AND PHILOSOPHIES FOR DEALING WITH THEM

Toy soldier prices

I have always been fascinated by the commercial economics of toy soldiers in the marketplace. As with most other products, there have since the start been various different qualities and styles of goods at widely differing prices. One of the nice things about collecting toy soldiers is that as I have experienced, it is possible to have just as much fun doing it whether you are operating on sixpence a week pocket money as a boy, with the advantage of a certain amount to invest as a single young man, or with fairly large other commitments in later life.

All prices that I quote in this book, unless I am quoting a specific occasion, are my opinion of what the price might be on average, based on my experience of current (2010) and past prices. Prices do, of course, vary widely. Half the fun of collecting is looking for bargains, or recognising WOW! where others cannot see it.

So what is the situation today, shopping at shows or auctions? Here are some examples of what you can get at various price points:

- **10p-£1.** Individual flats, other not very good looking figures, often home made, or interesting broken bits for conversion. Individual common plastic items, mostly unpainted.
- **£1-2.** Useful broken figures with not too much work needing to be done.
- **£2-3.** Common commercially painted plastic figures and less collected hollowcasts in Good to Fair condition.
- **£4-5.** Common individual New Toy Soldiers.
- **£5-10.** Individual relatively common hollowcast Britains on foot in good condition. Nice individual New Toy Soldiers in toy soldier style, new or second hand.
- **£10-20.** Individual CBG Mignot on foot. Good quality models second hand.
- **£20-50.** Individual good quality Britains, CBG Mignot or Heyde cavalry. Common sets of post-war Britains sometimes with boxes. Model quality individual figures brand new.
- **£50-100.** Individual rarities of old toy soldiers, and nice boxed sets of less rare things. Individual Lucotte figures are usually priced in this band.
- **£100-200.** The majority of Britains sets of hollowcast figures fall in this bracket. Auction lots of display figures containing 50 to 100 figures per lot. Very nice top quality finished models.
- **£200-500.** Most of the better sets for a reference collection can be obtained in this range. Larger models and other pieces often come into this bracket.
- **£500-1,000.** You start to be able to obtain rarities, here, and the only regular sets that start from this band are of Lucottes. Rare boxes of plastic figures have been known to reach this level. Commissioned models may well set you back this sort of money.
- **£1000-£3,000.** Incredibly rare individual figures sometimes reach into this price, but mostly we are talking iconic sets of Britains, large size Heyde and other German figures, immaculate large Hausser and Lineol vehicles and early CBG Mignot or Lucotte sets.
- **£3,000-£10,000.** The very ultimate rare sets of beautiful old figures. The most I ever heard of anyone paying for a set is **$50,000** for the largest Britains set, set 131, which had 275 pieces in it, and definitely rates WOW! factor 10.
- The most expensive toy soldier of all time, according to the *Guinness Book of Records*, was the 1963 prototype original G I Joe, which changed hands for **$200,000** in 2003.

How prices have moved over time

At start of sales at auction in 1968, a few pounds were able to buy some astonishing items. In the very first sale, a boxed set of Italian Cavalry was £12, and 190 pieces of Timpo clowns, soldiers, cowboys and others was £3. In 1972 the sale of the famous Pottier-Smith collection commenced, which ran through several auctions, and contained numerous lots of specially painted figures which he had commissioned from Britains in the late 1930s. One of my favourites was the US Cavalry in blue, of which I bought 21 figures for £42. At that time it seemed like a fortune, but when I sold my last group of five at auction in 1988, the price paid was £1,045, implying a 100-fold appreciation over 16 years. In 2002, this same set surfaced again at another auction, and the price paid this time was £862, so these 14 years produced a loss.

As this example illustrates, from the end of Britains hollowcast production in 1966 to 1987, there was an appreciation in second hand prices of an average of a hundred times, but as collectors rapidly became more knowledgeable over the years, certain categories of sets became known for their beauty and rarity, and together with a few other individual pieces have become the iconic Britains collector's want list.

Since 1987, when Britains collecting fever was at its peak, the trend of prices for the rare and exciting items has been only mildly upwards. Everything else has actually on average declined. The market has followed the general pattern for new and nostalgic collecting markets, in which there is an initial surge of interest, a peak, and then a gradual decline while the very top items retain their value, but everything else filters gradually downwards to a more or lesser degree. There will always be exceptions to this pattern, particularly as it is in the nature of auction sales that from time to time there is a freak price obtained (including some freakish bargains) but the civilian hollowcast toy market and the painted plastic toy soldier market in turn have appeared to follow this model.

The most collectable toy soldiers, in terms of investment value, have been William Britains from before the First World War, together with the rarer sets from the later years of hollowcast production. These sets include the Famous Regiment series, aircraft, set 1622 Royal Marine Light Infantry Band, large display boxes, Beiser game trays and figures by Britains and others, anything from the Paris Office and anything made or painted by Britains to special order.

The segment of Britains hollowcasts that has suffered the most decline has been that of post-war production (1948-1966), where common sets are now reaching only £50 to £100 per Very Good boxed set, when at one time the average was twice that. Now is probably a good time to acquire a beautiful collection of these. In many ways, they are still my favourites, from the nostalgia of them being the top soldiers when I was young. There are, however, plenty around, so there should be no expectation of appreciation in value, even though it could well happen.

Remember when buying that common figures will cost less in bulk at auction, but won't be on offer individually. Single figures (except for very expensive rarities) can only be bought at shows and from dealers. Rare things will be at fixed prices from shows, dealers and shops (though there is no harm in a bit of haggling) and may actually cost even more at auctions where collectors are competing for them.

Then there will always be the freak prices. In 1980 there was a sale at Sotheby's Belgravia at which only four serious collectors and dealers were present. On sale was the fabulous collection of a person domiciled in the Isle of Man. It was only the second collection containing a substantial number of Britains special paintings which has ever been put up for sale at auction, the first being that of Pottier-Smith in 1972. For £66, Burtt Erhlich bought a group of specially painted Royal Garrison Artillery in busbies that included a gun team at the halt with 4.7 inch Naval Gun and five mounted figures. This set went via Bill Miele's collection to the Ilyinsky collection, and was sold in 2002 for $9,000. In the same Sotheby's 1980 sale a red version slotted arm set 101, Mounted Band of the Life Guards was sold for £110, a set that often reaches £1,000 today.

At the other end of the scale, when the Forbes collection from the Palais Mendoub in Tangiers was sold at Christies in New York and London in December 1997, some astounding prices were reached, especially in New York, for figures which were in no way out of the ordinary apart from the fact that they had formed part of Malcolm Forbes collection. Forbes, one of the world's most influential and richest men, was a collector of many things from Faberge eggs to classic motorcycles. The Forbes sale attracted huge publicity and has been the largest and most expensive sale of toy soldiers ever, raising a total income of about three-quarters of a million dollars. As examples, a large lot of 168 common 1950s Britains American Civil War figures, estimated at $300-400 went for $10,350 dollars, or about £38 each, compared to today's normal show price of £5 to £10. Again, a perfectly ordinary set 162, Mauritius Royal Artillery (eight figures) from the Nostalgia collection was sold for $690, or $86 per figure, compared with the same set selling for about £40 in a lot of nine sets sold in 2009.

The market for different types of figure

Flats

These were the earliest toy soldiers to have mass distribution. They are still being made, and there are huge numbers out there. When found in their original boxes, they often look old and valuable, and occasionally they are old and valuable, but not often. At auction, it is unusual to be able to sell them for more than about fifty pence (a dollar) each. If worn, damaged, poorly painted or unpainted, this would be considerably less.

Picture 206: Greys Cigarettes

These unpainted flats were engraved by Frank for Ochel in the 1930s, who had been commissioned by Greys Cigarettes to do two series as an appropriate premium for the brand, as shown by the literature. The famous charges of the Scots Greys at Waterloo and Balaklava are the driving force behind these. The Russian cavalryman second from the right in the bottom row is in a pose very reminiscent of my first ever toy soldiers (see page xv) and makes me wonder if maybe those are also meant to represent Russian cavalry. Toy soldiers in card or tin (as shown in row three) were a popular alternative to the normal cigarette cards, although these Greys

are the only ones I know of in proper flat metal figures. The thin card or paper soldiers in the top row are part of sets issued as cutout sheets which can then be stuck to little wooden blocks to support them in standing upright. All of these, although interesting historically, have very little value.

173

Semi-flat

The nicest looking semi-flat figures are usually about 40mm in scale, well cast and finished in late nineteenth century best quality style paint. Made by Spenkuch, Haffner, Besold and other German makers, they can be quite charming in groups, and are often relatively inexpensive to buy at about £5 to £10 per figure, although the most attractive examples can go a lot higher. Semi-flat figures were the preferred option for home casting, and numberless moulds were sold by Schneider, Ideal (not the same as the plastics manufacturer in picture 11) or Prinz August and others throughout Europe and North America. From time to time, quite well marketed examples of these turn up in trinket shops, but for serious collectors of better quality toy soldiers, they are worthless. Should you wish to make a speciality of these, or indeed collect the moulds themselves, they shouldn't cost much to acquire.

Picture 207: Semi-flat Engineers

A lively group of 48mm scale semi-flat Prussian Engineers, dating from about 1875. These were the best quality toy soldiers of their time, and can often be sold for sums commensurate with their appearance. A group like this might fetch £100 to £200 at auction.

Picture 208: Semi-flat Zulus

I wonder if I will ever find out who made these lively 60mm scale Zulus. They are certainly German, but by which maker? They are nice enough that they should be worth around £10 to £20 each.

Solidcast

Traditional solid figures as sold from Germany and France from the late nineteenth century have always had a good following. The larger sizes of German figures from Heyde, Haffner, Heinrich and Noris among others are very collectable, but examples are relatively rare. In general terms, the larger and more detailed the figure, the more they will cost, allowing for condition. Size No.2, about 48mm scale, will sell for an average of £10 each for nice looking figures, rarities and boxed sets for much more. Elephants with riders, for instance can work out at about £1,000 each. Some of the very rare sets, such as the large Trojan War or Siegfried sets, are probably worth upwards of £10,000. Once the scale is up over 100mm, then it can be hundreds of pounds per figure. These, however, are high WOW! magnificent models, and look the price.

Lucottes and early CBG Mignot command good prices, the former starting at £50 for foot figures and £100 for mounted. The only comparable British figures are those by Richard Courtenay, although these are more like stylised models, mostly of medieval subjects. The charm and artistry of the heraldry is the attraction here, and mounted figures sometimes reach £500 each or more. All these have good WOW! factor.

Picture 209: CBG Mignot 40mm scale (No 2 size) semi-flat spring-mounted figures

Similar cavalry can be found from France and Germany mounted on thin springs, intended to give mounted models a lifelike movement when set in motion, for instance, by giving a table a nudge. I had once envied a beautiful set of German made lancers of this sort, so when I found these at a show a few years back, I probably paid a little over the odds for them at £200, as they are not in all that good condition, with some breakages. They are the only examples of this type of figure I have, and are quite unusual to find. The uniforms are of French chasseurs and dragoons from the early part of the First World War.

Hollowcast

Naturally among hollowcasts, Britains figures tend to command the best prices on average, but on the other hand Britains competitors, especially in the period 1893 to 1930, were producing far less quantity, and so are relatively rare. Many of the nicer figures from BMC, Renvoize, Reka, Fry and some early German and American makers will command £20 to £30 per figure, or a great deal more for extremely rare sets such as gun teams. To take this example, Britains gun teams were produced prolifically, and you can readily buy a very decent example for £500. I have only ever seen or heard about half a dozen examples of BMC or Renvoize gun teams,

Picture 210: Johillco Scottish soldiers in original box

I found this large boxed set of twenty figures in Wimbledon on one of my trips round London suburbs in the late 1950s. It has been a prized possession ever since. It includes an interesting if not very compatible selection of Scottish regiments, most having some problems with the selected uniforms, e.g. black horses for Scots Greys, red hackles for Gordon Highlanders. The box must have been made around 1954 at the latest, and they are still mint strung in from when I first purchased them. I managed to resist taking them out as they look better in the box than as a rather disparate group on the shelf. Today, this box should fetch between £100 and £200 at auction.

so they should from their rarity cost £5,000 or more each, should a good example ever come to auction. In reality, they might sell for about the same as the Britains equivalent, i.e. up to about £1,000, although this hasn't been tested in the market recently, they are so rare.

For pointers to general Britains prices see the paragraphs above, but you should be able to get common best quality figures in good condition from £5 for infantry and £10 for cavalry, with medium rare sets costing between £200 and £400. Items with a WOW! factor of 5 or more will normally cost more than this. The vast majority of things you see at shows, on the Internet or at auction will have WOW! factor of 4 or less. Second grade figures are worth a lot less, currently, even when they are quite rare.

Good original boxed hollowcast figures other than Britains are usually much rarer than Britains, but fewer people collect them, so they are relatively cheaper.

Picture 211: Britains second grade Infantry of the Line firing

These are a great deal rarer than you might suppose from the large amount of Best Quality sets using these castings. Dating from around 1940, they are actually difficult to find, and might well cost £10 each from a dealer. You might get lucky and pay half that or less if the dealer is not a knowledgeable specialist. Second grade and small size Britains are still not collected by many people as yet, and this has held the prices for them down.

Composition

The current market in composition figures appears to have followed right along with Britains, with good rare figures holding their value or even appreciating, while cracked or fair to poor condition items depreciating markedly. To buy nice originals should cost from £5-10 each for common figures, up to £20-£30 each for medium rare. From there on up, as with

Picture 212: British composition infantry.

The figures back and right were made by Brent Toy Products and/or Bell around 1945, when metal was unavailable for toy manufacture. The material used was advertised as Elastolene, a clear rip-off of the German Elastolin, although at the time I expect no-one in this country cared much about that. Thin nails are used to form part of the weapons, and there appear to be two different series in differing scales. Contrast these rather crude figures with the not much better ones to left front, the pilot definitely attributable to Timpo, and made of Timpolene in one of Zang's factories. The other two are an improvement on the rest. See also picture 166 for other early Timpo product. The figure to the left is a Dime-store like figure by an unknown maker, but clearly in British battledress. Because of the crudeness of these British composition figures, they are unlikely to have value for their aesthetics, and currently cost less than £2 per figure. As an historical curiosity, however, to my mind they are worth collecting, and after all, they are unlikely to break the bank!

Britains, high WOW! is expensive, reflecting their high collectability in both Germany and the United States. Most of the more expensive items are in the very best quality 70mm scale ranges. For a picture comparison in Highlanders, see picture 151.

Aluminium

The aluminium figures of Quiralu and its competitors in France have seen big price rises over the last twenty years, especially for near mint examples. Although this has sparked a certain interest from France in Wend-Al, the relatively poor design of the British company has meant that the price for common Wend-Al figures has remained under £5 each. Mounted lancers, hussars and Salvation Army, however, can be quite expensive.

Picture 213: Wend-Al infantry

The only original Wend-Al designs in this picture are the mortar party, where the angled base plate is an interesting departure from other depictions, and the machine gunner. The kneeling firing figure is evidently a copy of the Herald plastic model. The other figures are French infantry, probably by Quiralu, the man waving the machine pistol being particularly stylish. Some of the less flamboyant French figures were probably used by Wend-Al to supplement their very small range of combat infantry. Star of the show here is the mule with two casualties on stretchers. The mule could also take one of the piles of sacks in the foreground. The mule with loads is worth maybe £40. None of the other figures is individually worth more than £5, with the possible exception of the Frenchman with the machine pistol.

Models

In the 1950s and 1960s, models could be custom made for clients, at a cost in those days of about £20 per figure – the equivalent of £300 per figure today! (Top class fully painted models from the best makers, however, can easily cost £200 or so now, so custom made figures today would probably be relatively even more expensive than they were then.) Otherwise, back then, one could make them oneself from scratch, assemble and make a kit or paint a casting, all very costly in time and even then involving a fair outlay in materials. Since those days, production techniques and the opening of China to commerce has resulted in many models, from the perfectly passable to the utterly beautiful, being made available at prices ranging from about £5 for foot and £10 mounted to double or three times that. Average prices from Britains for a good model quality figure on foot are £20 to £25, still at that price only a twentieth of the cost of an equivalent model in 1950. Good models today can cost that much just for a new casting.

If you don't mind buying models second hand, maybe improving or repairing the work of someone else, then there is a huge amount of material out there for very little money. As always, it is the skills and patience which are at a premium, so that the completion of a finished work of art is still just as satisfying as it has always been.

Plastic

Plastic toy soldiers, painted or unpainted, started to be made in the late 1940s, and were ubiquitous by the late 1950s. By the 1980s and 1990s they were making good money at auction fuelled by the nostalgia of those that had played with them thirty or forty years before. Because of the relative fragility of plastic, and the propensity of the paint to flake, the relative difference in price of near perfect examples to the much more common fair or poor items is considerably wider than for metal soldiers.

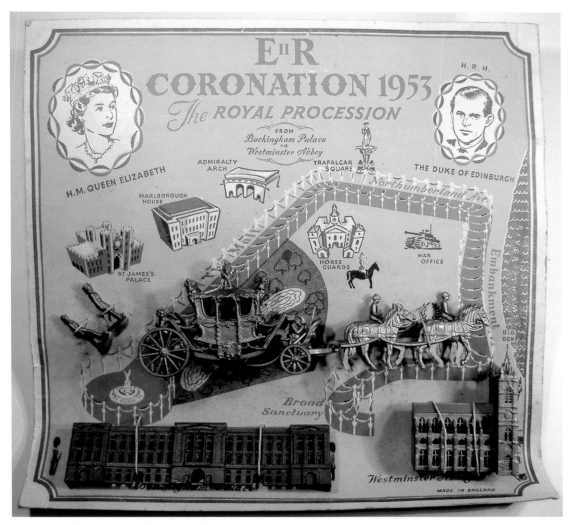

Picture 214: Plastic souvenir Coronation Card

What a splendid early plastic souvenir, which should be in every collection of coaches and Coronation memorabilia from 1953. I wonder how many survive. It is the more obscure plastic items such as this and the enormous variety of Hong Kong produced copies that provide much of the uncharted further reaches of plastic collecting. It may be that in years to come, some of these items, of which very few can survive intact, will become valuable. On the other hand, they may remain a backwater of collecting, of interest, but of no value, since there is no easy way to make a list of them for reference collection, and they don't fit readily into display collecting. Another item that might achieve a similar long-term rarity value is the Carcassonne souvenir header bag in picture 83.

I would not expect to pay more than £20 for this card, purely from the point of view that few people are currently collecting such items, and they are a nuisance to store, but this, along with other Coronation souvenirs, is an area that could well take off, for instance at the time of the next Coronation.

179

Equally, there was much less likelihood of the boxes for plastic soldiers surviving. Whereas the straightforward and quite sturdy tray and lid boxes that Britains and many other metal toy soldiers occupied were easy to keep and store with their soldiers inside, the 'cellophane fronted monstrosities' (to quote a leading dealer) in which plastic soldiers were often presented from the late 1950s onwards were fragile, difficult to open carefully and almost impossible to reconstruct with the soldiers in place inside. Thereafter, the ingenuity of packaging manufacturers to provide bubble packs, bags with carded headers or inserts, various slides, holders, rubber banded backing or vacuum formed trays knew no bounds, often taking the premise that since plastic was unbreakable, looks were much more important than durability. Essentially, the only guarantee of survival was not only that the boxes, even the outers, had never been opened, but also that they had received careful handling and that the plastic materials of which the figures were made had not deteriorated.

Following the above, the price of truly mint boxed plastic figures can be out of all proportion even to good condition loose examples. It would be wrong to set any guidelines, but thinking in the first instance of between five and ten times the combined price of the individual soldiers might not be out of order.

In the late 1970s a *Blue Peter* appeal for toy soldiers produced sixty or seventy oil drums full. Each oil drum contained about ten thousand toy soldiers, and all donations had been tipped in together (because plastic is unbreakable). Scores of volunteers separated the metal from the plastic, and I was called in as Phillips expert to pronounce on whether there were any gems among the metal figures. Unfortunately, although there was enough to make up a few auction lots, nothing really valuable had turned up. Nevertheless, the several hundred thousand plastic figures were bagged in quantities of five hundred and sold to dealers for about a pound a bag, the cheapest deal on toy soldiers ever, and actually a good return for *Blue Peter*.

One result of the use of plastic was that production methods had evolved, so that much greater volume was possible. The Timpo factory in Shotts, Lanarkshire, for instance, had a thousand full time and four hundred part time employees, and must have been churning out millions of models a month, sixty per cent of which were going to Germany alone. All of these models were likely to lose pieces and were subject to all the failings noted above and in Chapter 11, so that allowing for the greater volume on the one hand, and the lower likelihood of survival on the other, there would seem to be a similar number of original plastic soldiers in circulation for collectors as there are original metal ones.

So, collecting different plastic figures has just as much variety in price as there is for metal. 10p figures from a wide choice are readily available, with rare boxed sets regularly exceeding £1,000. As the market for plastic figures continues to mature, it will be perfectly possible that prices for the rarest and most perfect boxed items will go on up.

New Toy Soldiers

The production of so-called New Toy Soldiers started in 1973, and the most successful makers, Britains, King and Country, Blenheim, Ducal, Conte and Trophy, in various styles, have now had almost forty years of production. Because these were all made for collectors, in total contrast to original toy soldiers made for children, where attrition was always high, the vast majority of them have been well looked after and often survived complete with original boxes. The limiting factor for collectors thus became largely a matter of space.

Second hand collectors toys and models have, with a few exceptions, remained at relatively low prices. Early and discontinued King and Country are fairly well sought after, as are Trophy and some Britains. The Retail Price Index has gone up by roughly seven times since

Picture 215: Royal Navy machine guns

British expeditions to far flung corners of the world often relied on the Royal Navy for their heavy weapons. On the right is a Blenheim Gatling gun with four crew, made about 1978. The painted S on the base of one of the sailors denotes that this figure was a painting sample. A set like this would cost about £30 to £40 new from an equivalent manufacturer today – second hand at a show, it would probably cost between £20 and £30. Bought as part of a larger lot at auction, the cost might well be reduced to £10 to £15. To the right is a Nordenfelt machine gun by model makers Cavalier, made about 1978. Although the figures and gun are rather more detailed, they were supplied unpainted, and I painted them up myself in the toy soldier style, after which they looked very compatible with the Blenheim figures, and are worth a similar amount. Allowing for inflation, since they were sold into the model market, they would originally have cost new as much as the painted Blenheim figures.

Picture 216: Royal Navy armoured traction engine

Heavy artillery was always in short supply in far flung parts of the empire, so the Royal Navy famously supplied 4.7 inch guns for field service in the second Boer War. In spite of the usual depiction of these with long teams of oxen, a more usual means of moving these heavy pieces was by traction engine. David Bracey produced a whole range of slightly undersize 54mm scale vehicles to complement Britains, but only made a very few of these traction engines with their armoured rifle wagons. A pre-requisite to order one was to give him a pair of Britains 18 inch howitzer wheels. The result was simple and effective, as shown here with three Britains 4.7 inch naval guns and a variety of hollowcast and new toy sailors. Connecting with a connoisseur of Lancer vehicles who did not have one of these might result in a sale price of £150 for the engine and towed wagon alone.

Picture 217: Cranston Indian Army

Bill Cranston specializes in making one-off sets of the Indian Army in particular, and although they are done in the New Toy Soldier style, they are to New Toy Soldiers what Freddie Green conversions are to Britains, finished with such finesse that they stand out as something special. Add to this that there is only one set of each type, and it is really no wonder that they were making £100 to £150 per set of eight, double or three times the normal price of New Toy Soldiers, at auction. If you could find them, these may well be a good investment.

1973, so soldiers which cost about a pound then should be about £7 each today as new, and this holds approximately true for good quality figures, although the prices for model style tend to be a good bit higher. Second hand figures, on the other hand, can be bought at auction for between £2 and £5 per figure, and this is the best method of acquiring a good display collection quickly. They are also quite likely to hold their value against inflation.

Limited Editions

Many manufacturers of New Toy Soldiers, including Britains, tried to enhance the value of their product by offering them as limited editions. Britains quantities varied between 1,000 and 7,000 sets, and they always used the method of actually producing the specified number and then hoping that they sold out, whereas other makers would rather annoyingly announce an edition, and then make the number that they had sold, whatever that turned out to be, which made the whole idea of a limited edition somewhat meaningless. Nevertheless, to take the example of Nostalgia, Shamus Wade's famous series of British Empire colonial units, he had the moulds destroyed after each offer, which means that there are probably only 60 sets of some of the subjects in existence.

The fact of a limited edition does not of itself guarantee a higher price. The vast majority of Britains limited editions now sell at auction between £20 and £30 per box. This could

Picture 218: Britains die-cast Highlanders

Since these Highlanders were first issued in 1983, a piper was added in either bonnet or Glengarry in 1985, and these basic figures have been used in five Limited Editions, numerous different set combinations and some specials for Harrods, Hamleys and myself.

The Black Watch appear front right, with Drummers and some of the figures from Limited Edition set 5297. Behind them are a group of the figures I commissioned for my 1985 On Guard exhibition, for which only 500 officers and 2,000 men of the Argylls were produced. These now retail on their cards for about £40 to £50 per figure. Britains have so far kept their promise at the time not to do other Argylls with these figures, even though they have since gone through three further changes of ownership. At the back is the special Gordon Highlander Pipes and Drums produced as a 1,000 set special for Hamleys, followed by regular production Gordons, and finally by a group of figures that look as though they started out to become figures for Limited Edition set 5185, complete with fixed bayonets, but appear to have escaped from the factory floor before their final rubber stamping with the regular Seaforth tartan of red and white stripes. I bought them as a curiosity for two pounds apiece.

change later on, and according to what is in vogue among collectors, but it certainly looks inexpensive to me. They do need a certain amount of room to store, however.

Some makers, such as Bill Hocker, refuse on principle to limit or discontinue their production in any way. This is certainly currently holding down the second-hand price of his very stylish old Britains compatible troops. When he ceases production, I would anticipate a considerable movement in the price of his previous product.

Investment and the retail price index

The retail price index (RPI) works out approximately how much the cost of living increases over a period of years. In terms of the value of toy soldiers, it is only by adjusting price changes against the retail price index that meaningful comparisons can be made. I have extracted the following table from the retail price index to show how average retail values have changed since January1915, every five years.

To get the number of times that prices have multiplied between two dates, you just have to divide the index for the later date by the earlier date. Thus a shilling (5p) in 1915, which is what a box of Britains soldiers cost then, is the equivalent of fifty-one shillings today (£2.55). In 1965, however, a box of Britains cost twelve shillings and eleven pence (65p) so the price of a box of Britains hollowcast figures had increased thirteen fold, while the RPI had increased just three and a half times. If, on the other hand, you took the cost of a plastic toy soldier in 1965, typically 6d (2.5p) and compared that with the cost of an equivalent single figure in 1915, i.e. a penny (0.5p), the increase in the cost of toy soldiers had only been six times, not quite so severe.

To take the example further, and assuming that the box of Britains hollowcast soldiers

183

Date	Index	Date	Index
1915	4.1	1965	14.5
1920	8.1	1970	17.9
1925	6.5	1975	30.4
1930	6.0	1980	62.2
1935	5.2	1985	91.2
1940	6.3	1990	119.5
1945	7.3	1995	146.0
1950	8.3	2000	166.6
1955	10.7	2005	188.9
1960	12.4	2010	209.3

was a fairly common set, it might have fetched £5 in 1970, and been worth £150 in 1990. This would have been an appreciation of eight-fold between 1965 and 1970, and a further thirty times between 1970 and 1990. The equivalent rise in the RPI over these periods was 23% and 6.7 times, so the true appreciation between 1965 and 1970 was just under five times as opposed to nearly seven times, and between 1970 and 1990 was only four and a half times as opposed to thirty times!

These were nevertheless good gains, but then we come to the period between 1990 and 2010, when the RPI went up by 75%. If our £150 held its nominal value and is still worth £150 today, as many sets have done over that period, then its actual value has declined by 43%. If its value went down by £50, as happened with many sets of Britains from the 1950s, then it has actually lost 62% of its value rather than just a third. And even if its value appreciated by £50, which has happened to some more popular sets, the actual value would have declined by 24%. To have held its value, the set would have now to be worth £262.

Apart from those subjects that have continued to gain ground at startling rates, such as Zoo Animals and Garden, Britains have not proved a brilliant investment over the past twenty years. Otherwise, only with major rarities and on specific occasions have there been prices well outstripping inflation.

Costs in the second hand market

Every time that toy soldiers change hands, there is a transactional cost. In order to survive, everyone making a living from being a middleman needs to cover their costs, and this applies particularly to auctioneers and dealers. Expect today (2010) that auction houses will take up to 15% from the seller, 20% from the buyer and add extra charges for pictures and insurance. Altogether, this will be about a 40% margin between what the buyer pays and what the seller receives.

A dealer will generally need to mark up whatever he buys by between 50 and 100% in order to make a profit, although by operating on commission for others he can hold his costs down. In my youth, I used to take tables at shows and distribute postal lists of figures for sale, and as a result I have nothing but admiration for those who do this today. What with the storage, premises, packing, unpacking, travelling, table charges, listing, postage, individual packing, correspondence and telephoning (and this is just to sell things, let alone buying anything to sell and the money tied up in stock) I really wonder whether there is anything much left over to live on. There are, however, a number of well known people who have done it for many many years, and I take my hat off to them.

There are the people who take tables at shows to adjust their collections, and there is eBay. Operating in this way as a collector is very much a labour of love, and as always, any saving made by doing it yourself is only at the cost of a lot of bother.

Values and fashions, e.g. large Britains boxes

I still remember when I found my first large Britains box. I was touring Bristol on my dad's old bicycle, looking for old toy soldier stock. It was 1965, my twenty-first birthday. I found a leading toy shop in Kingsdown, and asked them whether they had anything in metal toy soldiers left. One has to remember that by this time plastic toy soldiers had been flooding the market for over ten years, so I was surprised and delighted to discover a box 73 that they brought out for me. This they must have had in stock for at least four years, and it was marked £5-10-0 in old money, five pounds, ten shillings. The box was a bit damaged, so I asked if they could give me a reduction, and they said OK, they would let me have it for a fiver. I paid them the cash, and asked them to keep it for me, as there was no way I could get it back to Wills Hall on my bike.

I pedalled home frantically, and got the bus back, which seemed to take hours, then back again on the bus. Finally I had it back in my room, and was able to take the time to very carefully unstring the figures and take them out, including the pieces that only ever appeared in this box, the Royal Artillery mounted officer at the trot, the 17th Lancers in full dress and the Black Watch officer and men marching. Magnificent. That for me was the most delightful and meaningful way to spend a twenty-first birthday I could ever have devised.

This set has remained in my collection ever since, and gave me the impetus to collect all the other large boxes. At one time, around 1987, large boxes of Britains commanded a premium over the value of their contents. My set 73 has been known to fetch £2,000 at auction. Now, the opposite is true. I tried to sell my set relatively recently, and it didn't even reach a reserve of £600. I am glad that I didn't succeed in selling it. Even if with its contents it is now only worth £500, let us say, at a hundred times what I paid for it, it is still showing me a reasonable return, though it is true to say that if I wanted to buy the contents in New Toy Soldier figures nowadays I would probably have to pay more like a thousand pounds for them. If I had invested the fiver in 1965, it would be worth £150 today, allowing for appreciation at double the RPI (2010).

The Holy Grail for Britains toy soldier collectors remains the gigantic set 131. I was recently talking to a collector who had tracked one down, and decided to pay the asking price of $50,000 dollars for it. That sounds like a lot of money, but compared to what one might pay for rarities even in other toy collecting areas, a little over £100 per figure for a set of which less than ten are known still to exist in the world (this is only the fourth one I have heard of) has to be good value.

Other than this, in double or more layer boxes, there are the even rarer, but not quite so attractive set 132, all the different versions of set 73, sets 129 and 130, two big Coronation Procession sets, the huge Wild West set, the popular Changing of the Guard set and a number of others, down to the Musical Ride, the complete American Civil War set, and the Arabs and French Foreign Legion box. Large Britains boxes make a brilliant very high WOW! cameo. With the exception of sets 131 and 132, their value has declined since the 1980s and 90s, but the fashion for them could easily return, so if you have the room to store them, this could be a good investment.

Best investment bets today

I put these highly speculative ideas forward without any promises whatsoever. My top principle for collecting is the WOW! factor, and these, like the big Britains boxes above, are the areas that I believe are undervalued at present. The first group is of already expensive items, and there is a risk that such items may include fakes (see page 80). While taking every precaution, such as trying to establish provenance, nevertheless the WOW! factor of these items is such that the WOW! payout should be worth the risk, even if the occasional mistake is made.

The second group is of areas in which there is still research to be done, and while there is, or may about to be, a focus of interest on them, the prices of them will have a good chance of increasing. As straws in the wind, I learned that a friend had recently been offered a not particularly rare second grade figure for £50. They are still available for a couple of pounds elsewhere. There remains just the one principle to bear in mind in what to put your money into, and it needs to be applied to each of the recommendations below. Buy what attracts you, and there is a good chance that other people will agree with you later. In the meantime, enjoy it, for that is the great dividend.

Picture 219: Lucotte Napoleonic French 3rd Hussars

This group of Lucotte cavalry are typical of the meticulous charm of the maker, at this point in the 1930s joined with CBG Mignot and being used as their premier brand. The chief difference between them and CBG Mignot cavalry, apart from the different moulds, is that the saddles with stirrups are separate pieces. The paintwork is intricate and delicate.

For many years in the toy soldier market, Lucotte figures have been worth a basic £50 each for foot, and £100 each for mounted, more for exceptional models. The effect of inflation means that their value has gradually been eroding, but they are still probably the most consistently expensive 54mm scale figures to collect.

Group one: high value items that may well appreciate further

- Britains boxed sets pre-First World War
- Britains horsedrawn vehicles with drivers in steel helmets
- Beiser sets using Britains or other figures
- Britains Paris factory products
- Britains special paintings
- Lucotte figures

- Heyde and other solidcast German figures in sizes larger than 48mm scale or in large, spectacular sets and groups

Group two: items where there is still research to be done
- German hollowcasts
- Best quality semi-flats
- Late 19th century wargaming figures
- Britains cheap and small size figures 1895-1959
- Britains' competitors 1893-1932
- Imaginative No.2 size Heyde groups and vignettes
- Large CBG Mignot displays
- Early New Toy Soldiers

Picture 220: Britains and Beiser Game Board sets

Charles W. Beiser was the inventor of a way of displaying toy soldiers in hinged clips attached to a baseboard, so that the soldiers could be knocked over by toy gunfire, and then by tipping the gameboard forward, they would all automatically stand up again in their right places. Britains made two sets of these under licence, 148, the Royal Lancaster Regiment, and 149, American Soldiers, the figures for which are pictured here. Evidently these sets were not very popular, and in spite of having taken the trouble to switch their entire production of infantry to rectangular bases suitable for the hinged clips (a legacy forever afterwards of this venture), Britains produced no more of this type of set. In the U.S., and often using imported Britains figures, Chas Beiser continued producing various sets for many years.

The sets are much sought after, and complete with baseboard, this one might well fetch £4,000 to £5,000. Without, of course, they are rather less interesting, and as shown here should be worth £1,500 to £2,000.

What is important in life?

To reach death with a rich experience, having pleased as many people as possible, i.e. to have good memories of them having been pleased with you. Two occasions come to mind, which started out as moneymaking occasions. The distribution manager who had served in AA artillery during WWII, to whom I ended up giving the magnificent model of the Astra 3.7 inch AA gun, and the colleague who remembered the Timpo Knights of King Arthur from his youth, to whom I ended up presenting a set. I remember these occasions with warmth not only because of the delight that the objects obviously gave them, but also that when they misunderstood that I wanted to give them rather than sell them, I managed to suppress my mercenary instincts and make them the gift, rather than disappoint them by insisting on payment.

Significance and the WOW! factor

In my previous book *Collecting Toy Soldiers*, I referred to three factors as determining the likely price of a particular item: these were Rarity, Desirability and Availability. In the twenty-five years that have elapsed since then, in my observations of collectors, one feature has been pre-eminent that I think I left out. Collectors like to explain their prize pieces to their friends in terms of why they are particularly special. Just as rarity and availability are not at all the same thing, though somewhat similar, so desirability is more dependant on appearance rather than any other factor, so the explanation of why a piece is special, which may indeed include rarity and desirability, usually also includes a further factor which I would term 'Significance'. The Significance of any piece in a collection may well involve a personal significance, for instance the circumstances in which the piece was acquired or whether it is a particular personal favourite. However, the sense that may affect the value is how significant the piece is in the history of toy soldier manufacture or collecting. Examples of this are firsts and lasts, pieces marking significant changes in manufacturing style or technique, or items known to have belonged to famous collectors. When Malcolm Forbes collection was sold, prices achieved were about three to four times higher than they would have been had they not been owned by a world famous celebrity. I would like to think that every toy soldier in my collection is there with a particular purpose along one or other of these lines. Certainly, whenever I have visitors, we seem unable to discuss more than a few of the items on show during the course of a couple of hours, which leads me to believe that many of them are sufficiently significant to be meaningful to many, expert in the subject or not. Thus Significance adds plenty to the WOW! factor, and therefore to the amount that collectors might be willing to pay when something changes hands.

Picture 221: King and Country: Normandy 1944

Allied troops advance into France in this Second World War diorama from King and Country. I have always been an admirer of the model making skills of fellow members of the British Model Soldier Society, and today, thanks to King and Country, Britains and Conte, among others, I have the opportunity to indulge in such items at a relatively reasonable cost, using ready finished components, rather than spending years of skill (which I never had) or a fortune (which I never had either) getting someone to do it for me.

BIBLIOGRAPHY

In *Collecting Toy Soldiers* I mentioned sixteen books and seven periodicals. During the subsequent twenty-four years, a steady stream of books, articles and websites have added an enormous amount of information. My father wisely taught me that it is not what you have in your head, but what you know how to look up that is important. Many of these books are now out of print, but today second hand bookshops have been supplemented by many amazingly useful websites that can be used to find copies.

I pick out here the books I now consider to be the most useful or the most fun to read, excluding those on civilian figure collecting, which is not part of the subject matter of the present book My full bibliography of what is available as literature about and in support of toy soldier and other figure collecting is on my website at *www.james-opie.co.uk.*

Books

Allendesalazar, Jose Manuel, *Coleccionismo de Soldates*, Everest, Madrid 1978. Essential reading on Spanish toy soldiers – in Spanish.

Asquith, Stuart, *The Collectors Guide to New Toy Soldiers*, introduction by James Opie, Nexus 1991. This book details hundreds of manufacturers with colour photographs. I wrote a 7,000 word introduction about the early days of the new (reproduction for collectors) type toy soldiers.

Blondieau, Christian, *Petits Soldats, Le Guide du Collectionneur*, Le Kepi Rouge, Paris 1996. An excellent collection of various toy soldiers, and as one might expect, strong on French makers.

Blondieau, Christian, *Soldats de Plomb & Figurines Civiles: Collection C.B.G. Mignot*, Le Kepi Rouge, Paris 1996. The best book so far on CBG Mignot – be sure to get the edition that includes English text unless you are a fluent French reader.

Borsarello, Dr J R, Alazet, R and Giroud, H, *Production Complete de Quirine & Cie*, private publication, Paris 1991.

Borsarello, Dr J, *Photos et Liste Des Figurines Quiralu Militaire*, private publication, Paris 1989. Exhaustive tomes on Quiralu production.

Bruun, Bertel, *Toy Soldiers From Ancient Times to Today's Most Exciting Toy Figures. Identification and Price Guide*, Avon, New York 1994. This one is a fun read.

Carbonel, Jean-Christophe, *Airfix Little Soldiers*. Imparts much of the excitement of wargaming.

Cole, Peter, *Suspended Animation* 2nd Edition, Plastic Warrior, 2004. Highly recommended for the understanding of what was going on at Britains from 1952 onwards, when plastic was taking over the world of toys.

Cowan, Peter, *Toy Knights*, private publication 2004. A fine book on medieval figures, covering different ground from Peter Greenhill's book.

Crahet, Bernard, *Gustave Vertunni: Catalogue Des Figurines Historiques*, private publication France 1996. A full resume of the products of Vertunni, complete with photographs.

Dean, Philip, *Wend-Al of Blandford*, AvalonImages.com 2005. A lovingly completed survey of Wend-Al.

Di Mauro, Orazio and Paoletti, *Italian Toy Soldiers*, Lazzaro, Torino 1994.

Doublet, Jean Bernard and Tisne, Jean-Michel, *Les Figurines in Plomb Creux Tome 1*, private publication 2010. Promises to be a fascinating catalogue of the French hollowcast manufacturers when complete in two volumes.

Fontana, Dennis, *The War Toys 2, The Story of Lineol*, New Cavendish London 1991. A good, if not exhaustive, survey of Lineol production.

Garratt, John G, *Model Soldiers: A Collector's Guide*, Seeley, Service 1959.

Garratt, John G, *The World Encyclopedia of Model Soldiers*, Muller, London 1981.

Garratt, John G, *Model Soldiers for the Connoisseur*, Weidenfeld & Nicolson 1972. The pioneer author for toy and model soldiers. Many of his insights and critiques still hold good today.

Greenhill, Peter, *Heraldic Miniature Knights*, Guild of Master Craftsmen Publications England 1991. A finely produced book on knightly splendour by the heir to the Courtenay legacy.

Grein, Markus, *With Heyde figures Around the World*, Edition Knannich 2003. Useful additional pictures and information about Heyde, text in German and English.

Hermida, Juan, *Historia del Soldadito de Plastico Espanol*, Private publication 2009.

Hornung, Bob, *Beton Basics: A Guide for Collectors*, private publication 1987.

Johnson, Peter *Toy Armies*, Batsford, London, 1982. The story of the Malcolm Forbes collection, the best attempt yet at a permanent public display.

Joplin, Norman, *The Great Book of Hollow-cast Figures*, New Cavendish London 1993. An invaluable book of British hollowcast production organised by manufacturer.

Joplin, Norman & Waterworth, John T, *Britains New Toy Soldiers 1973-Present*, Schiffer USA, 2008. An excellent compilation of data and pictures on the gloss painted metal military production of Britains 1973 to 2008.

Kurtz, Henry I, and Burtt R Ehrlich, *The Art of the Toy Soldier*, with a foreword by Roy Selwyn-Smith. New Cavendish 1985 New York: Abbeville, 1987. Probably the most visual of all toy soldier books, giving a magnificent flavour of old toy soldiers, particularly Britains, Heyde and CBG Mignot.

Maiotti, Gianni, *Faccetta Nera, Soldatini Italiani in Cartapesta 1936-1945*, Campione, Milan 1994.

Maughan, Michael, *The A to Z of Timpo 1960-1979*, private publication 1995. This is a definitive reference for the period covered.

O'Brian, Richard, *The Barclay Catalog Book.*

O'Brian, Richard, *Collecting American Made Toy Soldiers*, Krause (3rd ed) 1997.

O'Brian, Richard, *Collecting Foreign-Made Toy Soldiers*, Krause 1997.

O'Brian, Richard, *Researching American Made Toy Soldiers*, Ramble House 2010.

Opie, James, *Toy Soldiers*, Shire Album Shire Publications 1983. This was the first book that I wrote. It has 32 black and white pages, and explains simply what the toy soldier collecting hobby is. Great for introducing your friends for the first time.

Opie, James, *Britains Toy Soldiers 1893-1932*, Victor Gollancz 1985. Known as the Big Blue Book, this is a comprehensive study of the output of the Britains figures of the period, concentrating on contrasting the various changes of version which the figures in each set underwent. Can be read in conjunction with the publications of Joe Wallis, *Armies of the World and Regiments of all Nations*, to form a complete catalogue of Britains hollowcast toy output 1893 to 1966.

Opie, James, *On Guard*, New Cavendish 1985. The catalogue to my exhibition at the London Toy and Model Museum 1985-86. Illustrated with appropriate photos from *Britains Toy Soldiers 1893-1932* and *The Art of the Toy Soldier*.

Opie, James, *British Toy Soldiers 1893 to the Present*, Arms and Armour Press 1985. A black and white photo picture guide to Toy Soldiers by subject depicted, with price guide issued 1985 and 1987. A replacement for the classic book by Len Richards, which only covered early British toy soldiers. Known as The Pink Book.

Opie, James, *Collecting Toy Soldiers*, Collins 1987 (Hardback edition), New Cavendish 1991 (Paperback edition). A colourful book of advice to collectors, with some personal reminiscence. How to acquire, arrange and enjoy Toy Soldiers. Predecessor to the present book, but with different pictures, examples and anecdotes. Can be read as a prequel.

Opie, James, *Toy Soldiers*, Phillips Collectors Guide Boxtree 1989. A brief survey of the collecting field in 1989, with additional colour photographs.

Opie, James *The Great Book of Britains* New Cavendish 1993. Almost the book to end all books on Britains. 100 years of Britains production with 950 colour photos and a quarter of a million words, arranged in a year by year production sequence. 640 large format pages. Also, issued by Britains themselves, a specially bound edition with an exclusive set of toy soldiers.

Opie, James, *Opie's Pocket Price Guide to Britains Hollowcast Toy Soldiers*, New Cavendish 1994. The only checklist available for collectors with versions of the catalogued Britains set numbers, cross referenced to *The Great Book of Britains*. Although the prices in it are valid for 1994, in fact they have not changed a great deal over the ensuing twenty-five years, and the more valuable part of the book is the rarity rating which enables set rarity to be compared.

Ortmann, Erwin, *Model Tin Soldiers*, Studio Vista, London. This book, translated from the German, is mostly about flat figures.

Pielin, Don, *American Dimestore Soldier Book*, private publication, (2nd ed) 1986.

Pielin, Don, Joplin, Norman and Johnson, Verne, *Toy Soldiers and Figures: American Dimestore*, Schiffer USA.

Pietruscha, Andreas and Muller, Fritz, *Elastolin Kunstoff-Figuren*, Verlag Figuren Magazin Berlin 1993.

Piffret, Jean-Claude, *Figurines Publicitaire*, 276pp, Histoire & Collections Paris 1997.

Plath, Alfred, Timpo Toys Ltd, *Die goldenen Jahre einer schottischen Spielzeugfabrik*, 223 pp. private publication, Germany 2005.

Polaine, Reggie, *The War Toys (Kriegsspielzeuge): No 1, the story of Hausser-Elastolin*, New Cavendish Books, London.

Richards, Len, *Old British Model Soldiers 1893-1918*, Arms and Armour Press, London, 1970. This was the classic early black and white illustrated book of toy soldiers by the pioneer of systematic toy soldier collecting.

Roer, Hans Henning, *Old German Toy Soldiers*, Palagonia Verlag, Germany 1993. A very useful colour picture book on German made solidcast production by one of the leading experts, with dual German and English text for the articles.

Rose, Andrew, *The Collector's All-colour Guide to Toy Soldiers: a record of the world's miniature armies, from 1850 to the present day*, Salamander, London. An excellent book of large-size colour photographs of a miscellany of toy soldiers representing most of the main types. Many of the figures are from two of England's most noted collectors, Edmund Roche-Kelly and Peter Cowan.

Ryan, Edward, *Paper Soldiers*, New Cavendish London 1995.

Schenzle, Heinz, *Sigel-Bestimmungsbuch*, Friends of the Plassenburg, Kulmbach 1987. Exhaustive examination of the bases and markings of flat figures.

Schrepf, Norbert, *Militarisches Zubehor Katalog*, private publication 1998. An illustrated listing of the tinplate and other military equipment issued by Hausser-Elastolin and Lineol.

Schrepf, Norbert, *Lineol Military Figures*, private publication 2000. Exhaustive cataloguing of Lineol military production. Norbert Schrepf's website, *www.toy-soldier-gallery.com* has online versions of this and his equally meticulous research into Hausser-Elastolin.

Sinclair, A G, *Skybird Notes*, CWD Surrey, 1994. Excellent complete listing of Skybird output.

Sulzer, Alfred R, *150 Jaahre Feinste Zinn-composition Figuren, Ernst Heinrichsen 1839-1989*, 160pp, Zinnfiguren Museum, Zurich 1989.

Thomas, Alain, Meimoun, Jerry and Guillot, Philippe, *Starlux, Historique du Geant Francais de la Figurine Tome I*, (2nd Ed) private publication 2009. This is just the first part of a complete two-volume compilation of Starlux output.

Wallis, Joe, *Armies of the World: Britains Ltd. lead soldiers, 1925-1941*, private publication, USA 1993. Highly detailed listings of all Britains production 1925-1941. Black and white illustrations.

Wallis, Joe, *Regiments of all nations: Britains Ltd. lead soldiers, 1946-66*, 258 pp, private publication USA, 1981. With the preceding book, Joe Wallis has covered the second and third periods of Britains hollowcast production in as much detail as anyone could wish for. Complimentary to my own *The Great Book of Britains*, and essential for any serious collector.

Wells, H G, *Little Wars*, first published in 1913.

Periodicals (All current periodicals have websites)

The Old Toy Soldier Newsletter quarterly. This was the first toy soldier magazine, and majors on research and information articles. Runs the leading annual toy soldier show in the world in Chicago each year.

Toy Soldier Parade now discontinued.

Toy Soldier Review now discontinued.

Bulletin of the British Model Soldier Society quarterly. Majors on modelling, but also includes toy soldier collecting, news and auction reports. Has just celebrated 75 years of existence.

Collectors Gazette. For all types of toys, contains advertisements for shows and auctions, with news and reports.

Toy Soldier Collector Magazine. Mostly to do with New Toy Soldiers and similar models.

Toy Soldier & Model Figure Magazine. Bimonthly. Began in 1995. Particularly useful for new releases of models and New Toy Soldiers.

Figuren-Magazin. A German language magazine specialising in composition and plastic figures, especially Hausser-Elastolin, Lineol and Timpo. Also sells specialist publications.

Plastic Warrior Magazine. Bimonthly. A full run of back numbers would probably cover every plastic toy soldier ever produced, almost. The magazine also issues various compilations by manufacturer that are incredibly useful. Just celebrated 25 years of its annual show.

APPENDIX

New Toy Soldier manufacturers

Current manufacturers will usually have a website. For a snapshot of 180 manufacturers c.1991, see Stuart Asquith's book in the Bibliography. This selective list of past and present manufacturers since 1973 (some were even active earlier) is by no means definitive, and is inclined towards those I know by personal contact or by reputation. I should stress that the choice of a New Toy Soldier maker to collect is highly subjective, and there is no substitute for going to shows, shops or websites to make a decision.

Glossary

All these terms are used advisedly as the author's opinion only. Some manufacturers produce ranges in more than one category. The listing gives the shortened name by which collectors call the maker, rather than the official title. Where a particular well-known individual is connected with a make, his name is given in brackets. Where no terms are in use, my information is not sufficient for assessment.

- **CWB = Compatible with Britains Traditional Hollowcast Toy Soldiers.** ***You would need to look hard to see it isn't an old Britains. **Nice fit with old Britains. *Looks OK at a reasonable distance
- **ISO = In a style of their own, usually of a toy soldier nature.** These manufacturers will generally not fit well with anything much but other figures of their own making, but it is always possible to find some which are compatible with each other, and many look splendid massed in a grand display of their own. Some of the illustrations in this book show how far compatibility can be stretched, and this is anyway very much a matter of taste. ***Great standalone display potential. **Very acceptable. *Display with caution.
- **TTM = Tending towards a Model.** The more realistic the figure, the more they will fit with other models, assuming that the scale is similar. Many in this category are spoiled by not having ground modelled bases, but unless one is worried by altering them, this can easily be rectified with modelling materials! Obviously in this category, matt painted finish is an advantage, but gloss painting can always be covered with matting agent or repainted. ***Stands comparison with (and looks good alongside) models from the masters. **Will fit in well with models. *May or may not be to your taste.
- **Major, Medium, Minor = Scale of production.**
- Accurate plastic TTM**
- Alexanders (Nic Biberovik) UK ISO*
- All the Queen's Men (Derek Cross) UK 51mm Major TTM**
- Alymer Spain 56mm to 60mm Major ISO** TTM**
- Arkova (Allan Over) UK (Medievals) Minor ISO**
- Asset (Anne and Colin Randall) UK 52mm Medium ISO**
- BG of GB (Brian Gildea) UK Minor CWB*
- Bandsmen (John Ruddle) UK 54mm Minor CWB**
- Bastion (Andrew Rose) UK Medium ISO**
- Beau Geste Argentina Medium ISO**
- Blenheim (Jan and Frank Scroby) UK 55mm Major ISO*** (also Marlborough)

- Britains USA 54mm to 60mm Major CWB*** ISO*** TTM***
- British Bulldog (Mike Drewson and Peter Jones) UK 55mm Medium ISO**
- Bussler USA TTM*
- Caberfeidh (Graham Hilditch) UK 55mm Medium ISO**
- Campaign (Peter Johnstone) UK Minor ISO*
- Charles Hall (Charles Hall) UK Medium ISO**
- Conte (Richard Conte) USA 56mm to 58mm Major TTM*** also plastic
- Cranston (Bill Cranston) UK ISO***
- DB Figurines (Derek Brown) Australia Minor ISO*
- Del Prado 58mm Major TTM**
- Dorset (Giles Brown) 54mm to 56mm Major ISO*
- Ducal (Jack and Thelma Duke) 55mm Major ISO**
- East of India Company Hong Kong 60mm TTM***
- Frontline (Howard Swales) Hong Kong Medium TTM**
- Fusilier 56mm Medium ISO***
- GNM Miniatures (Graham Mollard) UK TTM**
- Good Soldiers (Alan and Susan Goodwin) UK Minor ISO*
- Great Britain and the Empire (Andrew Humphries) UK Minor ISO*
- HECO (Tony Williams) UK Medium 54mm ISO**
- HM of Great Britain UK Medium ISO**
- Hocker (William Hocker) 54mm Major CWB**
- Hornung Art (Bob Hornung) USA (Medievals etc.) Medium ISO**
- Imperial Productions (David Cowe) New Zealand 55mm Major ISO***
- Irregular Miniatures (Ian Kay) Medium ISO* TTM*
- Jankers (Hardiman) 55mm Minor ISO***
- King and Country Hong Kong 60mm ISO*** TTM***
- Lancer (David Bracey) 54mm Minor CWB***
- Little Legion (Mike Norris) UK Medium TTM*
- M J Mode UK Minor ISO*
- Mark Time (Peter Cowan) 54mm UK Medium ISO** (also Albion, Kingcast)
- Minimen (Jack Updyke) USA Medium TTM*
- Morgan Miniatures (Gareth Morgan) UK (Aztecs and Conquistadores) 60mm Minor TTM***
- Nostalgia (Shamus Wade) UK 55mm Major ISO***
- Pride of Europe (R. Dew) UK Medium ISO**
- Quality Model Soldiers (Ged Haley) UK 55mm Minor ISO*
- Replicants (Peter Cole) UK plastic Minor TTM**
- Rose (Russell Gammage) UK 52mm Major TTM***
- Sarum Soldiers 55mm Medium ISO**
- Soldiers Soldiers (John Tunstill) UK 55mm Medium ISO**
- Steadfast UK Medium ISO**
- Thomas Tin (Tom Loback) USA Minor ISO*
- Trophy (Len Taylor) UK Major ISO***
- Tradition UK 55mm Major ISO*** TTM***
- V.C. (Lyn Thorne) Minor ISO**
- Wailen (Derek Wailen) UK 54mm Minor CWB***
- White Tower Miniatures (Matthew Thair) UK Medium ISO**
- Whittlesey Miniatures (Keith Over) UK Medium ISO**
- Yeomanry (Brian Harrison) TTM**

INDEX

Entries are noted only where there is information or illustration offered, listing entries are excluded. Illustrations and captions are numbered sequentially throughout the book, starting with the jacket, and are given first, in **bold type**. Page numbers follow in normal type. B denotes features in the Bibliography. Looking up entries on the internet often provides interesting additional information.